Christian Counseling
and
Psychotherapy

Psychology and Christianity
Edited by David G. Benner

1. David G. Benner, ed., *Christian Counseling and Psychotherapy*

Christian Counseling and Psychotherapy

Edited by
David G. Benner

BAKER BOOK HOUSE
Grand Rapids, Michigan 49516

All chapters appeared originally in the Christian Association of Psychological Studies'
Journal of Psychology and Christianity (J) or *Bulletin* (B).

1. J 3, 1 (1984): 36–41.	17. B 3, 1 (1977): 8–12.
2. B 6, 2 (1980): 2–6.	18. J 4, 2 (1985): 12–14.
3. B 6, 3 (1980): 7–13.	19. J 4, 2 (1985): 86–90.
4. J 2, 3 (1983): 50–60.	20. J 4, 2 (1985): 26–28.
5. J 3, 1 (1984): 27–34.	21. J 4, 2 (1985): 15–18.
6. B 3, 2 (1977): 14–18.	22. J 4, 2 (1985): 76–82.
7. B 4, 1 (1978): 1–6.	23. J 4, 2 (1985): 71–75.
8. B 7, 1 (1981): 1–2.	24. J 4, 2 (1985): 9–11.
9. J 2, 2 (1983): 31–35.	25. J 4, 2 (1985): 19–21.
10. J 2, 1 (1983): 2–11.	26. J 4, 2 (1985): 98–102.
11. J 3, 3 (1984): 65–72.	27. J 4, 2 (1985): 95–97.
12. J 2, 2 (1983): 47–51.	28. J 4, 2 (1985): 48–51.
13. J 4, 2 (1985): 37–41.	29. J 4, 2 (1985): 5–8.
14. J 4, 2 (1985): 65–70.	30. J 4, 2 (1985): 52–56.
15. J 4, 2 (1985): 62–64.	31. J 4, 2 (1985): 42–47.
16. J 4, 2 (1985): 83–85.	

Contents

Part 3   Case Studies

Introduction to the Series

The Psychology and Christianity Series is published cooperatively by Baker Book House and the Christian Association for Psychological Studies (CAPS). Founded in 1952 in Grand Rapids, Michigan by a group of psychologists, psychiatrists, and pastoral counselors, CAPS is an international society of Christian helping professionals committed to the exploration of the relationship between psychology and the Christian faith.

Volumes in this series draw on CAPS publications, many of which are now out of print. From 1952 to 1974 the organization published the proceedings of its annual conventions. Then it replaced these proceedings with a quarterly professional journal, *The Bulletin of CAPS*, which, in turn, was replaced by the *Journal of Psychology and Christianity* in 1982.

This series will present psychological and theological reflections on basic issues encountered in helping, parenting, and educational relationships. After *Christian Counseling and Psychotherapy*, volumes in the series will include *Life-Span Growth and Development; Sin, Guilt, and Forgiveness; Psychospiritual Health and Pathology;* and *Personality and Biblical Anthropology.*

Further information about the Christian Association for Psychological Studies may be obtained from the main office:

Christian Association for Psychological Studies
26705 Farmington Road
Farmington Hills, Michigan 48018
(313) 477-1350

DAVID G. BENNER
Series Editor

Preface

One of the results of recent efforts to relate psychology to the Christian faith has been the development of a number of approaches to counseling and psychotherapy described as "Christian." Such efforts have not been without criticism. Noting the absence of a perceived need to develop distinctively Christian systems of architecture, accounting, bricklaying, or other human activities, critics have suggested that attempts to make psychotherapy Christian are misguided. They argue that while it is appropriate to speak of people as either Christian or non-Christian, it is inappropriate to designate human activities or professions as such. Consequently, that which makes psychotherapy Christian is a Christian psychotherapist.

What such an argument misses is the fact that the business of psychotherapy is closely related to the business of Christianity. In fact, the historical roots of modern-day psychotherapy appear to lie in the Christian tradition of the cure and care of souls. Psychotherapy and Christianity share a concern for assisting people in becoming whole. In this regard, they are both concerned with the question of salvation. The understanding of what it is from which we need to be saved as well as the methods of the salvation process may differ. However, both psychotherapy and Christianity are in the salvation business.

Viewed from this perspective, psychotherapy is either consonant with a Christian view of persons and the associated understanding of the process of growth toward wholeness, or it is at odds with it. This is not to suggest that psychotherapy, even when most successful, produces the same results as salvation or Christian conversion. But it does suggest the importance of efforts to develop approaches to therapy which are consistently Christian.

There is, of course, considerable room for difference of opinion within this broad understanding of Christian psychotherapy. Some authors in this anthology believe that the theory and techniques of psychotherapy should be derived directly from Scripture. Others suggest that therapy should be informed by major Christian themes and doctrines but that one should not expect to draw specific techniques from the Bible. These and other differences in the understanding of what it means to develop a Christian psychotherapy are much less important than that which the contributors to this volume hold in common—a desire to be faithfully Christian in their work as psychotherapists.

Part 1 of this anthology consists of six chapters which present various general strategies for developing and practicing "Christian" psychotherapy. The reader is introduced to some of the foundational theological and theoretical considerations necessarily involved in developing a Christian psychotherapy. A sample of the issues considered within this section include the place of hope in therapy; the concept of the ideal; the biblical themes of creation, the fall, and redemption and their impact on psychotherapy; and the biblical view of personhood and its implications.

The six chapters in part 2 present specific techniques or approaches to therapy judged to be useful for the Christian psychotherapist. These chapters draw on cognitive, behavioral, family and marital, hypnotic, and meditative techniques and approaches to therapy, revealing the breadth of practices in current Christian psychotherapy.

Part 3 includes nineteen case studies. The reader is given an inside peek at what happens in therapy when a therapist aspires to be both a faithful Christian and a responsible psychotherapist. The authors of these case studies are all experienced Christian psychotherapists. They represent a broad range of theoretical orientations and approaches (including family systems theory, object-relations theory, cognitive-behavioral psychology, Jungian theory, primal integration, and inner healing). They also differ in their understandings of what makes their therapy specifically Christian. However, all have the desire to be thoroughly Christian in practice.

It is important to say something about the people described in the case studies. Authors have done one of two things to preserve confidentiality. Either the identity of the patient has been suitably disguised and the article subsequently reviewed and released for publication by the patient, or the author has written a hypothetical composite based on a number of cases. Many of these cases are, however, real cases involving real people. In fact, two of them include the response of the patient to the therapy process. This provides an unusually rich opportunity to appreciate the inner workings of Christian psychotherapy. I wish, therefore, to particularly thank these people for sharing their experiences in this way.

The chapters in this volume confirm that there are as many ways of being a Christian psychotherapist as there are ways of being a Christian. Therapist and nontherapist alike strive to find and express the unique selves God has called them to be. The resulting pluralism, so clearly reflected in the present volume, demonstrates the health and vitality of the current efforts of Christian psychotherapists to be distinctively and thoroughly Christian.

Part 1

General Issues
and Approaches

1

Therapy with Theological Constructs and Tactics
Harold Wahking

Many bright, dedicated Christians are working diligently to develop explicitly Christian approaches to psychotherapy. This book testifies to what has already been accomplished. This chapter is a contribution to this effort. It is not an attempt to describe *the* Christian psychotherapy for all practitioners, but to describe a method some therapists may wish to use in their own form of Christian psychotherapy.

First, a definition of Christian psychotherapy is in order. The term should denote something quite different from the model that may be called "biblical preachment counseling," which refers to the use of Scripture to advise a person as to what he should do about a problem. This approach, lovingly used, may provide some biblical guidelines to an individual facing a specific, conscious, and rational problem. "Christian psychotherapy" is also intended to denote something different from another model, which may be called "secular therapy done by a Christian." In this approach, Christians help people change their lives by use of secular concepts, tactics, and theories, perhaps as screened by the counselor's Christian moral value structure, but making little use of biblical methods for life change or repentance. Even though this approach may benefit persons in need, it is not structured by biblical insights for repentance and personal renewal.

In contrast to these two uses of the term, "Christian psychotherapy"

15

denotes a personal relationship between two or more people, in which the therapist, at least, is a Christian. It involves face-to-face communication focused on the dynamic psychological processes of that relationship and other relationships in the light of biblical concepts and values. The goal of such therapy is that the participants become more whole, joyful, and Christ-like.

Most psychotherapies emphasize face-to-face communication focused on the dynamic processes of relationship. A special Christian contribution to therapy can be that the therapist is a Christian, the framework of communication is biblical, and the goal is Christ-likeness, that is, the development of personality traits modeled by Jesus (Gal. 5:22–23).

Compared with strictly secular psychotherapies, there are a number of advantages and several important limitations of this model of Christian psychotherapy. Christian therapists directly use the power of faith God has given therapist and client to make necessary changes. This can be facilitated in therapy through prayer, worship, commitment events, and biblical assurances. Also, the participants can choose directions for personal change and growth based upon the ultimate model set by Jesus and upon time-tested and inspired Christian values. In addition, Christian psychotherapists can make use of immensely helpful biblical concepts which do not have clear parallels in most secular psychotherapies. Some of the most important of these biblical contributions are: the practice of seeking and giving forgiveness; dealing with guilt through contrition, confession, restitution, and repentance; grace; and the experience of spiritual rebirth or conversion for those who have not previously put off the old self and put on the new (2 Cor. 5:17). Another advantage of Christian psychotherapy is that new clients, who are themselves Christians, may more quickly establish rapport with a therapist whose framework is biblical and whose values are familiar.

Three important limitations of Christian psychotherapy must be noted. First, clients who are not Christians may have negative reactions to explicitly Christian terminology, and clients who are Christians may be alienated from God and hostile toward the church. This antipathy will likely hinder therapeutic work unless the therapist is willing to use more secular language. Second, some individuals develop problems by processes which they express in theological language. Their religion may not make them "sick" but they may use religious concepts to describe and maintain their pathology. If so, they may be inclined to argue theological points with the counselor as an evasive tactic for avoiding the work of therapy. Third, theological concepts have most often been presented to people as answers to life's problems rather than as aids to the dynamic process of inner self-discovery. If the client hears the therapist giving answers in this manner, he may shift his focus from discovering his own self-answers to passively receiving the theological answers of his therapist. If this is allowed to happen, the dynamic process of therapy is shut down.

Having described some of the advantages and limitations of Christian psychotherapy, we may now proceed to develop some specific tactics for constructing therapeutic processes and interventions. Different therapists will likely develop models for their work according to the way they relate most authentically, and yet, all models may have much in common.

The researchers known as neurolinguistic programmers (NLP) identify three factors which all presently known forms of psychotherapy have in common (Bandler and Grinder 1979). These form a metamodel of therapy. (The latter three listed below are taken from the NLP research findings. The first is an addition made by this author.)

All psychotherapies share the following characteristics:

1. A relationship between the client and the therapist which is personal, accepting, and perhaps even loving
2. A means of sorting out the various antagonistic, denied, and distorted parts of the client's personality and behavior
3. A means of developing dialogue between these sorted parts
4. An integration of those formerly antagonistic, denied, and distorted parts

Any model of psychotherapy using Christian structures seems likely to include these four stages which can be termed *relating, sorting, dialoguing,* and *integrating.* The construction of techniques and therapeutic interventions may now proceed in an orderly fashion by developing specific tactics for each of these four steps.

Relating

Relating is generally thought to be the most important therapeutic task of the therapist. Relating is much more than the proper use of techniques. Relating is as much a matter of who the therapist is as it is what he or she says or does. The therapist-client relationship is founded upon explicit statements of professional ethics, is free of negative countertransference, and involves honest, caring concern for the client's well-being. One way of describing this ideal in relating is as skillful, unconditional love.

The biblical basis for the relating dimension of therapy can be taken from Ephesians 4:15. Therapists "speak the truth in love" that clients may grow into the fullness of Christ. Therapy is one form of an I-Thou encounter, a relationship between two persons in which both grow in personhood through response to each other and to God. The Christian counselor may love his clients much as a secular therapist might, but he also loves because he is aware that he has first been loved by Jesus (John 13:34–35). He may also love out of the awareness that as he loves one of the least of God's people, he is loving Jesus himself (Matt. 25:40). Other biblical qualities of a dynamic relationship in therapy are those known as the fruit of the Spirit: love, joy, peace, patience, kindness, goodness, faithfulness, gentleness, self-control (Gal. 5:22).

Some techniques which a therapist might use include hugs, words of encouragement, smiles, honest confrontation, careful listening, and attention to the ongoing quality of the therapist-client relationship. Some extra ways Christians may show love in therapy are praying for clients before they come in; praying with clients; reminding clients of God's loving presence in the counseling session; and relating to the client, not from a position of superiority, but as a fellow pilgrim on the way.

The therapist might ask the client, "Do you have a faith which might help you in the work you intend to do with me? How might your faith be of help? Do you believe God is present in this room as we meet together? How might his presence help us? Do you believe God will love you regardless of whether you do effective work with me today or any day?" These questions may help Christian clients establish rapport and hope, and identify specific resources they may use to reach their therapeutic goals.

Sorting

Clients normally report some internal conflict as they deal with external realities. These internal processes distort their perceptions of external events and inhibit their creativity in devising solutions. Psychotherapy involves sorting out these internal processes as well as possible responses to external events.

Therapists have developed many sorting techniques, such as inviting clients to sit in different chairs to represent different "parts" of themselves. Or, they may put a part of themselves in their right hands and a part in their left hands and dialogue between the two. Sometimes clients are asked to visualize first one part of themselves and then another. When clients are ready to make decisions for change, they may be asked to generate numerous options and then choose which are satisfactory to all their parts.

A biblical basis for sorting in therapy can be observed in the model set by Jesus. He asked individuals questions. He intuited their inner divid-edness and invited his "clients" to confess their inner struggles (e.g., Mark 9:24). Confession, as used in Scripture, seems to mean a pouring out of one's heart, whether confessing sin or faith (Matt. 16:16; 1 John 1:9). This laying out of belief and unbelief, sin and hope, guilt and grace, is a biblical model for the sorting done in psychotherapy.

Once therapist and client have prepared for sorting or confessing, then specific sorting techniques may be used effectively. A person may be asked to share a favorite Bible story that is especially meaningful and to be each character, identifying his feelings and values expressed through that character. Clients may be asked to pray from that part of themselves that is scared, then the part that is confident, then the part that is resentful, and so on, through all the parts they have identified.

Once the internal elements of conflict have been sorted out, clients may be asked to sort out what they are willing to change in their lives. These questions can be expressed clearly in theological language. "What do you believe the Holy Spirit is leading you to change in your life? Do you believe this change is God's will for you? How might your faith help you make this change? What kind of victory will you have when you make this change? How might you let sin block you from completing this change? How will you keep from doing that to yourself?"

Another valuable sorting technique using theological language is to ask clients, "What sinful behavior do you want to reduce today? What positive quality does some part of your personality hope to gain by this sinful behavior? How might you get that same positive good without sin-ful behavior? Will you commit yourself to getting that need met in a way which is congruent with your Christian faith?" In this way clients are invited to redeem sinful behavior rather than to reject or disown it only to have it plague them again in another form.

Other methods of sorting are greatly needed in order to enable Chris-tian therapists to draw upon a wide range of sorting techniques as they do their work. They will thus be able to use tactics that are chosen specifically for individual clients and which they are excited about them-selves. Using the same sorting techniques over and over often results in reduced emotional responsiveness in both client and therapist.

Dialoguing

Once clients have formed a loving relationship with the therapist and have sorted out the various parts of themselves which are related to the changes they plan to make, dialogue between various aspects of the cli-ents' personalities may proceed to deeper levels. Usually, the deeper the emotional expressiveness in dialogue, the more change of inner heart will likely occur in integration. Clients therefore need the assurance that they can express all kinds of feelings in therapy, not just ones which they or the therapist approve. One necessary limitation is that there must be no damage done to any person or property during the release of feelings.

A biblical basis for the dialoguing aspect of therapy may be found in Jesus' words, "you will know the truth, and the truth will make you free" (John 8:32) and "proclaim release to the captives... to set at liberty those who are oppressed" (Luke 4:18). Dialoguing is the release of such powerful emotions as fear, guilt, rage, lust, doubt, and despair. Dialoguing is contrition—heartfelt expression of grief and need. Scripture encourages us not to repress our inner conflicts but to open ourselves to the love of Jesus (Rom. 7:15, 19, 24–25). Therapists may encourage dialogue between ego states (Berne 1961), between "Top Dog" and "Underdog" (Shostrom 1967), or between two polarities (Bandler and Grinder 1975). In these and other dialoguing tactics, clients are encouraged to go for "feeling" words, to repeat more intensely expressions of feelings, and to put into words the feelings behind various spontaneous gestures they may make.

Once the client feels secure in the therapeutic relationship, the Christian psychotherapist may well use dialoguing techniques from secular therapy based upon biblical teachings. The client may be asked to pray about his need; the therapist may then make interventions during the prayer to heighten affect and to increase the fullness and depth of the feelings being expressed. Another dialoguing tactic using prayer is to ask the client to express his feelings in prayer and then to "play Jesus" and respond to himself. This alternation between roles may be carried on for some time and with considerable emotional depth.

Some clients report painful memories which haunt them even though years have passed since the events. Healing of these memories can be accomplished by asking the client if he will close his eyes and recall in detail the distressful event. He is asked to recall where this event took place, what the room looked like, what people looked and sounded like, how they felt and how he felt. Once the client is feeling all the painful emotions associated with this event, he is then asked to be aware that Jesus is present somewhere near him. The client is to see and hear Jesus relate to him and to the others in the scene in ways which invite healing and reconciliation. Jesus may be seen to talk with people, touch them, and to encourage them to talk with each other so that the ending is different from the original one.

Another dialoguing tactic gives clients the opportunity to change early childhood decisions about the way they are to be (*script redecisions;* Goulding and Goulding 1979). One way to do this is to use any of the widely used relaxation techniques to enable the client to become calm. In this state he or she may be more imaginative, have better recall of events, and be more ready to experience emotion than in the usual state of tension. Once relaxed, the client is invited to see, hear, and feel the presence of parents and other authorities at a time when he or she was hurting. As he or she recreates this early childhood scene, the client will likely express the original script decision such as, "Daddy, you get mad at me every time I want to get on your lap. I'll just stop trying to be close to you." After the client has re-experienced the original script decision, he can take into the scene the wisdom and power he did not have in childhood. He can announce to the people in the scene how he will live from now on. This new decision is usually made with deep affect.

The common theme of all these therapeutic tactics is to give verbal expression within a loving environment to all the antagonistic, denied, and distorted feelings, beliefs, and ideas the client is experiencing. As the client accepts these as parts of himself, that is, redeems or reowns them, he is preparing for integration.

Integration

In this phase the client experiences resolution of inner conflict. As a result he may feel new energy and hope for dealing with whatever outer conflicts he may have. Integration is the result of deep dialoguing in the context of accepting love or grace.

One biblical basis for integration is the concept of wholeheartedness. Jesus announced that he came to care for those who needed to be made whole and righteous (Mark 2:17). Wholeness is achieved whenever a person can overcome inner dividedness and act with healthy singleness of purpose. In biblical perspective the heart is the seat of the will and motivation. Therefore, if a person acts with his whole heart, his outward behavior and his inner attitude will be congruent or integrated.

An example of a tactic for working toward integration is to ask a brash and bossy client to let his left hand represent that part of himself which is tender, intuitive, and cautious. His right hand can then represent that part of himself which is powerful, tough, and action-oriented. When the client clearly associates these two polarities with his two hands, he can then be invited to bring his hands slowly together, and when he has done so, to verbalize his feelings. An integrated response might be, "Together they are strong, competent, and caring." By actively relating his two polarities instead of emphasizing one and denying the other, he has moved toward being a more whole and balanced person.

Some explicitly Christian forms of inviting integration might be to ask such questions as: "What is Jesus-like about those parts of yourself that are fearful, cautious, and skeptical? What is Jesus-like about those parts of you that are rugged, powerful, and ready for action? Visualize Jesus taking those parts and bringing them together creatively so that you have the best of both of them. How do you feel as you see and feel Jesus doing that?"

Another tactic for inviting integration is to ask the client to dedicate to God his strong moral sensitivity which by itself has led him to be overly critical of his teenagers, and his joy in seeing them become thinking and self-directing persons. By recognizing the godly values of these personal tendencies, he accepts both and integrates them.

Clients often benefit from a reinforcing experience immediately after an integrative decision. They may stand up and do a "go around," telling other members of the group how they are going to be from now on. They may lead in a prayer of thanksgiving for their new selfhood. They may practice with the therapist the new behavior which they have just given themselves permission to use. Celebrating the new decision is also helpful. A client may repeat the words of Jesus, "You will know the truth, and the truth will make you free" (John 8:32) and then declare, "I am free! I am free from now on to. . . ."

Conclusion

As we develop more principles and practices for a truly Christian psychotherapy, we will become increasingly clear with clients about how to relate, sort, dialogue, and integrate. By helping people draw upon their faith and upon the loving power of God, we can help them become the people God created them to be.

References

Bandler, R., and J. Grinder. 1979. *Frogs into princes: Neuro-linguistic programming.* Moab, Utah: Real People Press.

———. 1975. *The structure of magic.* Vol. 1. Palo Alto: Science and Behavior Books.

Berne, E. 1961. *Transactional analysis in psychotherapy.* New York: Grove Press.

Goulding, M., and R. Goulding. 1979. *Changing lives through redecision therapy.* New York: Brunner-Mazel.

Shostrom, E. 1967. *Man, the manipulator.* Nashville: Abingdon.

2

Biblical Themes in Psychological Theory and Practice

J. Harold Ellens

During the last five years the American evangelical community has given birth to an important dialogue in the helping professions: integration of psychology and theology. This dialogue demonstrates a serious concern to relate faith to life. On the theoretical level, it concerns the question of the essential nature of science. On the practical level, it concerns the question of responsible discipleship in applied disciplines. The enterprise seems pregnant with new insights, new routes across the frontiers of both theology and psychology, and new potentials for doing both theology and psychology more wisely and creatively at the theoretical and applied levels. The motivation driving the dialogue is the realization that there is a necessary rather than accidental relationship between being an imager and celebrator of God in his grace, on the one hand, and being a psychological scientist or therapist on the other.

There are inherent difficulties in this dialogue. One of these is the difficulty of basic definition. In *Mind and Madness in Ancient Greece*, Bennett Simon declares that the difficulty in talking about psychology is that of getting a commonly agreed upon definition of it, even among specialists in the discipline. Difficulties in definition complicate the evangelical dialogue considerably. The complexity of summarizing such theoretical constituents of the dialogue as sound theories of personality and pathology is one. Achieving a responsible, faith-oriented critique and appreciation of classical psychological formulations and models such as those of the diverse psychotherapeutic systems is another. This paper addresses two problems, two principles, eight possibilities, and twelve practical applications.

Two Problems

The first problem in the direction this evangelical dialogue has taken is rooted in the conceptual model that the term *integration* implies. Models or paradigms are usually difficult to construct. The way faith relates to science or Christian commitment to psychological theory and practice is far from self-evident.

Holmes (1977) contends there are three ways science and religion relate:

1. Both use models to explain reality.
2. Conflict is never ultimately over empirical data but concerns a priori principles or philosophical assumptions (faith commitments).
3. Properly conceived, all science, as all human experience, finds its ultimate meaning in religion, that is, in faith perspective.

But the integration model suggests two disparate entities, psychology and theology, essentially alien to each other, which must be lined up or force fitted to each other in order to insure decent or responsible evangelical work in the helping professions. This poses an epistemological problem on the theoretical science level, a structural problem on the applied science level, and a problem of psychodynamic dissonance on the experience level.

The integration model presents an inaccurate picture of reality on two counts. First, it holds at its base the essentially fundamentalist notion that truth comes only through Scripture by the special revealing action of the Holy Spirit of God. Such a view devalues God's general revelation in the world studied by the natural and social sciences. Integration suggests that science, our reading of God's book in nature, is at war with our reading of God's other book, the Bible.

Such a notion is a residuum of old-time fundamentalism in the schizophrenic way it sets the natural and supernatural worlds at odds, the apocalyptic way it demarcates the domain of God and of the demonic, and the pagan suggestion that lies at the bottom of this dichotomy, that is, that God does not live here but must invade alien territory to enter the domain of "this world" and its scientific truths.

Scholars who stand more consciously in the historic tradition of the Reformation recognize that God lives here. However, in view of their extremely limited contribution to current evangelical dialogue, such scholars give the distinct impression that they are not sure that God's living here really makes that much difference. There are, however, evangelicals of both traditions who are beginning to understand the problem with the integration model and reach beyond it.

A second problem with the integration model is that it tends to suggest that psychology must be absorbed into theology or vice versa. In *Rebuilding Psychology* (1977), Collins suggests that psychology and theology remain aliens to be aligned but never really integrated, disparate fields to be worked in by individual psychologists and believers, but not quite a place for either to be at home. In so far as a Christian feels at home in psychology while retaining his faith commitment, he does so by forcing psychological notions into his belief categories and proceeds as though the science of psychology has no prerogatives of its own.

Carter and Narramore in *The Integration of Psychology and Theology* (1979) suggest that one must either have theology absorb psychology or psychology absorb theology. One is either a psychologist who happens incidentally to be a believer and a kind of theologian, or one is a theologian who happens incidentally to be a kind of popular psychologist.

However, theology and psychology are both sciences in their own right. Both stand legitimately on their own foundations and both read one of the two books of God's revelation. They are not inherently alien. When they seem paradoxical or disparate, it must be because of some dysfunction. The professional has failed perhaps to read the Bible well enough or do the sciences of the natural world thoroughly enough; or he has distorted the science of the theological or natural world by arbitrary dogmatism, not properly constrained by sound investigation of God's Word in creation or Scripture; or he has drawn erroneous conclusions in either of those investigations.

Wherever truth is disclosed it is always God's truth. Whether it is found in general revelation or special revelation, it is truth which has equal warrant with all other truth. Some truth may have greater weight than other truth in a specific situation, but there is no difference in its warrant as truth.

The integration model will be a dead-end street in the quest to relate psychology to the Christian faith unless these problems are solved regarding the essential alienation of psychology and theology, and the need for absorption of one into the other. To solve them will require discarding both the term *integration* and the conceptual model which it implies.

The real issue in the quest for Christian responsibility in the helping professions is the search for a method of doing theology from a psychological perspective and doing psychology from a theological perspective. Such a perspectival model of theoretical and applied professional work takes seriously the legitimacy of both sciences and acknowledges that they are generically one. The perspectival model assumes the universal lordship of Christ and God's sovereignty in all things.

Two Principles

There are two principles which must be taken seriously in laying the groundwork for such a perspectival model. First is the principle regarding what constitutes the distinctiveness of being Christian in the helping professions. In the realm of psychological theory development, the first principle of being Christian is not that our scientific achievement supports, reinforces, or coordinates with our theology or faith; but that our science reflects God's truth from his created world. To be distinctively Christian requires that psychological theory development produce warrantable scientific theory. In the realm of psychological practice, the first principle of being Christian is not that our psychology conforms to our theology but that it is the most superbly sound psychotherapy possible. To be a Christian therapist requires first of all that I be a thoroughly effective therapist. Otherwise one may be both a Christian and a therapist but not specifically a Christian therapist.

Everybody is tempted to sometimes substitute comfortable private philosophy for the demands of sound psychotherapy, but that human error is less excusable in those who seek God's truth in science and experience. John Gardner believes that most people cheat in the pursuit of excellence. But sometimes it appears that evangelicals especially cheat in this pursuit.

Sound psychological theory and practice is that which genuinely enhances the patient's progress from pathology to full-orbed personhood. Christians perceive this in varying degrees. Full-orbed personhood may be achieved by patients to varying levels of completeness or functionality. Sound psychology which brings the patient, for example, out of depression to emotional resilience and stability is just as Christian at that level, as that which affords the final stages of maturity—spiritual certainty and peace as a "person in Christ." Even if that deliverance from depression is done by a secularist, it is a kingdom act and a Christian enterprise, though it may never achieve the completeness it could under a comparably effective Christian therapist.

What makes practice in the helping professions Christian is less the imparting of biblical information or religious practices to the patient, and more the enhancement of healthy functionality of the person in the direction of completeness of body, mind, and spirit. That practice of the helping professions which is preoccupied with the final step of wholeness—spiritual maturity—will usually short-circuit the therapeutic process and play the religious dynamic of the patient or therapist straight into the typical religious patient's psychopathology. Such practice tends to reinforce, for example, neurotic guilt, depression from repressed anger and low self-esteem, compulsivity, and the psychotic decision of the schizophrenic to exchange the real world for his own.

The second principle regarding being Christian in the helping professions is the necessity of the incarnational style of the professional in his role. As in all forms of incarnation, that of Jesus Christ supremely so, the import and impact of the role are more direct and life-shaping for the incarnating one than for the recipient of that person's ministry or service.

The Christian therapist incarnates for the patient healing expectations, direction, and certification from a Christian perspective. The therapist's values, attitudes, goals, insights, techniques, and passions are conditioned in terms of the divine claims of sound faith and sound science. The impact upon the client is indirect. Being a Christian psychologist has more to do with what is happening in the therapist's professional and personal attitudes, thoughts, and experiences than it has to do with what happens to the patient. The impact upon the patient should manifest itself in the way the Christian therapist's perspective and nature enter into the patient's experience of the therapist as a person and professional. The therapist's patient-handling technique and expectations regarding what health means must incarnate sound Christianity and sound science. Perhaps ultimately the desired impact is that of the therapist's worldview seeping into his patient's experience.

Eight Possibilities

The possibilities for the therapist's incarnational role as a Christian are found in eight biblical themes. These themes ought to be incorporated into the Christian professional's conceptualization of life and work. The themes are the biblical concepts of personhood, alienation, grace, sin, discipline, "the wounded healer," mortality, and celebration as a way of life. These concepts illumine psychological theory and practice.

The biblical theology of personhood is surprising and profound. Unconditional grace is clearly the central biblical theme from the Pentateuch, through the psalms, to the covenant theology in the prophets, especially

Isaiah, Hosea, Zechariah, and Malachi, and into the gospel tradition of how Jesus handled people. In the Bible one thing is overwhelmingly clear: Humans are unconditionally cherished by God, in spite of themselves. God so loved the world that he created it. He made humans imagers of himself. He invested all persons with an unnegotiable and inviolable dignity. From the outset he imputed to each the status of compatriot. The Eden story does not speak of man as child, servant, or subordinate of God but as a divine compatriot. God visited Adam and Eve in the cool of the evening, and they helped God keep the garden and name the animals. Adam was placed in a complimentary relationship with God.

That imputed status was never abrogated despite Adam's declaration of independence. God's response to the fall was to change the ground rules at his expense and to reaffirm humankind's kingly status and destiny. In that inviolable status every person has only two potential conditions: to be in a posture which rings true to that God-given status and, therefore, true to self; or to be inauthentic in perspective, disposition, or behavior, and suffer the dissonance and disease inherent in that inauthenticity.

God remains preoccupied with human need not human naughtiness, with human failure of destiny more than of duty, and not with the sinful past but with redeemed potential. If God confirms patients and therapists in that quality of personhood, Christian psychological theory and practice must be based upon it. Patients are free to be what they are for the sake of what they can become before God.

The biblical theology of alienation starts with the fall. It describes the human person as a child who has lost touch with the Father. Paul developed his anthropology around three stages: primordial man in Eden, fallen man in history, and the man in Christ in salvation.

The state of fallenness is expressed in Augustine's prayer, "Thou hast made us for thyself and our souls are restless until they rest, O God, in thee." The fallenness of humanity is obvious. Its psychological consequences are evident everywhere. The brokenness and disjointedness of the psyche of all humans is the empirical expression of our longing for our Father's hand, the primal anxiety permeating everything. The many compensatory strategies incited by all of that are frequently additional dynamics which produce pathology. Religion, particularly the Judeo-Christian religion of divine grace, is a significant anxiety-reduction mechanism. The uniqueness of the Judeo-Christian theology of grace is that it reveals God as unconditionally gracious; all other religions represent him as a threat. Moreover, the anxiety-reduction factor in all other religions is legalistic self-justification—forcing God's favor through the performance of liturgical or ethical requirements, devised by religionists, for measuring up to God's standards. In the Judeo-Christian religion the anxiety-reduction mechanism is exclusively that of grace—God's "unconditional positive regard" for the sinner. That anxiety reduction is reinforced, of course, by the opportunity for the life of gratitude that follows so great a salvation. So the theology of alienation is critical to the Christian professional's perception of self and others and the recognition of God's way of dealing with that as the Christian's analogue for handling people.

The biblical theology of grace therefore, is critically important to any sound psychological or psychotherapeutic concept or strategy. In the Bible, grace is unconditional and radical. It is unconditional as in the parable of the prodigal son, and it is radical in that it cuts through to the center of human alienation, whether humans like it or not. Moreover, God's grace perpetually reaffirms the compatriot status of all humans with him, in spite of themselves. That has been a difficult perception for the believing community to grasp. People have a proclivity to try to get their own hands on the controls of justification because accepting free grace is scary and nearly unbelievable for those who perceive themselves as "not-okay children." The Christian's model of pathology and patient care needs to be formed and informed by the radical realities of this biblical theme.

The biblical theology of sin is likewise crucial to the perspectival model of Christian professionalism. Sin, contrary to popular opinion, is a failure in achievement of authenticity to self and of full-orbed personhood in Christ. It is a distortion and distraction to lesser achievements. It cannot be compensated for. It can only be converted from. *Metanoia* is the only solution. That is possible only to the person who has heard the announcement that he is forgiven and accepted unconditionally. Nietzche said the courage to be in this hopefully tragic world is the ability to stand at the brink of the abyss of nothingness and hear without flinching the announcement that God is dead. Actually, the courage to be in this fractured and alienated world is the ability to stand in the middle of the hopelessness of human alienation and hear the announcement that God has embraced us in spite of ourselves and realize that if God is for us no one can be against us (Rom. 8:28). Ultimately, each person cannot even be against himself or herself as an obstruction to divine grace and acceptance. Human destiny is to realize in full-orbed personhood the palpable experiences of the regal status of compatriot, which God has imputed to humans in spite of themselves. God never abrogates that status. He simply waits for us to achieve the self-actualization which expresses it. Sin is falling short of that divine expectation.

God's law is not a threat, implying a conditional relationship with him, infraction bringing loss of favor. His law is rather a constitution for the kingdom of *shalom*—peace and prosperity in all facets of life. It is interesting in this regard that Jesus was preoccupied, as were the prophets, with social-psychological wholeness, not practices of private piety and personal purity. Preoccupation with the latter is idolatry, manufacturing out of self a plastic doll, as opposed to celebrating the compatriot status grace establishes. Sin is bondage and pathology because it is a distraction to a distorted destiny, a constrained striving, compared with maturity in God's grace, which is the glorious freedom of the children of God. Thus Luther could say, "Sin boldly," and mean it.

The biblical theology of discipline is the theme of discipleship. Discipline is the endeavor of beginning down the road of forgiveness of self and others, acceptance of self and others, unconditionally caring for self and others, reflecting the divine analogue. Discipleship is a troth with self and God to incarnate that divine grace dynamic that infuses the universe. It is the troth to forsake all other foci and keep thee only to the kingdom destiny. Jesus urged people to such discipline in the way he handled them. He said to the adulterous woman, "I do not condemn you. Go and do not do it anymore. It is untrue to yourself" (John 8:11, paraphrase). To the Samaritan woman he gave the insight that spirituality, not religiosity, is the issue (John 4:19–24). Christ ordained Peter, the denier, to build the church, and Matthew reports that in the garden Jesus grabbed Judas and said, "Friend, how did it come to this?" (Matt. 26:50, paraphrase). Biblical discipleship means being bound to Christ, to be free in grace. It means to live eschatologically "before the face of God." Since that is what life is designed to be, Christian expectations for therapists and Christian possibilities for clients will be shaped by such discipleship.

Henri Nouwen focuses on the biblical theme of the wounded healer (1975). He takes the suffering servant notion of the Old Testament (which is also epitomized in the messianic theology of the New Testament), and points out that there are four doors for God and the Christian into the heart of humanity: the woundedness of the world; the woundedness of any given generation; the woundedness of the individual; and the woundedness of the healer. He points out that this wounded healer theme implies that all grace, growth, and healing is communicated or incited by starting where the healer and the person to be healed are. The humanness and brokenness of both must be affirmed. The healer's role is not to remove the pain of life but to interpret it. Moreover, the evidence in the healer of woundedness and pain and of the transcendence or constructive endurance of it helps to heal the patient. Carl Jung's notion of the archetype healer projected by the patient upon the therapist and the value of the healer sharing his or her own growth dynamics in therapy are relevant here. The wounded healer can become the model and the incarnation of risk taking in growth and healing.

The biblical theme of mortality is directly related to the idea of the wounded healer. The Bible gives little support to perfectionist notions that building the kingdom will bring the elimination of the mortality and brokenness of the world. The Bible, instead, affirms our mortality and the world's brokenness and emphasizes the strategies for making godly sense in that setting. That, after all, is what grace is all about. Brokenness, humanness, and pathology are affirmed: We are dying men and women in a generation of dying men and women. Scripture acknowledges both the magnificence and malignancy in the universe. The persistent malignancy is pathologically denied in our cultural idealization of the "bigger and better." The Bible says it is okay to vary from the idealized norm. It is acceptable to age, wrinkle, decrease, distort, weaken, become more dependent, and even die. In fact, "to die is gain," according to Paul (Phil. 1:21). Youthfulness is not the focus of meaning in the biblical concept of mortality but maturation is. Patients need to see in therapists the fact that it is a supportable and perhaps even a celebratable condition to be a human, mortal, dying person before the face of God.

The finest biblical illumination of what it means behaviorally to be Christian in our work and world is the theme of celebration. It is a revealing clinical and biblical fact that people who can be grateful can be healthy and people who are incapable of generating spontaneous and authentic gratitude are unable to be healthy. They do not have the interior machinery or dynamics for it. The German Reformers knew that four hundred years ago and wrote it into *The Heidelberg Catechism*, with its focus upon gratitude as the Christian way of life. Celebration as gratitude may take the form of worship, or the childlike posture before our Father which we call prayer. Celebration may be exhilarated joy for the providence of God in life. To be a Christian means to be like a child celebrating a father's beneficence. A Christian therapist who sees life as that kind of enterprise will incarnate for the patient crucial elements of celebration.

Twelve Practical Applications

The twelve practical applications of biblical theology to the psychotherapeutic setting can be detailed briefly. First, recognition of the biblical themes leads to the assumption of a pre-established identity for the patient. It is the identity of one whom God affirms as compatriot. That identity needs to be recovered or enhanced in therapy. The therapist is in that sense a priest of God for that needy person.

Second, the biblical themes imply a certified and secure destiny for the patient which is infused with clear purpose for self-realization in the kingdom context. Third, they insure for the patient the experience of acceptance in keeping with the analogue of God's unconditional grace for the patient and the therapist. The biblical themes introduce into the therapeutic milieu a dynamic which can work toward the defusing of neurotic guilt, unproductive remorse, hopelessness, unresolved grief, self-pity, compulsivity, and some of the need for schizoid ideation. The Christian perspective also potentially decreases the need for the defeating processes of masking, denial, self-justification, self-affliction, and conversion reactions. Moreover, the insight afforded by the biblical themes free one for informed and constructive self-acceptance.

Fourth, the perspective the themes give the therapist and potentially the patient provides the foundation for a life-style of dignity; not a life-style of self-abnegation and demeanment but of being cherished and affirmed. Fifth, the biblical perspective can take the panic out of therapy for the therapist. Since God is God and grace is grace, even when we are not experiencing it, the therapist need not feel as though the weight of the world is on him or her and as though the therapist's own personhood or destiny hangs on the outcome of a particular case. Sixth, these themes afford the relief, affirmed self-esteem, and certification as a person that are likely to take the form of a sense of worthiness imputed and inherent in the patient as a person, rather than worthiness earned and dependent upon the patient's behavior.

Seventh, these biblical perspectives can reduce the therapist's anxiety with which the patient has to deal. Eighth, they provide a broad base of insight and perspective for building wholesome transference and countertransference. Ninth, they afford a coherent context for all of life, healthy or pathological. That context is God's disposition of inviolable goodwill, not divine threat. Tenth, they expand the potential for risk taking toward growth and integrated maturity, by means of constructive anxiety reduction. The entire mode of these themes is that of freedom. They afford relief from constraints that distract from the patient's Christian self-actualization.

Eleventh, the biblical perspective frees the therapist to be human without being careless; to play God as necessary in therapeutic decision making and method without losing sight of his real stature and role; and to exercise a sound sense of humor about himself, God, the patient, the pathology, and the fragile enterprise of therapy.

Twelfth, the biblical perspective releases persons to die "well." That relief attacks the ultimate panic that stands as a specter behind all pathology.

Conclusion

Theology and faith are cognitive-emotive processes. Therefore, their function for ill or good must be relevant and applicable to disorders which are cognitive or emotive in source. That means that healthy dynamics and perspectives in theology and faith will affect the potential health of the therapist and patient in such psychosocial disorders. Religious dynamics may be somewhat less relevant in psychopathology which is of a body-chemistry nature, though even then, healthy theology and faith may be invaluable in management of the symptomatology.

However, with increasing evidence for the two-way switching function of the hypothalamus in channeling or controlling the impact of endocrine disorders and of the effects of psychic disorders on endocrine function, the role of healthy or pathological theology, faith, or spirituality becomes increasingly interesting with regard to the role in or impact upon even those psychopathologies which appear to root in distortions of body chemistry.

Therefore, concerns about theological perspective, faith commitment, religious experience, and spiritual maturity are becoming increasingly vital therapeutic issues.

References

Carter, J. D., and B. Narramore. 1979. *The integration of psychology and theology.* Grand Rapids: Zondervan.

Collins, G. R. 1977. *The rebuilding of psychology.* Wheaton: Tyndale.

Holmes, A. 1977. *All truth is God's truth.* Grand Rapids: Eerdmans.

Nouwen, H. 1975. *The wounded healer.* New York: McGraw-Hill.

3

Toward an Integral Mode of Psychotherapy
Arnold H. DeGraaff

Integration is becoming a popular theme in the development of a Christian perspective in psychology and psychotherapy. This reflects a growing desire to bring different dimensions of our experience into greater harmony: our faith experience and our feelings; our findings in theology and those in psychology; our view of human nature and that of the different modes of therapy. It marks our uneasiness in living with two different kinds of knowledge and experience and reflects a deep resolve to live more integral lives.

However, the word *integration* has a misleading implication, namely, that there are two or more aspects of life that we must harmonize. The implication is that the act of integration requires special effort and that the results will probably be partial and tentative. In the background is the notion that there is an inherent duality, opposition, or tension between two or more dimensions of our experience.

However, we need to approach this problem from an opposite perspective. Instead of a tension or duality, let us assume that there is an integral unity and harmony between our faith and our feelings, between the findings of theology and those of psychology, between our view of the person and that of therapy. Let us also assume that the human person is an integral, unified, spiritual creature, rather than a unity of body and soul or body-soul-mind-spirit. If this assumption has any validity, then our task with regard to integration is not so much to construct a unity as it is to discover the integral unity that is already there. If human life is integral then our main task is to allow ourselves to experience that integrality and to discern that unity.

I experience my own life as integral and the lives of the persons I contact also manifest that integrality. This is not to say that my experience of the unity of life and that of others is not painful at times. It is painful to be aware of how immature our feelings and our faith life can be as adults. It is tragic to see how a certain approach to therapy can both bring a measure of healing to a client and at the same time lead that person into another kind of distortion, for example, that of absolutizing human sensitivity or of affirming a materialistic way of life. But these painful immaturities and distortions highlight the integrality of life rather than reveal a duality. What happens in one dimension of life deeply affects all other aspects. An immature emotional life results in an immature faith life and vice versa.

Scripture affirms our experience of the integral unity of life and that it points us back to our experience as revelatory of the inner coherence and unity of the different dimensions of human existence. Biblical/theological studies of the last decades have brought to light once again the scriptural proclamation concerning the spiritual unity and centeredness of the human person. From whatever point of view we look at the person, according to Scripture, we are always confronted by the whole person in relation to God (DeGraaff and Olthuis 1978). Moreover, to understand God's order for the many dimensions of human life, Scripture points us back to our experience. In such passages as Genesis 1, many psalms, John 1, Colossians 1, and Hebrews 1, Scripture makes it clear that God reveals his will in and through his creation, in and through our experience. If we are to develop an integral model of psychotherapy and the human personality, we must focus on psychotherapy itself in the belief that it will reveal its orderly and coherent character to us.

In keeping with this approach I have entitled this chapter "Toward an Integral Model of Psychotherapy," rather than "A Model for Integrating the Different Modes of Psychotherapy." Psychotherapy has an integral coherence. Its spiritual or normative character is inherent in the very process of therapy itself. We do not have to add a spiritual dimension at some point; it is there all along. Likewise, the different modes of therapy constitute an integral unity. It is up to us to discern that integrality. Our experience of the regularities and the integrality of life reveals God's intentions for our existence.

Psychotherapy as a Specific Type of Counseling

The specific problems and conflicts people hope to resolve through counseling reflect concrete, existential, total, integral human situations and relationships. Problems are not merely physical, emotional, social, cognitive, or spiritual. Rather, every dimension of a person's life is affected by a specific conflict.

Although the whole person is affected by a specific problem, not all difficulties a person encounters are the same. This diversity of problems is reflected in the many kinds of counseling that exist. There is pastoral counseling, marriage and family counseling, child therapy, child-welfare care, legal aid, financial counseling, vocational guidance, rehabilitation services, medical care, physiotherapy, speech therapy, school counseling, special education, nutritional counseling, psychotherapy, and so on. There are as many kinds of counseling as there are dimensions of life and problems people encounter.

Although all the aspects and effects of a conflict upon a person may have to be dealt with in time, the core of a problem as the client presents it and as it comes to the fore during initial counseling sessions determines what kind of counseling the client needs. For example, a legal problem calls first of all for a legal solution, even though the conflict may affect many other dimensions of the person's life as well. To have a legal conflict means first of all that the norm for justice has not or cannot function in a particular situation and that the client needs help in resolving that conflict. Of course, it may well be that the difficulty has deeply affected the person's faith life or physical health, and the legal counselor may advise the person to seek help for those problems as well.

In each type of counseling we are called to let ourselves be guided by our understanding of the norm that holds for that dimension of life. The norms of certainty, troth, justice, stewardship, respect, style, clarity, unfolding, consistency, sensitivity, and well-being are our provisional guidelines. In this concrete way God's revelation, as it comes to us in our experience and as our eyes are opened to it from Scripture, serves as the basis and directive for all forms of counseling.

All human problems and conflicts have an emotional side to them as well. Sometimes that emotional side stands out and constitutes the core of the problem. In this chapter I want to focus on counseling that offers help with regard to emotional disturbance. For the sake of clarity I will use the term *psychotherapy* specifically for this type of counseling.

The orderliness and interrelatedness human sensitivity reveals demand and allow for an integral approach to psychotherapy, which, in turn, is fully in keeping with the inner structure of psychotherapy as a process of guiding. To develop this thesis I will first describe the regularities and interrelatedness human sensitivity manifests. Then I will summarize my understanding of the structural features of psychotherapy as a process of guiding. Finally, I will consider how the different modes of therapy are based on these regularities both of our sensitive life and the guiding process, and call for a more integral approach to psychotherapy.

The Sensitive Dimension of Life

The sensitive dimension of life includes such phenomena as sense perception, feelings, emotions, dreams, and so on. These phenomena manifest a certain orderliness or regularity. It is this regularity of the development and function of our sensitive life in its interrelation with all other functioning that researchers and therapists attempt to describe.

Our sensitive way of being in the world involves acting and reacting. Through our sensing we become aware of and seek to determine the sensory configurations that present themselves to us. In our feelings we appraise whether something is pleasant or unpleasant, and respond with like or dislike. In our emotional reactions we live out and express the sensed and felt meaning of an event and respond with joy, excitement, fear, or disgust. Our feeling reactions and our emotional responses constantly accompany our sensory perceptions. When looking at a garden we sense the quiet beauty of a sunny spring morning; we feel the pleasure of being alive and are moved with a joy that may rise to ecstasy. Thus, feelings are immediate, spontaneous, appraising reactions to what we sense. And in the emotions our sensations call forth, we bodily live out and express the meaning of an experience. In this manner our sensing, feeling, and emoting are inseparably related. They constitute the different modes of our sensitivity.

Sense and Perception

Through our sensing we perceive the world around us and its immediate meaning for our existence. It is the world we can see with our eyes and experience in the present moment. The distances we sense, for example, are not those of the road map but the distances bound by our senses. Likewise with regard to our sensory awareness of time, it is the experience of the present moment and not the time of history or future plans. We sense the redness of the cherries that invites us to eat them or the unknown movement in the distance which frightens us.

Sense perception is the immediate, nonreflective awareness of our surroundings. In our sensing we scan the horizon of our immediate environment for meaningful gestalts or configurations. Sensing a movement at the edge of the forest, we cautiously change position so that we can look at it from different angles and determine whether it is the play of the sunlight on the rustling leaves or an approaching animal. Thus we seek to grasp each sensory gestalt in its meaning for our existence.

Given this basic meaning of sense perception, research can direct itself to the development of the structural features that characterize the different types of sensing. In their integral unity, the types of sensing enable us to orient ourselves and to explore and determine the sensory gestalts that present themselves to us.

Unlike animal sensing, human sensing is completely open to the whole range of human activity—thinking, socializing, working, judging, loving, believing. We sense the difference, for example, between a tree and a sculpture in a park and respond accordingly. We sense the presence of a celebrity and the touch of a friend. Our sensing manifests historical and cultural features and is subject to conditioning and learning or lack of nurturing (sensory deprivation). Most important, in our sensing we act as subjects, not as passive objects that merely respond to environmental stimuli. We surrender ourselves in our sensing. With intentionality we actively scan our horizon for sensory meaning or we withdraw and close ourselves off.

Our feeling reactions are direct responses to what we have become aware of and have identified by our sensing. Being aware of something, we experience either pleasure or displeasure, liking or disliking, acceptance or rejection. Thus, to feel is to appraise. When we taste something bitter, we feel repelled. When we are enjoying a hot bath, we feel relaxed. When we experience physical well-being after a good sleep, we are inclined to respond, "I really feel good today!" Or, when we hear about a tragic situation we may react by saying, "That makes me feel sad." Our feeling reactions constantly accompany our sensory perceptions.

Our feelings manifest differences according to the dimension of life to which they are directed. As with sensing, our feelings are completely open to other functions. Depending on our sensitive openness to reality, our feelings are appropriate or inappropriate, balanced and authentic or exaggerated and distorted. Our feelings are not merely instinctual reactions. Rather, they are an integral part of our human response to reality as it is ordered by God.

Body Expression

Emotions are immediate, spontaneous, overwhelming, intense reactions that deeply affect our entire physical and organic functioning. They mobilize us and make us pull away from or move toward someone or something. In our emotions we surrender bodily to how we feel in a particular situation.

Certain sensory gestalts can call forth specific associative memories and as sensory symbols give rise to strong emotional reactions. Thus the sensory image that once horrified us can be reawakened and haunt us through associated images. Unresolved, suppressed primary emotions, for example, that we could not or dared not live out in the past, can be projected onto present sensory images and make us tense with anger or devastated with grief.

Because of their embeddedness in the whole of the personality, human emotions always have varied manifestations. Joy, for example, may be religious joy, the joy of ultimate surrender and entrusting, the joy of commitment and bonding; or aesthetic joy; or the joy of caring for someone or of making something; or the joy of sharing; or the joy of thinking through and solving some problem, and so on. With regard to anger, it may be righteous indignation, or anger about broken promises, or wastefulness, or rejection. We are not merely physical, organic, and sensitive organisms but we are spiritual creatures that respond to the normativity of life in all our functioning. Our emotional reactions are an integral part of our spiritual awareness and response to the norms that govern our lives.

Normativity

Without an awareness of the normativity of life, we cannot judge whether an emotional reaction is appropriate and in keeping with the reality of a given situation. To respond with joy when confronted by hurt and brutality is perverse and abnormal. To react with an outburst of anger when inadvertently passed by in a social gathering is inappropriate and shows suspicion or inordinate neediness. An emotional reaction functions as a foundational moment of a normed, total response and must be evaluated accordingly. Without awareness and acknowledgment of the norms of certainty, troth, justice, stewardship, respect, care, unfolding, style, clarity, and consistency, we cannot know whether an emotional reaction is good or bad, appropriate or inappropriate, normal or abnormal. Our emotions are human emotions, and their very development and structure reveal that they are an integral part of our total response to the normativity of life.

A healthy emotional life requires that a person experience and express the whole range of primary emotions. Interest or excitement, for example, helps us to attend to the new or the necessary. Enjoyment or joy binds us to the familiar and the agreeable and prolongs and enhances contact. Surprise interrupts an ongoing activity and forces us to attend to a new situation. Distress or sorrow enables us to cope with loss or helps us to turn away from the painful. Shame or humiliation inhibits our interest or helps us to turn away from the bad. Contempt or disgust helps us to cope with the poisonous and turn away from the harmful. Fear or terror helps us to become aware of and flee from the threatening and the dangerous. Anger or rage enables us to cope with and confront the hurtful and destructive. All these primary emotions and their variations are essential for responding appropriately to our various life situations.

Preliminary Summary

In summary, through our sensing, feeling, and emoting we are pulled toward or away from things, depending on whether we appraise what we have sensed as appealing or threatening and react to it with the appropriate emotion.

The Biblical View of Personhood

The biblical view of personhood suggests that our sensitive actions and reactions are prerequisite for fulfilling our calling to care for the creation and for one another. Through our sensitivity we come in immediate, vibrant contact with our surroundings and experience in the present moment and their significance for our lives. If we are not open and responsive to reality we tend to distort, deny, or suppress our experiences and engage in selective inattention, rationalization, or projection. Our sensing, feeling, and emoting constitute an essential and inseparable part of our awareness, appraisal, and response to our environment—of coming to know and do the truth with regard to life. Knowing and doing the truth involve the whole person in all dimensions, including the sensitive.

The first way we come to know our environment is through our bodies. Our physical movements and reactions and our organic pulsations orient us and give us a first indication of what our environment is like and what response is required. We shiver from the cold and our stomachs contract with hunger. Our posture and movements reveal who we are and they communicate our intentions. We come to know and do the truth with regard to life first of all by our physical way of being in the world.

The second way we learn to respond appropriately to life is through our sensing, feeling, and emoting. Specifically, in our sensing we become aware of, in our feelings we appraise, and in our emoting we live out the meaning of an event in the immediate moment. When we sense an unjust situation and react with anger, we know in a most basic way the meaning of injustice and are deeply moved to do the right if we are open to reality as normed by God. Without this sensitivity and this experience of frustration and anger, we can easily minimize or ignore the injustice and accommodate ourselves to the situation or compromise our beliefs. To the degree that we do not allow ourselves to be in touch and be emotionally moved by an event and suppress or deny our feelings we tend to distort the reality we face. Suppressing the truth in unbelief and distorting the truth happens in earthy, creaturely ways.

Thus, our sensitivity is an essential foundation for our awareness, evaluation, and response. Our sensitivity undergirds and motivates us in our calling to love God and our neighbor and to understand and care for the creation. Human sensitivity is prerequisite for and an integral part of coming to know and do the truth with regard to life. Knowing and doing involve the whole person in integral unity as a spiritual creature.

The integral function of human sensitivity in the whole of the personality also points out the responsibility we have for the way we express that sensitivity. Our sensing, feeling, and emoting are immediate, spontaneous actions and reactions, but the way we express ourselves sensitively is learned. Our sensitive life is subject to our self-forming, the modeling of our parents and other adults, and the formative influence of our culture. In this formative process we ourselves play a determinative role. We surrender ourselves in sensing, feeling, and emoting, or else we hold back. We are either sensitively open to our environment as it presents itself to us or else we ignore or distort what is there. We react either appropriately or inappropriately in our feelings, reactions, and emotional expressions.

Since our sensitive actions and reactions are not merely instinctual, automatic, or conditioned responses but the expression of our selfhood and the result of our self-forming, we bear responsibility for the way we act and react. In other words, human sensitivity as embedded in and expressive of the whole of the personality is always a part of a normed activity. We are called to surrender ourselves to our sensing, feeling, and emoting; we are called to be open and receptive to what we perceive and to react authentically and appropriately, in order that we may know and do the truth. The words *surrender, open, receptive, authentic,* and *appropriate* give us an idea of the God-given norm for human sensitivity and our calling with regard to the formation of our sensitive life. Our sense perceptions ought to be in keeping with the identity of things and our feelings, and emotions ought to be oriented to reality. Thus, the identity of things, the true state of affairs, and the norms for life (certainty, troth, justice, and the like) determine whether or not our sense perceptions are truthful and our feelings and emotions are appropriate. If not, our responsibility is to grow, to change, to mature, or, if there has been maldevelopment, to seek the healing and renurturing of our sensitive life.

Some Structural Features of Psychotherapy

Psychotherapy can be seen as a particular kind of human form-giving or the exercising formative influence over one of more dimensions of a person's life. Child rearing, schooling, and the learning of a particular skill or craft are other examples of human form-giving. They involve the development and the nurturing of the various ways of human functioning.

In distinction from the different forms of education, counseling, including psychotherapy, involves a relearning or a renurturing. Relearning is necessary because of some kind of malfunction, disturbance, inability, conflict, or repression which affects the entire personality. For whatever reasons, there is an inability to live out God's good order for life. The different kinds of counseling offer guidance with regard to the normativity of life and offer clients help in regaining physical or emotional health. Counseling, therefore, always presupposes that clients find themselves in situations in which they no longer wish to be. They want to change, heal, integrate, or resolve their present condition and they look for help or guidance in this process of relearning. Old ways of functioning or responding must be unlearned and new ways must be mastered. Thus, counseling offers people help in learning to follow God's good order for life.

In this context, psychotherapy can be described as the renurturing and reintegrating of a person's emotional life. Psychotherapy offers clients help in learning to live out God's norm for their sensitive functioning, namely, the call to be sensitively open to all experience as ordered by God's Word and to respond appropriately to that which is sensed.

There are a number of structural features that seem to characterize all forms of psychotherapy as well as other kinds of teaching and learning.

First, human form-giving, including the reforming of a person's sensitive life, involves a process of differentiation, individuation, and harmonization. The child is born as a sensitive creature but depends entirely on the modeling and guidance of the parents to unfold or differentiate that given potentiality so that it can take on its specific individuality, and become an integral part of the child's other ways of being in the world. Likewise with regard to the renurturing of a person's sensitive life, the potentiality is given. The therapist's task is to help the client become more sensitively open and to learn to respond more appropriately to present situations. This renurturing involves a process comparable to the original formation of the child's sensitivity.

Second, human forming involves the use of certain methods or techniques. In child rearing we take a particular approach to help the child achieve maturity. These means or ways of guiding either help us to achieve the goal or they frustrate us and lead us astray. In the case of psychotherapy the approach we take and the methods we employ prove helpful depending on whether or not they are in keeping with the nature of human sensitivity and whether or not they are expressive of the other features of human forming.

Third, human forming involves a coordinate, correlative, or cooperative relationship and actions. From the very beginning the child is a subject who is called to surrender to the guidance offered. If there is to be healthful unfolding and maturing, parents intuit that they must appeal to their children's personal responsibilities and seek their active cooperation. With regard to psychotherapy, clients must renurture their emotional lives. Opening themselves up to God's good order for emotional well-being and surrendering themselves to this calling is a personal, conscious, willful, and subjective activity. No one can dissolve their defensive and inappropriate ways of reacting for them. Psychotherapy finds its limits in the freedom and responsibility of the client as a unified, centered, spiritual being—as a subject active in his or her own behalf. In this light, providing therapy and seeking emotional well-being are truly correlative activities that require mutual respect, equality, and cooperation.

Finally, human forming involves purposeful "forming unto" or "according to," in which our vision and way of life play a directing and integrating role. When we nurture and guide a child, we let ourselves be guided, consciously or subconsciously, by what we consider healthy development and maturity. In the case of psychotherapy, our guiding reveals our view of emotional well-being and integration and our view of human life as a whole. There is direction and purpose to the guidance we provide and our clients experience our view of human nature as it directs and gives perspective to the therapy we provide.

Preliminary Summary

In summary, human forming, including psychotherapy, is characterized by the facilitating and guiding of an unfolding process that results in a differentiation, individuation, and harmonization of given potentialities by means of appropriate methods or techniques within a correlative and cooperative relationship with a view to a certain goal. Whichever approach to or mode of therapy we look at, these characteristic features are highlighted.

Therapeutic Methods or Techniques

Many therapists consider the question of which therapeutic approach or method to adopt a matter of personal preference or choice. Others advocate an eclectic approach using whatever methods seem most appropriate for a particular client. It is difficult to move beyond personal preferences and eclecticism in deciding which therapeutic techniques to use. However, if we approach psychotherapy from the viewpoint of the regularities of our sensitive functioning and human guidance, then a number of criteria for evaluating the relative merits of the different modes of therapy emerge.

A particular therapeutic approach or technique constitutes the technical means by which a therapeutic climate is created and the therapeutic process is facilitated. Carl Rogers, for example, uses a nonjudgmental, genuine, warm, and empathetic attitude and responses to create a safe environment which encourages clients to explore and become conscious of their feelings. Rogers uses a nondirective, client-centered, person-to-person approach. He has no other methods apart from this way of responding to clients. Fritz Perls's method, in comparison, consists of challenging clients to develop uninterrupted awareness or a clear gestalt of their present feelings in order to find creative solutions to their unfinished emotional conflicts. Confrontation, interruption, encouraging the client to speak in "I" sentences, staying with present feelings and perceptions, role playing, imagining, and pursuing and resolving polar opposites constitute Perls's therapeutic technique for developing clear gestalts.

Each school of therapy has developed its own specific techniques for facilitating emotional well-being and integration based on its particular view of human sensitivity, emotional disturbance, and relearning.

Criteria

Confronted by the array of techniques the various schools of therapy advocate, there are two fundamental criteria we can use in evaluating the relative merits of the different methods. First, with regard to the regularities of human guidance—the pedagogical norm—we can ask: What view of learning does this particular method embody?

To illustrate, Carl Rogers insists upon a total self-discovery method of learning. Certain forms of behavior therapy, in contrast, making use of a system of rewards and punishments, are almost entirely therapist directed. Many other methods embody views of learning that can be placed on a continuum between these two poles of client self-discovery and therapist-directed learning.

Contrary to a common view (Ausubel and Robinson 1969), however, the key question to be asked is not whether a particular technique embodies a self-discovery or a therapist-directed view of learning, or a more "balanced" view. Rather, the basic question is whether or not a specific method in some way allows for personal involvement and responsibility and fosters a correlative and cooperative relationship. Carl Jung, for example, encouraged his clients during the course of their therapy not merely to talk about their dreams but to paint what they had dreamt about in order to encourage their personal and active involvement and independence in resolving their life conflicts and in developing inner harmony. In this emphasis on active participation Jung struggled with the correlative nature of forming that involves the self-forming of the client.

In view of this pedagogical criterion, the more preferable methods would seem to be those in which the therapist sees his or her task as the guiding and facilitating of the client's self-therapy. Thus, a high level of therapist and client involvement would seem optimal. In short, the first question we can ask with regard to any method is whether or not a particular therapeutic approach or technique in some way appeals to and develops the client's responsibility in self-forming.

The second criterion has to do with the focus of our forming, namely, our sensitive way of functioning. Influencing others, if it is not to be an expression of arbitrary power or absolute control, not only requires a genuine person-to-person relationship but also a therapeutic method that is in keeping with the regularities of human sensitivity. In psychotherapy, both the therapist and the client direct themselves to the arrested, repressed, or disturbed aspects of the client's sensitive life. Thus, the second series of questions we can ask with regard to the different methods is: What structural aspect of our sensitive development and way of functioning does this particular technique make use of, and does it do so in isolation or in relation to all the other aspects of our sensitive life? Does this technique help harmonize our feelings with the whole of our personality or does it tend to deal with feelings and emotions in isolation?

A few examples may illustrate the point. Carl Rogers's method of creating a free and safe environment is entirely geared to encourage clients to break through their defenses so that they can come to grips with their suppressed feelings. The Rogerian therapist's communication of genuineness, warmth, regard, and empathy helps clients break through their defenses. In making use of these attitudes and feelings as a therapeutic method Rogers attempts to recreate the emotional climate necessary for healthy development in early childhood—feelings of safety, trust, and independence based on provisions for attachment, sustenance, and exploration. It becomes apparent that Rogers has taken hold of only one characteristic feature of our sensitive way of functioning, namely, the conditions or climate necessary for healthy development.

When we compare Fritz Perls's method to that of Carl Rogers the difference is striking. Perls takes hold of a fundamental moment of sense perception, namely, the figure-ground phenomenon that he considers to be characteristic of all forms of sensing. Out of the ground of a myriad of images, sounds, and odors, we focus our attention on one particular image in order to satisfy some basic need. More than anyone else, Perls has underscored how our anxieties interfere with our ability to form clear sense perceptions. Consequently, if a client can be challenged and helped to develop an uninterrupted, clear awareness or gestalt of an anxiety-producing experience, including the strong emotions it evokes, some anxiety is dissolved and some new sensitive openness to experience is generated. Thus, Perls's primary method makes use of the structural possibility to form clear, uninterrupted sense perceptions in the immediate present.

Since Perls's basic technique was developed in reference to one structural feature of human sensing, he had to develop a number of additional methods to deal with the emotional anxiety of clients, helping them to break through their defenses and explore their repressed feelings. Rogers, however, does not provide us with any additional techniques for dissolving the client's disturbed sensing, feeling, and emoting and for harmonizing the sensitive life into the whole of the personality. These changes, he assumes, will take place automatically if the therapeutic climate is sufficiently free and safe.

Some further comparisons may be helpful. Alexander Lowen, in his bioenergetics or body therapy, makes use of the structural given that emotional responses involve total bodily reactions. Through specific physical exercises clients are encouraged to let go of chronic muscular tensions that are an integral part of their defense against anxious feelings. By means of a process of tension and relaxation this physical and psychic armor is broken through.

This method usually releases strong feelings, allowing clients to dissolve chronically suppressed emotions and to learn new responses to their life situations. For the analytic or interpretative part of his therapy Lowen relies heavily on his psychoanalytic training. Other bioenergetic therapists make use of whatever other therapeutic modality they have been trained in for the interpretative and directive side of their counseling.

While bioenergetics and other body therapies make use of the close interaction between our sensitive and physical-organic functioning, different cognitive therapies like rational-emotive therapy or transactional analysis appeal to the interrelation between our sensitive and analytical functioning. Art therapies, in contrast, by means of music, dance, painting, sculpturing, or drama, appeal to the emotionally symbolic meaning different colors, forms, sounds, and actions have for us as a result of childhood experiences.

Eclectic or Integral?

It appears that every characteristic feature of our sensitive life has given rise to a particular technique for evoking and working through unresolved emotional conflicts. Since each method is integrally related to a therapist's view of human nature, most therapists present their method as the only or the most successful method. These claims have given rise to many competing and conflicting schools of therapy. However, if we see each method as an attempt to make the most of a specific structural feature of our psychic functioning, then each method is of importance and becomes complementary to all other methods.

Such an approach allows us to develop an integral technique in which different methods are blended together to form one unified and consistent approach. As it is now, the various methods are the exclusive domain of radically different and opposing therapies (see fig. 1).

The different methods in this diagram can be incorporated in one unified and integral approach. It is possible to do so in more than an eclectic way or by means of addition because the various dimensions of life constitute an integral unity, which in turn is reflected in the unity of the different moments of our sensitive life. For example, the moment of "openness," "trusting," "surrender," or "risking" anticipates and reflects on a psychic level our common tendency to entrust ourselves to what we believe to be the ultimate meaning of life. Thus there is an integral unity of emotional trust and ultimate trust or surrender. We cannot have one without the other. A mature faith life requires a mature emotional life. Likewise within the psychic dimension, the moment of entrusting ourselves opens up all the other moments of our sensitive life. When we are sensitively open to all experience without reservations and defenses, we can sense and express what we feel, and experience our emotions fully in appropriate ways.

Figure 1

Various Therapeutic Methods

Dimensions of Human Life	Therapeutic Methods Dealing with Emotional Disturbance in Terms of One or More Dimensions of Life
Ultimates of Life; Belief; Values; Meaning	Existentialist Therapy; Humanistic Therapy; Logotherapy; Christian Therapies
Symbolic; Playful; Imaginative, Suggestive	Art Therapies; Psychodrama; Play Therapy
Intentional; Formative; Habitual	Will Therapy; Reality Therapy; Behavior Therapy
Cognitive; Analytical; Discerning; Remembering	Psychoanalysis; Rational-Emotive Therapy; Transactional Analysis
Psychic; Sense Perception; Feelings; Emotional	Gestalt Therapy; Rogerian Therapy; Primal Therapy
Physical; Organic; Visceral Organs; Muscular System; Posture; Body Types	Body Therapies; Bioenergetics; Bio-Feedback
Interpersonal	Group Therapy; Family Therapy

The different schools of therapy and the various methods they employ make use of this inherent unity. What we are proposing, however, is that we relate our therapeutic technique to every moment of our sensitive life and, implicitly, to every dimension of our experience instead of one or two. In the development of such an integral therapeutic technique, the primary characteristics of our sensing, feeling, and emoting as described in the section on human sensitivity can be our guide and criterion.

Integral Techniques

Given the physical and organic basis of our sensitive life, the bodily living through of what we sense and feel, some physical movement, gesture, expression, posture, or sound will constitute the first or foundational moment of an integral therapeutic method. There can be little awareness, resolving, and renurturing if we do not actively experience our anxiety-provoking emotions within the therapeutic setting. For that to happen there must be some heightening of the client's physical and organic functioning so that repressed and anxious sensations, feelings, and emotions will be evoked. This moment of movement or emoting of our sensitive life suggests that we involve our clients in some physical activity or expression.

However, the physical and organic movements or expressions must be grasped in their emotional significance. It is not sufficient to engage the client in some physical exercises, encouraging him to make certain sounds or to breathe more deeply. The psychic meaning of the physical and organic events must become evident to the client, for we are dealing with the physical basis of our sensitive life or the emotional meaning of physical expressions. Thus the therapist can ask, "How does it feel?"

Emotional awareness of the physical and organic events calls for a broader cognitive understanding as well if there is to be a conscious integration of repressed feelings. The client needs to become his or her own analyst for there is a discerning dimension to human sensitivity that wants to be incorporated in our various ways of conscious knowing. To aid this process we can ask, "What do you make of that?"

The fourth moment that we can incorporate in an integral technique is the formative or intentional moment and the awareness of the habitual side of emotional reactions. Sensitive expressions manifest a certain form and tend to be repeated once learned. The question to be asked is, "Can you let yourself experience that again?", and perhaps later on in the session or the course of therapy, "Can you do that again and let yourself feel that again, but this time can you react differently to that experience?"

Our sensitive life also anticipates and reflects our symbolic way of responding to life. To bring out this symbolic moment we can ask our clients, "What does this remind you of?" or, "Does this suggest anything to you?" or, "Can you act that out or give expression to that in some way?"

Anxious sensations, feelings, and emotions are usually repressed and require conscious awareness through understanding, expression, and communication. However, allowing oneself to become consciously aware of long-standing, habitual patterns of reacting requires a lot of trust and surrender. To aid the process of becoming aware and of dissolving we can incorporate the entrusting or certitudinal moment in our technique. We can ask our clients at specific times, "Can you surrender to that feeling?" or, "Can you give in to that emotion?" or, "Can you let go?" or, "Can you let yourself experience that emotion without holding back?"

Three Additional Dimensions

There are other aspects of our psychic life that we have not referred to, but this brief description of the physical, emotional, cognitive, formative, communicative, symbolic, and certitudinal moments may be sufficient to illustrate how we can develop a unified and integral therapeutic technique. A number of other dimensions that underlie these core moments call for our attention, namely, the developmental, the interpersonal, and the ultimate meaning dimensions.

Awareness of the developmental dimension will continually make the therapist and the client move from the present to the past and to the future. Maldevelopment, particularly at the early stages of emotional development and at critical periods in life, needs to be "repaired." To complete some of the incomplete gestalts of childhood, the client can be encouraged to regress and go back in time. Regression, however, must be followed by progression, that is, by a process of relearning in the present and by developing an openness toward the future if new patterns are to develop. Particular physical and organic activities will tend to put a client in touch with sensations and habitual emotional reactions that have come about as a result of childhood trauma. Basing our technique in physical and organic movements and expressions will bring this developmental side to the fore. Questions like, "Do you remember feeling anything like that before?" and "Can you respond differently to that situation now?" tend to bring out this developmental side.

We live in relation. This dimension of human life also comes to expression and can be utilized in the process of therapy. The communication and sharing of feelings that we referred to earlier is one side of this dimension. The personal relationship with the therapist or a group represents this interpersonal and communal side of life and can be utilized accordingly. We can ask the client, "Experiencing this, how do you feel toward me or the group right now?" The integration of feelings and the renurturing of emotional reactions toward others presents still another side of our communal way of being in the world.

Finally, the ultimate meaning or guiding dimension of the therapeutic process calls for our attention. The questions about the ultimates of life are never far away from any therapy session. "Why did this happen to me?" "Why should I re-experience this despair?" "Is there any reason to do so?" "Is there any hope?" "Can I really start over?" Or clients may ask, "How can life be different?" "What is fair and just?" "Are commitment and love really possible?" "Can one really care?" Vision and way-of-life questions tend to permeate, direct, and integrate the entire therapeutic process.

Throughout this description we have illustrated our approach by questions that started with "Can you . . . ?" "How do you . . . ?" "Will you . . . ?" This form was chosen to illustrate concretely how the pedagogical norm can come to expression in our technique. The regularities of human forming call us to form and guide in such a way that it evokes and involves the self-forming and the reguiding of the client. In this way clients remain free to respond from out of their own inner selfhood. Genuine change requires that clients be personally involved in the therapeutic process. The following diagram (see fig. 2) illustrates the proposed therapeutic method.

Figure 2

Toward an Integral Therapeutic Method

Moments of our sensitive life in reference to all other dimensions:	Forming that leads to self-forming
The entrusting or certitudinal moment	"Can you surrender to that feeling?" "Can you give in?"
The symbolic moment	"What does this remind you of?" "Can you act that out?"
The communicative moment	"Can you say that once more and look at me?"
The formative moment	"Can you let yourself experience that again?" "Can you react differently?"
The cognitive moment	"What do you make of that?"
Sensations, feelings, emotions	"How does it feel?" "What are you aware of?"
Physical and organic movement or expression	"Can you do this?" "Can you express that in some way?"
The developmental dimension:	"Do you remember feeling like that before?"
The interrelational dimension:	"How do you feel toward me?"
The ultimate meaning dimension:	"Why?" "How?" "Is there?"

In this presentation I have limited myself to a description of the modes and techniques of therapy to illustrate my main thesis. However, the other dimensions of therapy, namely, the types of emotional disturbance, the process and goal of therapy, the interrelationship between therapist and client, the integrating vision of life, and the organizational structure of therapy as a social institution show a similar integral picture manifesting the orderliness and integration of our sensitive way of being in the world and of human formation.

Reference

DeGraaff, A. H., and H. H. Olthuis. 1978. *Toward a biblical view of man: Some readings.* Toronto: Institute for Christian Studies.

4

Christian Counseling and Human Needs

Edward W. C. McAllister

The counselor who desires to integrate Christian teaching and psychological theory has the opportunity to use the truths of God's perception of reality. These truths are those that are specifically revealed in Scripture and those that are learned from God's created world, fallen though it may be. Since God is complete, what he has said is in harmony with what he has made. Collins (1977, 152) claims that an integrated approach is based upon one major premise: *God exists and is the source of all truth.* A corollary is derived from this: *Man, who exists, can know the truth.* Carter and Narramore (1979, 103) indicate that since humanity has fallen and therefore God's image in us has been affected, "the integrationist does not assume that all the truth claims made by psychologists are valid." Neither can it be assumed that all interpretations of Scripture are infallible. If humans can discover, through observation and research, some of the basic aspects of their nature and behavior, these should not be in disagreement with what God says to us in the Bible. If a conflict exists, and we are sure of what God has said, God is the authority. As integration develops, these conflicts should be few.

The Bible does not claim that Christians are immune from psychological problems. As Schaeffer (1971, 132) affirms:

> Let us be clear about this. All men since the fall have had some psychological problems. It is utter nonsense, a romanticism that has nothing to do

with biblical Christianity, to say that a Christian never has psychological problems. All men have psychological problems. They differ in degree and they differ in kind, but since the fall, all men have more or less a problem psychologically.

Some of the problems that humans experience come from the fact that we have fallen bodies that are not functioning as they should physiologically. Other problems may relate to our spiritual search for meaning in life. Still other problems may reside in a person's mind or thought processes and be caused by a misunderstanding of the world because of inadequate conceptual schema. Since a person is a unity or a whole, the best way to approach the problem may not be immediately known. In counseling and psychotherapy there can exist a variety of opinions among equally committed believers regarding the best approach—even among integrationists. Carter and Narramore (1979) state:

> At first glance this seems surprising. Shouldn't Christian therapists who are committed to the authority of Scripture be able to agree on one general model of counseling? Isn't the Bible sufficiently precise to show us *the* biblical approach to counseling?
>
> As desirable as this may be, for a variety of reasons, we doubt that this will happen. To begin with, the nature of people's adjustment problems dictates the counseling style that will be most helpful. Short-term directive counseling is ready made for a variety of situational problems and certain personalities. Long-term therapy may be very helpful for others. Behavioral methods are clearly successful in relieving a variety of symptoms. And many people respond well to nondirective counseling. The variety of effective therapeutic styles suggests that no one counseling methodology will serve all purposes.
>
> Jesus demonstrated a very flexible approach to other people's problems. (113–14)

The counselor, therefore, should examine all aspects of functioning. He or she may refer a client to medical experts if it appears that the problem comes from the physical level. He or she assesses the client's relationship with God to determine the client's spiritual orientation. Finally, using clinical methods, the counselor tries to discover the thoughts of the client that direct the client's behavior and feelings. In many cases, the counselor may have to work simultaneously with all three aspects. As medical treatment can bring "substantial healing" to the body, counseling can bring "substantial healing" to the mind (Schaeffer 1971, 132). Biblical or psychological counseling can certainly contribute greatly to a person's well-being, but the integrated approach recognizes that special revelation does not deal with every problem that the counselor faces in practice. In addition to biblical principles, the integrationist recognizes that God has placed people in a world of general revelation (Ps. 19; Rom. 1:18–20; 2:14–15). It is our responsibility to use both general and special revelation to fulfill the goal God has set for our lives.

Counseling is an activity composed of three interlocking dimensions: content/theory; technique/process; organization/institution. The *content/theory dimension* encompasses that conceptual orientation which the counselor uses to define the goals and objectives of the counseling process and through which the counselor "hears" the client and comes to understand the client's dilemma. The *technique/process dimension* involves the way the counselor chooses to interact with the client. This interaction includes listening style, type of questions asked, and other related factors. Counselors with the same theoretical orientation may counsel with different types of techniques and those using similar techniques may have different content/theory orientations. The *organization/institution dimension* is made up of those parameters that are defined by the particular organization or institution in which a counselor works. Such factors may include guidelines for intake sessions, scheduling of appointments, places of meeting, record keeping, and other practical issues.

Basic Human Needs

Vernon Grounds has listed a series of human needs that he believes both psychology and theology have addressed from their respective data bases and that are applicable to understanding people. This list can provide a content/theoretical basis for practice in counseling. Since these needs can be considered from both a theological and psychological perspective, using such a list of needs leads to the development of a counseling system that uses the fundamental assumptions of the integrative position, namely, that all truth is God's truth (Carter 1980) and acknowledges that the scientific method and its data are available to the Christian counselor as he or she seeks to integrate this data with information from the Bible (Cosgrove and Mallory 1977, 13).

The basic needs of humans identified by Grounds are as follows:

1. Meaning
2. Forgiveness
3. Courage
4. Love
5. Community
6. Power to cope
7. Hope

Both the Bible and the writings of psychologists have made extensive and profound statements regarding these human needs. The integrationist brings the contributions of both areas into the existential arena of counseling where the people involved, through the working of the Holy Spirit, can jointly move toward a fuller understanding of God's will for each life. While these are needs of all people, the integrationist should find them particularly useful as both psychology and theology have addressed such issues. In order to explore these possibilities, further consideration of these needs is useful.

The Need for Meaning

Ligon (1942) pointed out that achieving purpose or meaning in life is one of the best ways to promote healthy-mindedness. He believed that the explanation for this was that a sense of meaning brings about integration in a person's life. Powell (1975) writes:

> In the wake of the industrial revolution, man somehow slowly lost the ability to relate this skill and knowledge to the progress of mankind, to the skill, knowledge, and efforts of other men. His own work and person became devalued in his own eyes. He began to lose a sense of meaning and importance of his own life. And once the sense of inner worth and outer meaning go out of a man, all real values and sense of dedication also go . . . man not only loses a reason to live and a reason to die, he loses all appreciation and sense of himself. (39–40)

When a person adopts this particular attitude, life seems absurd and incomprehensible, causing "symptoms" that may lead to counseling. In some cases, a client will have perceptively noted that the need for meaning contributes to his or her problems. Powell and Ruitenbeck (1964) have noted the common relationship between work and meaning. Unemployment often triggers the search for meaning since work has often temporarily supplied meaning to a person's life. The Christian therapist may find the client open to the possibility of turning to Jesus Christ to meet the need for meaning. Tournier (1976) points out that we all share in the divine adventure of doing something useful, which has meaning in the bringing forth of fruit (John 15:5). Life is in us allowing our fruits of work—all we do, feel, think, and believe—to ripen in us (Tournier 1976, 236). The ultimate solution to the search for meaning in life is to obey God. Clinebell (1979, 116–17) points out that a viable belief system concerning the purpose of existence helps provide a foundation of meaning and that a meaningful future is a central motivation for growth. A foundation need of each person is a need for meaning that is internalized and not subject to change due to environmental variables.

The Need for Forgiveness

Each person must answer the question, "What do I do with my guilt?" The counselor is likely to meet people with differing problems related to forgiveness and guilt. The questions that come immediately to mind are: What is guilt? From where does guilt come? Anna Freud believed that the superego develops through an internalizing of the moral values shown to the person by people with whom that person identifies. This developmental process allows the person to internalize a sense of right and wrong. When the person's behavior transgresses these internalized moral values, internally produced anxiety results in guilt feelings (Muuss 1968, 26–27). Sigmund Freud believed that guilt becomes a factor in neurosis when it is false or unrealistic. This is basically a result of oversocialization. A person internalizes a value structure that cannot realistically operate in accord with his behavior. This results in the repression of basic energies which cause guilt problems for the individual.

The key implication of this concept is that guilt is a feeling unrelated to the real world. The feeling of anxiety present is because of what the person wants to *do*, not because of what he *did*. The solution, therefore, is to release the person from these feelings by weakening the overly strict superego to allow proper balance and ego control. This viewpoint is particularly appealing because it sounds so logical. It sounds logical because of the assumption that the internalized rules are solely a result of the process of interacting with those with whom the person identifies. It can be seen, therefore, that different people internalize different moral structures because they identify with different types of people. The all-encompassing success of this concept in our culture has left a legacy of conviction that, in fact, moral values are relative and involved in the emotional areas of development. As Mowrer (1961, 20) explains:

> The resolution of a conflict between instinct and moral scruple by means of repression is thus unstable and debilitating and from this it followed, reasonably enough, that the sovereign aim of therapy was to undo repression and permit sexual and hostile impulses to find freer, less encumbered routes to gratification. Such a program called upon the psychoanalyst to align himself with and to speak for the instincts, in opposition to the moral or pseudomoral forces within the personality which have instituted the repression.

Some counselors have tried to show their clients that they have no guilt and hence need no forgiveness. These counselors try to show their clients that their guilt is self-constructed and that they only need to reevaluate their own moral perspectives to redefine matters so that they can eliminate their guilt. While some clients may, in fact, have inappropriate guilt feelings, they must also face up to the possibility of true moral guilt and seek forgiveness from God and other people. As Mowrer (1961, 100) writes:

> Now is the moral law less demanding than civil and criminal codes? Does conscience have less rectitude than a court? Unless we answer the question affirmatively, it follows that in the moral realm, no less than in law, confession is not enough and must be accompanied by restitution. This possibility has been greatly neglected in our time and may account for widespread confusions and misdirected therapeutic and redemptive effort.

For the Christian counselor, Christianity can become directly involved in counseling. Through the atoning action of Jesus Christ, the client can deal with real moral guilt through repentance, forgiveness, and belief. Mowrer (1961, 191) quotes from Dietrich Bonhoeffer's *Life Together* where he relates release from guilt and sin to the community in the church:

> "Confess your faults one to another" (James 5:16). He who is alone with his sin is utterly alone. It may be that Christians, notwithstanding corporate worship, common prayer, and all their fellowship in service, may still be left to their loneliness. The final breakthrough to fellowship does not occur because, though they have fellowship with one another as believers and as devout people, they do not have fellowship as the undevout, as sinners. The pious fellowship permits no one to be a sinner. So everybody must conceal his sin from himself and from the fellowship. We dare not be sinners. Many Christians are unthinkably horrified when a real sinner is suddenly discovered among the righteous. So we remain alone with our sin, living in lies and hypocrisy. The fact is that we are sinners! (110)
>
> In confession the breakthrough to community takes place. Sin demands to have a man by himself. It withdraws him from the community. The more isolated a person is, the more destructive will be the power of sin over him, and the more deeply he becomes involved in it, the more disastrous is his isolation. Sin wants to remain unknown. It shuns the light. In the darkness of the unexpressed, it poisons the whole being of a person. This can happen even in the midst of a pious community. In confession, the light of the Gospel breaks into the darkness and seclusion of the heart. The sin must be brought into the light. The unexposed must be openly spoken and acknowledged. All that is secret and hidden is made manifest. It is a hard struggle until the sin is openly admitted. But God breaks the gates of brass and bars of iron (Ps. 107:16). (112)

The church and the psychologist are closely related in dealing with the client who is struggling with guilt and doubt about moral values. Through faith, guilt can be forgiven. The client must accept this through a mature understanding of who Jesus Christ was and what he did. The counselor must exercise great care in this area to determine the status of the client. If the client is, in fact, guilty and needs forgiveness, then action must be taken to begin the process. The client must try to re-establish the relationships involved, be they human to human or human to God. Involved in this process will be an attempt to actively repair the damage done in relationships. Action may also be necessary to set right environmental factors. Finally, the client must ask for and receive forgiveness as the basis for re-establishing any relationship.

For some clients, the problem might involve the granting of forgiveness. It is not uncommon to hear a client say, "I just can't forgive. . . ." Yet, the Bible makes it clear that to be the kind of persons that Christ would have us be, we must forgive (Eph. 4:32; Col. 3:13). It may, in fact, be that the client finds it very difficult to forgive another person for some action. However, God has forgiven us our transgressions and, in like manner, we are to forgive others. We have a need not only to be forgiven but also to forgive. By not forgiving, clients are injuring themselves, for they are not allowing themselves to have the kinds of relationships that people need to have. Lack of forgiveness may lead to far more harm for clients than the harm done to them by others. Counselors must carefully explore the sources of an inability to forgive.

Finally, there are those who have difficulty in accepting the forgiveness of others. This may be a problem of pride. The client refuses to accept the fact that someone else could forgive him or her because he or she has been so "bad" that no one could be "good" enough to forgive him or her. Perhaps this is why it is helpful to recognize a completely guiltless and perfect man personally gave his life up in a painful and bloody death to allow us to re-establish a relationship with God. We must acknowledge Christ's death as a payment for our sins; when we accept God's forgiveness of us, we learn how to accept others' forgiveness.

Others have difficulty with forgiveness because they believe that God is punishing them. They confuse the process of living and learning—the road of discipline—with punishment for unforgiven sin. The Bible points out that God will discipline us but he will not punish those whom he has already forgiven (Rom. 8:28–30; Heb. 12:4–13). Discipline is necessary for our future (Jer. 12:5), not to punish us for our past.

The Need for Courage

There is a need for courage in life to overcome anxiety. Vernon Grounds (1976) writes that "Christians, unfortunately, are not automatically exempt from the anxiety which troubles their non-Christian contemporaries. The undeniable fact is that some Christians seem to worry just as much as worried non-Christians" (24–25). In particular, a person needs courage to face three basic areas of anxiety and fear.

Courage to face situational fear

We have all faced situations that have required courage. It is not easy to convince a client to believe that he or she has the resource of courage. Yet without the courage to move onward in daily life, the client will be in need of continual counseling. We all have experiences where anxiety has frozen us in inaction. In order to live as God would have us, we must have the courage to follow his will for us.

Situational fears may be one of the areas where psychology has been most helpful. Situational fear is a persistent and irrational fear that causes a person to avoid certain social situations or objects. Various well-documented procedures have been developed for dealing with various neurotic phobia (e.g., Lazurus 1971).

Courage to face neurotic anxiety

Jourard (1974, 99) states that "anxiety differs from fear in that with the latter one can see the source of the danger, and can, perhaps, cope with it by combat or flight." When people cannot escape from anxiety or cope with it, they may develop neurotic life-styles. When the anxiety becomes strong, the person falls back into a limited mode of functioning, withdrawing from the world to a position where functioning is possible. This is not a place where the creative powers in us can develop. Tillich (1952) has written of the need for the "courage to be" in order to develop a healthy personality. Some anxiety is necessary for growth. As Tillich (1952) has discussed, it is often necessary for a person to have someone who can encourage him or her to face life.

Courage to face existential anxiety

The courage to face existential anxiety comes from the answers that God has given us about life and death. This area is the one in which psychology is least prepared to provide answers. The need for courage relates to our needs for meaning and love. The Bible provides a framework of answers to the basic questions of existence. The counselor and the client may not fully understand all the factors in this enterprise, but there is sufficient revelation to provide real answers and real courage for real anxiety. Working with clients in this area is likely to involve the counselor and the client in mutual learning. The counselor may, in fact, serve as a role model for the client in this area. The Christian counselor has answers that many secular counselors do not. Adams (1977, 413–25) suggests that the source of courage and the answer to fear is love. He points us to 1 John 4:18 to see that perfect love drives out fear. The love of God has provided an eternal answer to the existential anxiety of humanity. Love is to be the source of our courage in living.

The Need for Love

Every person has the need to be loved. Many clients seek out a counselor because the withdrawal of love has caused them to question the very meaning of existence. They seek out counseling because they have symptoms of low self-esteem, anxiety in interpersonal relationships, and, perhaps, questions regarding the nature of their heavenly Father. People must see that God loved them so much that he provided the solution to their existential anxieties. God sent his Son so that humanity might be in fellowship with him (Gal. 2:20). By example, God showed that love is self-giving and moves toward others.

Once a person has recognized that he or she is the object of love, that person must learn to express himself or herself as the agent of love. A person, as a created imager of God, has a basic need to love. This has been warped by the fall but the need to love still exists. While God is by nature love (1 John 4:16), a person has a motivational predisposition to love. All people show love to some degree. Perhaps it is only some small and obscure object that the person loves, but the love is there. To live a full life one must love God and others.

The Need for Community

Humans are social and desire to escape from loneliness. This trait is another that reflects their created nature. People were created by God to have fellowship with him. Although fallen, people still show this trait in seeking out others. Many clients who come to see a counselor are lonely. They feel rejected by others. They are afraid to establish social relationships. They believe that they are of so little worth that others do not want to associate with them. The counselor's greatest resource in working with such clients is (or should be) the church. The church is, or at least should be, a caring community. The Bible teaches that each person has gifts that God will use in the fulfillment of his purpose. These gifts and talents are to come together in a corporate body called the church. Counselors should be able to refer their clients to a church where they will be accepted and loved. In this community they should be able to learn that others do, in fact, care for them and that they are able to care for others. Unfortunately, not all churches are functioning in ways so that this can happen. Yet some churches have established a ministry to their people through small group Bible studies, fellowship groups, prayer and praise gatherings, and are actively reaching out into their community to incorporate all people. People need the church and the church needs people. Too many people believe that all they need is to hear a sermon on television. This only fosters the impersonal and does not allow the opportunity to express real love to another person, to receive acceptance from a group, or to share the difficulties of living with other Christians. Counselors should be alert to recognize that the church could provide a valuable therapeutic environment for their clients.

The Need for Power to Cope

Vernon Grounds (1976) writes:

> People have problems. No statement is more trite than that, yet no statement is more tragically true. Without exception, people have problems. All of us who belong to the human race are sinful creatures living East of Eden in a world under God's curse. Frail as well as fallen, and fallen as well as frail, we are exposed to error, pain, failure, tragedy and death. Life has its joys, to be sure, its experiences of delight and ecstasy; but life is also plagued and blighted by loneliness, disease, hate, depression, boredom, anxiety, grief, inferiority and despair. (17)

What we need in this world is the power to cope with that which comes our way. Coping is a process of contending with the world in such a way as to maintain a healthy level of adjustment. Fundamentally, most clients seek out a counselor because they believe that they lack this power to cope with their problems. They come to a counselor hoping that somehow, by some magic, perhaps the counselor will be able to supply the answers that will allow them to cope with life. They do not wish to be totally adjusted. They only wish a little help, a way to cope with the problems of life that are about to overwhelm them. This is, I believe, the most difficult of tasks in counseling. The counselor, in fact, has no such magic wand to wave to supply the power to cope. Only by working together can the counselor and client attempt to resolve the difficulties that the client must face. Yet identifying this as a key problem area allows the counselor to marshall his skills and to seek the aid of the Holy Spirit in developing coping mechanisms.

The Need for Hope

Although this need is discussed last, it may well be the first that the counselor must help the client meet. The client must see that there is hope. No matter how dark the way looks, no matter how deep the pit seems to be, no matter how complicated the situation, no matter how weak the client, there must be hope. The client comes primarily to hear that there may indeed be a way out. That way may be long and difficult, but somehow there is the possibility that an answer may be found. Every counselor should be sure that early in his or her involvement with each client, the possibilities of resolution are discussed. If the counselor cannot offer the client some hope, what motivation to continue with counseling remains? Hope is the first step. Hope promises that an answer to problems does exist somewhere, in some form. Hope is the foundation of the counselor's work. The client must recognize that when things go wrong they usually continue to do so for a while even though the client may be seeing a counselor. Once a start is made toward making things better, they often go on getting better and better. This recognition may help the client to work during those early days of counseling when an instant solution does not appear. The counselor can turn to the basic teaching of Scripture to provide a basis of hope from the life and work of Jesus Christ and the power of the Holy Spirit.

Implications for Diagnosis and Treatment

The content/theory dimension of counseling is the foundation that should guide the counselor's work with the client. The seven needs of humans are essential to this counseling process. The counselor should use the assessment of the client's need structure as a diagnostic step at the beginning of counseling. A technique/process dimension similar to Carkhuff's and Berenson's (1977) may help to accomplish this goal (see fig. 3).

Figure 3

Summary of Carkhuff and Berenson's Technique/Process Model

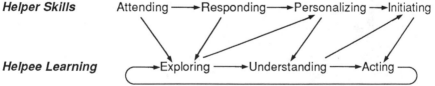

Through an attending process the counselor can begin to discover the needs expressed by the client. Appropriate responding to the content, feelings, and meanings of the client's communication will stimulate the client to explore his or her own needs structure. As the counselor begins to personalize the experiences, problems, and goals of the client (e.g., "You feel depressed because you recognize that your experiences suggest to you that there is no real meaning to life") he or she can help the client come to understand the sources of symptoms, attitudes, and behaviors. As the client comes to understand these sources, the counselor can then work with the client to initiate specific steps to meet the needs that are being expressed. This will eventually lead to action that can help the client change.

Having identified the needs status of the client, the counselor can introduce a program to help the client better meet those needs that are not currently being met and are producing symptoms. The counselor's role is to use the technique/process dimension with which he or she is most comfortable to work with the client to facilitate the meeting of needs. In addition, the counselor's function is to teach the client skills that will allow the client to act to meet these needs as they are expressed in different forms throughout the life-span.

Counseling sometimes fails because the client only learns how to temporarily meet needs. Unless the client has established a personal relationship with Jesus Christ that becomes the center of that client's identity, changes in life will once again lead to unmet needs. Even those clients with new identities in Christ will experience periods when certain needs will express themselves in symptoms or inappropriate attempts at problem solving. However, those with a real understanding of their needs, and with skills to channel their energy, will move toward appropriate solutions.

One key skill that clients should learn is how to use the Bible to discover God's Word regarding the actions required to meet their needs. The Bible speaks about both attitudes and behaviors. When particular symptoms appear, the counselor should work with the client to find if there are solutions to such symptoms in the Bible. The counselor should also work with the client to discover the underlying needs of particular symptoms. I have found that clients have responded well to Ward's *The Bible in Counseling* (1977). This workbook deals with such symptoms as despair, depression, hopelessness, fear, suffering, weakness, and anxiety, as well as the seven basic needs of humans. For the Christian client the Bible becomes a major source of support because the Christian has the power of the Holy Spirit to aid in understanding God's message.

Another area of skills that can be taught by the counselor is more psychological in nature. The teaching of relaxation skills can be of major benefit to some clients. Clients can be taught to relax in order to facilitate the ability to handle stress and to think clearly to determine what the next step should be. Many clients report knowing that they can reach to God for the power to cope, for hope, for courage, and for meaning, yet under the stress of the moment, are unable to call upon this resource.

Relaxation techniques and perhaps Christian meditation using God's Word are vital tools for the client.

An implication for treatment is that the counselor should make greater use of the church to aid in meeting the client's needs. Clients should be taught to look to fellow believers for support. They should also recognize that they have a responsibility in the community to help others as well. Psychologists and counselors ought to give serious consideration to the possibilities of working with churches as well as with clients in developing an overall framework to meet the basic needs of all people. Churches can be key institutions to aid clients in exploring, understanding, and acting.

Counselors need to develop an integrated model of content/theory to use with their choice of technique/process in working with clients. Basic human needs can be used initially as a diagnostic tool. Clients can then be encouraged to explore their relation to these needs in order to understand their feelings and behaviors. This understanding of their needs allows clients to work with the counselor to develop action plans to alleviate problems.

Summary and Suggestions

In this chapter it has been argued that counselors should have an integrated approach using psychology and theology in their practice. Seven needs which all humans strive to meet throughout their life-spans have been identified. When these needs are not satisfied, people will develop symptoms of maladjustment and unhappiness that may lead them to seek counseling. Whatever the counselor's organization/institution affiliation or technique/process of treatment, this foundational content/theory dimension is a useful guide to the counseling process. The needs that are not satisfactorily met must be identified. The counselor and the client can work together to allow the client to develop or obtain the skills required to satisfy these unmet needs. These skills, ideally, should be general enough to allow the client to continue to find solutions to unmet needs as they express themselves.

In addition, counselors should consider working with the church to allow the community of believers to be effective in helping people meet their needs. People are continually trying to satisfy these needs and generally, will seek counseling only when symptoms become severe. The church should function in a preventive way to help the majority of people as well as those seeing counselors. This will also require the church to function in an integrated knowledge framework and suggests that counselors should work with churches as consultants to develop a structure and process to achieve this goal.

References

Adams, J. E. 1977. *The Christian counselor's manual*. Grand Rapids: Baker.

Carkhuff, R., and B. Berenson. 1977. *Beyond counseling and therapy*. 2d ed. New York: Holt, Rinehart and Winston.

Carter, J. D. Toward a biblical model of counseling. *Journal of Psychology and Theology* 8 (1980): 45–52.

Clinebell, H. 1979. *Growth counseling: Hope-centered methods of actualizing human wholeness*. Nashville: Abingdon.

Collins, G. R. 1977. *The rebuilding of psychology*. Wheaton: Tyndale.

Ellens, J. H. 1980. *God's grace and human health*. Nashville: Abingdon.

Grounds, V. 1976. *Emotional problems and the gospel*. Grand Rapids: Zondervan.

Jourard, S. M. 1974. *Healthy personality: An approach from the viewpoint of humanistic psychology*. New York: Macmillan.

Lazurus, A. A. 1976. *Behavior therapy and beyond*. New York: McGraw-Hill.

Ligon, E. M. 1942. *The psychology of Christian personality*. New York: Macmillan.

Mowrer, O. H. 1961. *The crisis in psychiatry and religion*. Princeton, New Jersey: Van Nostrand.

Muuss, R. E. 1968. *Theories of adolescence*. New York: Random.

Powell, J. 1975. *A reason to live, a reason to die*. Chicago: Argus.

Ruitenbeck, H. M. 1964. *The individual and the crowd: A study of identity in America*. New York: Mentor.

Schaeffer, F. A. 1971. *True spirituality*. Wheaton: Tyndale.

Thiessen, H. C. 1963. *Introductory lectures in systematic theology*. Grand Rapids: Eerdmans.

Tillich, P. 1952. *The courage to be*. New Haven: Yale University.

Tournier, P. 1976. *The adventure of living*. New York: Harper and Row.

Ward, W. O. 1977. *The Bible in counseling*. Chicago: Moody.

Wolpe, J. 1973. *The practice of behavior therapy*. New York: Pergamon.

5

Hope in Psychotherapy
Hendrika Vande Kemp

Pedestaled on a rock in front of Hope College's historic Graves Hall rests the Anchor of Hope, the college's symbol. President Albertus C. Van Raalte said of the school's founding, "This is my anchor of hope for this people in the future" (Vanderzee 1976, 24). Since reading *The Inflated Self: Human Illusions and the Biblical Call to Hope* (Myers 1980), my thoughts on hope have diversified. My mind has been teased by questions concerning the nature of true hope and its place in mental health, the dynamics of hopelessness, and the stigma of false hope. I have asked myself repeatedly, while reviewing my current psychotherapy cases, how the dynamics of hope and hopelessness are expressed in these lives. While I am writing this paragraph, I am interrupted by the ringing of the telephone, and I spend nearly an hour talking to a young woman whose hopelessness and despair are so deep that she holds a razor blade and fights the temptation to cut her wrists. While I listen to her and grope for words of comfort and clarification, I wonder if the hope I offer is a false hope, if perhaps she ought to surrender to the realm of hopelessness, if I ought to know a more direct way to make the living Christian hope real in her life.

Biblical Conceptions of Hope

The place of hope is poignantly explored in Psalms 42 and 43. Here the psalmist raises himself from the depths of despair to fullness of trust and peace of soul, moving from pathos to praise in three resurgent movements, illustrating the fact that people move through life in cycles of ecstasy and depression, of hope and despair. In the first movement, there is a predominance of gloom, unrelieved until the writer rings out the clear notes of trust and hope in that well-known refrain: "Why are you cast down, O my soul, and why are you disquieted within me? Hope in God; for I shall again praise him, my help and my God" (Ps. 42:5).

But the relief is only temporary, and in the second movement the psalmist expresses the conflict of opposing emotions: the turmoil in the depths of his soul which constitutes his deep affliction, and the upward-looking prayer to God whom he trusts and whose love he remembers. Again he voices the refrain of hope in the presence of God who helps and delivers (42:11). In the third movement (Ps. 43) the psalmist's lonely prayer is transformed into a prayer for vindication by God in whom he takes refuge. And in his grasping of God's truth and light he claims an undisputed victory over his despondency as he jubilantly repeats the refrain: "Hope in God; for I shall again praise him, my help and my God."

This concept of hope is easily assimilated into dynamic psychology. The psalmist assumes that hope is an active process involved in the journey out of despondency and despair. He also assumes that hope has a proper object in God and his light and truth. The psalmist's hope is also relational, involving a God who helps. As William Lynch (1965/1974, 40) has noted, this is an important aspect of truth:

> The truth is that hope is related to help in such a way that you cannot talk about one without talking about the other. Hope is truly on the inside of us, but hope is an interior sense that there is help on the outside of us. There are times when we are especially aware that our own *purely inward resources* are not enough, that they have to be added to from the outside. But this need of help is a permanent, abiding, continuing fact for each human being; therefore, we can repeat that in severe difficulties we only become more especially aware of it.

As pointed out in *The Interpreter's Dictionary of the Bible* (1962, 641), the Old Testament concept of hope was multifaceted. At least four different attitudes were implied:

1. Trust in God, which led to a commitment of one's cause to the Lord, holding fast to him and living in serenity and peace under his pro-

tection. Although hope no longer tends to have this connotation, this definition highlights the intimate relationship between hope and faith, which is deeply rooted in such reliance and trust.

2. A ready eagerness to take refuge in the Lord from one's foes and to rely on him for speedy deliverance.
3. The confident expectation of future gladness which creates the possibility of present rejoicing. This attitude of anticipation and expectation serves as the occasion for eschatological hope.
4. A patient and courageous waiting for the Lord to bring his salvation while enduring in the face of present adversity.

Such a complex concept of hope led to the possibility of at least three different, related sins:

1. A lack of trust in God's guidance, which we may interpret as a lack of faith
2. Despair in refusing to believe that God is ready to forgive a contrite soul, which may be understood as a lack of basic trust
3. Presumption, which involves abuse of God's mercy by relying on him while continually offending him, thus avoiding one's responsibility for reciprocity in the relational context (Steinmueller and Sullivan 1956, 475)

While Van Raalte's choice of a motto reflected the Old Testament notion of hope, his choice of a symbol involved the adoption of a New Testament metaphor.

> So when God desired to show more convincingly to the heirs of the promise the unchangeable character of his purpose, he interposed with an oath, so that through two unchangeable things, in which it is impossible that God should prove false, we who have fled for refuge might have strong encouragement to seize the hope set before us. We have this as a sure and steadfast *anchor* of the soul, an hope that enters into the inner shrine behind the curtain, where Jesus has gone as a forerunner on our behalf, having become a high priest forever after the order of Melchizedek (Heb. 6:17–20, italics added).

As C. D. F. Moule (1953, 23) points out, hope is described in this passage with different metaphors. As fugitives seeking asylum in ancient Israel grasped the horns of the altar, we can hope with certainty because of God's Word and his almighty oath. Thus, hope is grounded in history and promise, in agreements that have been honored. Hope is also likened to an anchor which can neither slip nor drag (thus losing ground) because its flukes take a solid hold at "rock bottom." This metaphor takes us to the heart of the meaning of hope, as Moule comments:

> I have associated this chapter with "the anchor," and it is here that, in more senses than one, we touch "rock bottom": certainly in the sense that we have to plumb the depths in order to reach this hope, and in the sense that this is the security into which the flukes of our anchor bite, and in the sense that, once here, distress can only deepen our hope. For a striking fact emerges here, namely, that "affliction," "endurance," and "tried worth of character" are ideas which the New Testament closely associates with "hope," suggesting that it is precisely *de profundis* that hope begins to be understood. (28–29)

Hope connects us with the invisible world of the Holy, where Christ himself has entered to make intercession for us. Thus, hope allows us to transcend the human situation.

These metaphors make clear the fact that true Christian hope is grounded in the past, in salvation history, but also looks toward the future, in Christian eschatology. And through the action of the Holy Spirit this solid past and certain future transform present reality. All true hope pervades time in this way. It is grounded in the past, in history, through the action of memory. As David Woodyard states (1972, 39–40):

> ... There is a relationship between hope and memory. The man who hopes passionately longs for something new in the future because he remembers promises which have been honored in the past and which yield intimations of the coming future. ... In the Biblical faith, hope is defined not by what has been but by what will be. This not only sets the viability of hoping but suggests the qualities for which one may indeed hope. The coming future is not altogether unknown; while remaining unpredictable and startlingly new, it has yielded glimpses that are often only recognized in retrospect. While the past is never more than provisional, it contains announcements of what is forthcoming. Thus one can say that "hope exists in the mode of memory and memory in the mode of hope." In the promissory history of Biblical faith, man hopes because he remembers, and he remembers because he hopes. Memory is the internal form of hope and hope the actualization of memory. Hope has a history that is the basis of confidence in the coming future.

Woodyard's comments are of great significance to the clinical psychologist, for many who come to us for therapy or healing do not have hope, because they do not have the memories of kept promises to sustain it. Hope is generated and nurtured in relationship. Christian hope comes from a relationship with a trustworthy God, and hope in general emerges from a relationship of mutuality and trust (Giovacchini 1978). Hope involves the appropriation of help offered in mutual relationship. Thus, we cannot give hope to those who have none by mere pieties relating the content of Christian hope. We must actually demonstrate to the hopeless that help *is* available from the outside. This process is, in essence, the task of psychotherapy. The therapist realizes that it is a relationship of love that makes trust or the process of hoping possible.

It should be no surprise to the theologian that hope is intimately related to love, for the New Testament joins these two repeatedly with faith into a dynamically related triad (1 Cor. 13:13). *The Interpreter's Dictionary of the Bible* (1962, 642) points out several aspects of this relationship. In Paul's writings it is clear that hope is regarded as the ground of faith's expectancy, implying that true hope has a definite theological content. In Hebrews hope is held up in the same way—as that which produces and vindicates faith, which consists in the subjective appropriation of objective hope. Erich Fromm (1968, 9–12) also discusses the relationship between faith and hope, speaking first of the attitude of hope and then of its place in the life of faith:

> It is neither passive waiting nor is it unrealistic forcing of circumstances that cannot occur. It is like the crouched tiger, which will jump only when the moment for jumping has come. . . . To hope means to be ready at every moment for that which is not yet born, and yet not become desperate if there is no birth in our lifetime. There is no sense in hoping for that which already exists or for that which cannot be. . . . To hope is a state of being. It is an inner readiness, that of intense but not-yet-spent activeness.

The opposite of apathy, hope is the mood that accompanies faith—the certainty of the uncertain.

> Faith, like hope, is not prediction of the *future;* it is the vision of the *present* in a state of pregnancy. . . . It is certainty about the reality of the possibility—but it is not certainty in terms of man's vision and comprehension; it is not certainty in terms of the final outcome of reality. We need no faith in that which is scientifically predictable, nor can there be faith in that which is impossible. Faith is based on our experience of living, of transforming ourselves. Faith that others can change is the outcome of the experience that I can change. (13–14)

Fromm continues by applying this to human relationships, where the building of trust is of critical importance:

> In the sphere of human relations, "having faith" in another person means to be certain of his *core*—that is, of the reliability and unchangeability of his fundamental attitudes. In the same sense we can have faith

in ourselves—not in the constancy of our opinions but in our basic orientation to life, the matrix of our character structure. (14)

While hope is the mood that accompanies faith, hope can have no base except in faith, which concerns itself with the content of hope. In some mysterious manner, love is involved in the dialogue between faith and hope in a manner that is of concern to every psychotherapist. Carl Jung, in his assessment of the human condition, attributed all neuroses to a failure of this dynamic triad and its relationship to understanding, which may be beyond the comprehension of the nonreligious therapist:

> As a doctor he is not required to have a finished outlook on life, and his professional conscience does not demand it of him. But what will he do when he sees only too clearly why his patient is ill; when he sees that it arises from his having no love, but only sexuality; no faith, because he is afraid to grope in the dark; no hope, because he is disillusioned by the world and by life; and no understanding, because he has failed to read the meaning of his own existence? . . .
>
> These four highest achievements of human effort are so many gifts of grace, which are neither to be taught nor learned, neither given nor taken, neither withheld nor earned, since they come through experience, which is something *given*, and therefore beyond the reach of human caprice. . . . The way to experience . . . is a venture which requires us to commit ourselves with our whole being. (1933, 225–26)

Clinical Implications

One solution Jung suggests to cure spiritual and psychic ills is the life of fantasy:

> . . . "Meaning" is something mental or spiritual. Call it fiction if you like. . . . Whether the fiction rises in me spontaneously, or reaches me from without by way of human speech, it can make me ill or cure me. Nothing is surely more intangible or unreal than factions, illusions and opinions; and yet nothing is more effective in the psychic and even the psychological realm. (224)

Hope is intricately wrapped up in the life of fantasy and the imagination, as Lynch so clearly points out in *Images of Hope:* ". . . hope imagines and it refuses to stop imagining (or hypothesizing), and it is always imagining what is not yet seen, or a way out of difficulty, or a wider perspective for life or thought" (23). Fantasy has the capacity to dissolve problems, as James Hillman asserts in *Re-visioning Psychology* (1975, 135):

Psychologizing tries to solve the matter at hand, not by resolving it, but by dissolving the problem into the fantasy that is congealed into a "problem." In other words, we assume that events have an outer shell that we call hard, tough, real, and an inner matter that is epiphenomenal, insubstantial, strange. The first we call problems, the second fantasies. Problems are always "serious." One is stuck with them; they don't go away. Whereas fantasies are hard to catch. They are said to be "just fantasy" or "mere fantasy," "silly" or "far-fetched." They are never considered "thorny," "weighty," or "basic" like problems.

Fantasy permits a "seeing through" and beyond the problem, which is exactly what hope permits us to do. J. R. R. Tolkien, a Christian master of fantasy literature, regarded fantasy as a form of "subcreation" which is unique to humanity and a special but natural gift of God:

> Fantasy is a natural human activity. It certainly does not destroy or even insult Reason; and it does not either blunt the appetite for, nor obscure the perception of, scientific verity. On the contrary. The keener and the clearer the reason, the better fantasy it will make. If men were ever in a state in which they did not want to know or could not perceive truth (facts or evidence), then Fantasy would languish until they were cured. If they ever get into that state (it would not seem at all impossible), Fantasy will perish and become Morbid Delusion.
>
> For creative Fantasy is founded upon the harder recognition that things are so in the world as it appears under the sun; on a recognition of fact, but not a slavery to it....
>
> Fantasy can, of course, be carried to excess. It can be ill done. It can be put to evil uses. But of what human thing in this fallen world is that not true?... Fantasy remains a human right: we make in our measure and in our derivative mode, because we are made: and not only made, but made in the image and likeness of a Maker. (1966, 54–55)

Tolkien attributes to fantasy three hope-giving functions which might also be attributed to psychotherapy: recovery, escape, and consolation. *Recovery* includes a return and renewal of health and consists in the regaining of a clear view, in "seeing things as we were meant to see them— as things apart from ourselves" (57). This is especially true for those things which are familiar and which we regard as "problems." Often the therapeutic task consists in "the gentle art of reframing":

> To reframe ... means to change the conceptual and/or emotional setting or viewpoint in relation to which a situation is experienced and to place it in another frame which fits the "facts" of the same concrete situation equally well or even better, and thereby changes its entire meaning. The mechanism involved here is not immediately obvious, especially if we bear

in mind that there is change while the situation itself may remain quite un-changed and, indeed, even unchangeable. What turns out to be changed is the meaning attributed to the situation, and therefore its consequences, but not its concrete facts—or, as the philosopher Epictetus expressed it as early as the first century A.D., "It is not the things themselves which trouble us but the opinions that we have about these things." (Watzlawick, Weakland, and Fisch 1974, 75)

Thus, one way that psychotherapists can offer hope is to transcend the fact that "our beliefs about the social world are frequently influenced more by our theories and expectations than by observable facts. Our processing of information is 'theory driven' " (Myers 1980, 54).

A second hope-engendering function of fantasy is *escape,* by which Tolkien implies the "escape of the prisoner" rather than the "flight of the deserter" (more properly labeled *escapism;* 60–61). We need to escape at times both from our lives and from our present time and self-made misery. But even more important than our need to escape from "the noise, stench, ruthlessness, and extravagance of the internal-combustion engine" is our need to escape from things which are more terrible, such as "hunger, thirst, poverty, pain, sorrow, injustice, death" (65).

Such escape points to another therapeutic function discussed by Lynch—the need to distinguish the realm of hope from the realm of hope-lessness. He states that "the plain fact for all of us is that many things are without hope, many people we are inclined to depend on cannot give hope, and many isolated moments or periods of life do not themselves contain hope. I repeat that hope is not absolute in its range. Part of reality belongs to hopelessness" (Lynch 1974, 54). Hopelessness is the realm of despondency and despair, the experience of "too-muchness" and apathy and the sense of impossibility. The developmental process includes learning to differentiate between the possible and the impossible. In neurosis, the person is trapped in a world in which

> . . . some thing or wish or situation or pattern or person has become absolu-tized and fixed. In this context, we can equate the idea of entrapment and the idea of an absolute—a false absolute—of course. What is clearly lack-ing in every such case is flexibility, freedom, imagination. What is also present is some degree of hopelessness. Hope never quite gives up imagin-ing, but the neurosis is an entrapment and a failure of the imagination. (64)

In such situations, the therapeutic goal prescribed by Lynch is to help the person learn to tolerate ambivalence. We must fight such absolutiz-ing tendencies as the expectation that there is a single, simple way of thinking and feeling in a given situation, or the belief that it is possible to love others without a shade of hostility. Such beliefs and expectations belong in the realm of hopelessness. One thing that certainly must be said of "do-it-yourself psychic repair," of some forms of counseling and psychotherapy, and of the varieties of "therapeutic religion" is that they all to some degree tempt us with tidbits from the well-stocked shelf of false absolutes, which include power, love, sexuality, good feelings, and self-fulfillment. While it is the goal of psychotherapy to develop the capacity for imagination and hope, this therapeutic process is not implicitly related to its goal, and psychologists often trap their clients in the sin of presumption. It is especially in the area of terminal goal setting that the therapist must turn to the teachings of Christianity to determine what constitutes a proper object of hope. Thomas Szasz (1961) has pointed out that, even from the point of view of a nonreligious therapist, the Christian faith may offer the "best" object for faith:

> These few comments merely offer a glimpse into the exceedingly complicated subject of the psychology of hope in relation to religious faith. The core of this problem is: What should man be *hopeful about*? In what should he *invest his hope*? Disregarding the broadly existential character of these questions, I wish to emphasize only that investing hope in religious faith is, psychoeconomically speaking, one of the best investments one can make. This is because by investing a small amount of hope in religion—especially in a Christian religion—one gets back a great deal of it. After all, let us remember that religions *promise* hope and gratifications of all sorts. Few other enterprises, other than fanatical nationalisms, promise as much. The rate of return on hope invested in religion is thus much higher than on hope invested in, say, work-a-day pursuits. Hence, those with small capitals of hope may do best by investing their "savings" in religion. From this point of view, religion could be said to be the hope of the hopeless. (287)

There is but one catch in this contemporary restatement of Pascal's famous wager: the assertion that religion engenders hope is to some extent a tautology, "for it is circular to argue that religious belief gives man hope, because it is also necessary to have hope that religion will be satisfying before he can believe in it" (287). This poses a major problem for the psychotherapist: How does one engender hope in a person who has no memories of a helpful, hopeful relationship? It is exactly when the therapist has such a complex goal that the results of psychotherapy must be elusive to the scientific psychologist. Although the completely hopeless person is probably a psychological impossibility, as asserted by the old Latin proverb *Dum spiro, spero* ("As long as I breathe, I hope"), measuring the quantity and quality of hope is a serious challenge to the therapist.

The third function Tolkien attributes to fantasy is that of *consolation:*

... I will call it Eucatastrophe. ... The consolation of fairy-stories, the joy of the happy ending: or more correctly of the good catastrophe, the sudden joyous "turn" (for there is no true end to any fairy-tale): this joy, which is one of the things which fairy-stories can produce supremely well, it is not essentially "escapist," nor "fugitive." In its fairy-tale—or other-world— setting, it is a sudden and miraculous grace: never to be counted on to recur. It does not deny the existence of *dyscatastrophe*, of sorrow and failure: the possibility of these is necessary to the joy of deliverance; it denies (in the face of much evidence, if you will) universal final defeat and in so far is *evangelium*, giving a fleeting glimpse of Joy, Joy beyond the walls of the world, poignant as grief. (1966, 68)

This function is epitomized in the message of the Christian gospel:

The Gospel contains a fairy-story, or a story of a larger kind which embraces all the essence of fairy-stories. ... But this story has entered History and the primary world; the desire and aspiration of sub-creation has been raised to the fulfillment of Creation. The Birth of Christ is the eucatastrophe of Man's history. The Resurrection is the eucatastrophe of the story of the Incarnation. The story begins and ends in joy. It has pre-eminently the "inner consistency of reality." There is no tale ever told that men would rather find was true, and none which so many skeptical men have accepted as true on its own merits. For the Art of it has the supremely convincing tone of Primary Art, that is, of Creation. To reject it leads either to sadness or to wrath. (71–72)

Thus, Tolkien makes it clear that the rejection of true hope is one of the things that leads to hopelessness and despair. But it is also clear, from our previous discussion, that hope involves much more than a proper object. When we ask "Where is hope?" our answer must include a large portion of life. Hope includes a feeling that what is wanted will happen, a desire and anticipation or expectation which presupposes memory and a capacity for loving. This capacity is in itself a criterion for mental health, and its presence is morally and ethically and theologically neutral, because its presence is the result of experiences beyond a person's control. Such hope includes an object, which may be a person or a goal. Here we enter into the realm of ethical decision making, for we may place our hopes in a relationship that is unattainable or in an object that lies in the realm of hopelessness or false absolutes. Hope also includes a person or thing from which something may be hoped, and this aspect may again lead us into the worship of false gods or the striving after false absolutes. This aspect also implies that hope is relational, so that the notions of trust and reliance are implicit in the concept of hope.

The possibility for hope is everywhere, but the potentiality must become actuality, which presumes an act of grace, whether human or divine, and an atmosphere of love. Some may be led to true hope through an act of divine grace. Many others lack the inner resources or the interpersonal relationships which mediate the divine grace, offering the hope and help necessary to claim the *evangelium*. For them, the best initial investment may be in the therapeutic relationship, where the capital for the final investment may be discovered and actualized. Only then can the flukes of the anchor grasp "rock bottom."

References

Briggs, C. A., and E. G. Briggs. 1906. *A critical and exegetical commentary on the book of psalms*. Vol. 1. International Critical Commentary. Edinburgh: T and T Clark.

Buttrick, G., ed. 1962. *The interpreter's dictionary of the Bible: An illustrated encyclopedia*. Vol. 2. New York: Abingdon.

Calvin, J. 1949. *Commentary on the book of psalms*. Translated by J. Anderson. Grand Rapids: Eerdmans.

Fromm, E. 1968. *The revolution of hope: Toward a humanized technology*. New York: Harper and Row.

Giovacchini, P. 1978. *Treatment of primitive mental states*. New York: Aronson.

Hillman, J. 1975. *Re-visioning psychology*. New York: Harper and Row.

Jung, C. G. 1933. *Modern man in search of a soul*. Translated by W. S. Dell and C. F. Baynes. New York: Harcourt, Brace and World.

Lynch, W. F. [1965] 1974. *Images of hope: Imagination as healer of the hopeless*. Notre Dame: University of Notre Dame Press.

McCullough, W. S., and W. R. Taylor. 1955. *Psalms and proverbs*. Interpreter's Bible. Vol. 4. New York: Abingdon.

MacLaren, A. 1903. The psalms. In *The expositor's bible*. Vol. 2. New York: Armstrong.

Moule, C. F. D. 1953. *The meaning of hope: A biblical exposition with concordance*. Philadelphia: Fortress.

Myers, D. G. 1980. *The inflated self: Human illusions and the biblical call to hope*. New York: Seabury.

Szasz, T. S. 1961. *The myth of mental illness: Foundations of a theory of personal conduct*. New York: Dell.

Steinmueller, J. E., and K. Sullivan. 1956. *Catholic biblical encyclopedia*. New York: Wagner.

Tolkien, J. R. R. 1966. On fairy stories. In *The Tolkien reader*. New York: Ballantine.

Vanderzee, A. 1976. Hope presidents look ahead. *Hope College Magazine* 29(2):24.

Watzlawick, P., J. Weakland, and R. Risch. 1974. *Change: Principles of problem formation and problem resolution.* New York: Norton.

Webster's new world dictionary of the American language. 1966. College ed. Cleveland: World Publishing.

Woodyard, D. O. 1972. *Beyond cynicism: The practice of hope.* Philadelphia: Westminster.

6

The Concept of the Ideal: Therapy for Christians

C. Markham Berry

Man finds the concept of the ideal, that internalized measure of the utterly perfect, both his best friend and his greatest tormentor. At one moment it seems good and is seen in an aura of ultimate reality, and as such is a goal which tantalizes his pride with grandiose promises of becoming the very best. It was in this sense that Joseph Conrad described an ideal as "a flaming vision of reality." In another moment man feels condemned because he falls so short of its standard, and it becomes the anvil upon which the conscience hammers into him depressing guilt and a sense of worthlessness. Nations, under the banners of various ideals, have called for his greatest sacrifices and highest sense of service on behalf of the best causes. Other nations, equally zealous, have by revolutions, tyrannies, and inquisitions crushed out man's basic humanity under the same banners.

The ideal becomes a frequent issue in the care of people with emotional problems, and here the same paradox exists.

A middle-aged man spends an hour pouring out a pitiful lament over an indiscretion committed in his college years. "It's like I have a factory in me manufacturing guilt, and I'm trying to corner the world market!"

A chic young commercial artist, seeking help for her troublesome compulsiveness, describes the scene which took place in her home when she reported she had made 798 on the language portion of her college entrance examinations. Both she and her parents became obsessed about her failure to make two more points which would have meant that no one in the country had made a higher score than she did.

A successful businesswoman has lain awake nights and become helpless because a fine scar on her face (which can barely be seen) mars the perfect smoothness of her skin.

A recently divorced woman expresses her relief at being out of a bad marriage, yet she grieves because now she will never be the virgin bride of her fantasy.

Such clients are generally treated by bending their models more into conformity with the reality of their lives. This makes one more comfortable with his guilt but at the same time removes some of the vitality from his existence. The person still finds himself in the dilemma Dostoevski describes in *The Brothers Karamazov:*

> Beauty! I can't endure the thought that a man of lofty mind and heart begins with the ideal of the Madonna and ends with the ideal of Sodom. What's still more awful is that a man with the ideal of Sodom in his soul does not renounce the ideal of the Madonna, and his heart may be on fire with that ideal, genuinely on fire, just as in his days of youth and innocence. Yes, man is broad, too broad, indeed, I'd have him narrower.

The Christian sometimes finds living with this broadness even more difficult since the claim that he has a vital identification with Christ undeniably carries with it an imperative to the pristine righteousness which makes his being merely human an uncomfortable state.

The charismatic movement within the church, among other things, attempts to recover this ideal in life. In a somewhat different way, legalistic movements do much the same thing. One is pressed from both sides to become either pure by being filled with the Spirit or to maintain a saintly walk by keeping all of the rules. It is difficult to remain aloof from the simplistic charm of such solutions.

The Christian who does counseling will get little theoretical help from his studies in psychology and theology. This chapter frames some of these issues and makes proposals relevant to both therapy and biblical theology.

In this regard, it will be helpful to briefly review some of the Freudian thought on the development of the superego since psychoanalysts have considered this a central problem for many years. In addition, there is a propensity for pastoral theologians to rely heavily on the unconscious in their formulations (Flew 1934; Sangster 1943).

Psychoanalytic Thought

In "On Narcissism" Freud first proposed an element within the personality which served as a standard (1914). He developed it more fully in *The Ego and the Id* (1923), and summarized it again some years later (1938). He frequently commented on this ideal, and made it a central part of his formulations. Initially, he seemed to reserve the term *ideal*, or *ego ideal*, for the standard which "finds itself possessed of every perfection that is of value," and separately described another "faculty that incessantly watches, criticizes and compares . . ." (1920, 428). Later he compressed these two concepts, the ideal and the conscience, into a single structure, using the terms *ego ideal* and *superego* interchangeably (1921; Sandler 1963, 142). Still later, he apparently reinstituted the distinction (1933). Since Freud, psychoanalytic thinkers have moved generally in two directions. One group maintains this distinction (Sandler 1963; Novey 1955; Lampl-de Groot 1962; Reich 1954). Most, however, have gone on to emphasize combined function, especially in reference to the Oedipus conflict (Jones 1926; Schafer 1960).

Either way, most writers base the ideal in the life of the infant, who experiences a primary narcissistic bliss. The judgmental, cruel aspects of the conscience initially begin in the anal-sadistic period, but find their final configuration under the threat of castration in the Oedipus conflict.

The ideal has two roots: one is internal (primary narcissism) and the other is more external, coming from a complex identification with parents, especially centering around paternal criticism, but also buttressed by training, education, and the culturalization process (Freud 1923; Sandler 1960).

Freud pointed out, though, that it was not the parent's ego which was transferred to the child but his superego (1933). The model, then, is transferred, not the experience. This, then, still leaves open the theoretical question of where this mental model of the completely perfect originated. Freud saw guilt as coming ultimately from an epochal, prehistoric murder of the father-patriarch by his maturing sons (1930, 85). This would presuppose, however, an existing standard of morality which troubled prehistoric man but did not trouble the wolf pack on which this behavior was modeled.

Contemporary analysts have shown renewed interest in the relevance of our earliest infantile experiences, especially those involved in object relations. Of these, the most pertinent, for our purposes, is the thinking of Heintz Kohut. He sees the narcissistic ideal of early infancy taking two forms. A blissful, euphoric perfection nurtures the infant's positive self-concept while his internal parent-image (or *imago*) is idealized as the ultimate of what is admirable. In a favorable environment, both of these primordia become integrated into the adult personality and provide the pleasure one derives from being good, the ability to set and preserve reasonable goals, and the capacity for the mature admiration of others (1968).

This narcissistic experience might conceivably be one source of esthetic, affective, and perhaps functional perfection, but it is still hard to see how it contributes the original ethical righteousness which is at the heart of the problem. In other words, developmental experiences (Spitz 1958; Sandler 1960; Reich 1954) may help us to understand how an internal model might be fleshed out and clothed with the character of our family tradition and culture, but the question is still open as to where this skeletal nidus of innocent moral perfection comes from.

 Other psychologists from different perspectives are no more helpful. Hobart Mowrer (1960) emphasizes the learning process. Carl Rogers (Mowrer 1953) pragmatically shifts the focus onto the "self-ideal" as being something "the person wants to be, which in many instances is very different from what he feels he should be." Ausubel (1955) thoughtfully dismembers the popular distinctions between shame and guilt in the culturalization process and concludes that "the capacity for experiencing guilt is conceived as so basically human and so fundamental to the sanctions by which social norms are maintained and transmitted to the young that under minimally favorable social conditions, it should develop in all cultures" (1955, 390).

These various approaches, then, all see the discordance between primitive, archaic ideals and the fallibility of our real existence to be a major problem. The superego tends to be rigid, unrealistic, and punitive, the ideal, distant and unobtainable.

Three general approaches to management are suggested. The superego becomes less ominous when insight is given into its roots in parental and social norms. It can be made less cutting by behavioral methods of desensitizing our responses to guilt and shame. It becomes less threatening if one can remodel it into something closer to our actual behavior, thus allowing it to painlessly enrich our adult personalities. The problem with all of these approaches is that the association with a transcendent perfection is lost and one is orphaned from the loving and beloved character of the superego (Schafer 1960).

Is there some way in which we can maintain the ideal as a lively element in the personality without being defeated by the shame and guilt which come from falling short of its standards?

Whereas religious concepts can aggravate these problems, the additional resources of faith give one the opportunity to explain the origin of this phenomenon and to offer more satisfactory resolutions. The author speaks from the Christian tradition and regards the Bible as having a unique reality of its own comparable to that of the personality and one which can be applied to the human experience. It is as part of an ongoing effort to seek out and elucidate common themes which are presented both in the human personality and the pages of Scripture that these proposals are made.

The term *structure* as used in the following pages should be considered more in the sense of the structuralists (Piaget, Levi-Strauss, and Chomsky) than as it is used by the psychoanalysts (Hartmann 1947). It implies an innate structural element of the human mind which is both skeletal and developmental (Piaget 1970). However growth and experience might develop or elaborate such a structure, in essence it remains a part of the equipment with which a human being begins his life, and it is around this axis, extended in time, that various mental and emotional elements form during development.

Proposals

The ideal is a given element of man's essential nature, not something which derives from his history. It was first realized in his earliest generic experience which was that of being part of a perfect creation. God created Adam in his own image and placed him in a garden which was esthetically pleasing, functionally good, and morally pure. God built into the human personality a skeletal structure around which the ideals of rightness, beauty, and innocence formed. Since that time, man from generation to generation, from culture to culture, has fleshed out this structure with those qualities valued by his family and society. The ideal, then, can be a constant factor within the human personality but at the same time vary in the form that it takes.

It is clear that at some point man lost this perfection of experience but maintained the essence of it in his ideal. God's response to man's fall was to continue interacting with man. From this we must assume that God's original purposes in the creation of the ideal Adam continue in fallen man. The consideration then moves to what the intent of God was and continues to be in human life.

In the first place, it is clear that sinlessness, righteousness, and even goodness are the properties of God and not man as he now is. They are possessed only through faith in Christ (Phil. 3:9). Jesus confronts the man who would call him "good" with the statement "One there is who is good" (Matt. 19:17). Man finds himself a sinner who falls "short of the glory of God" (Rom. 3:23), and can partake of righteousness only by identification with Christ. This is variously described as a covering (Gen. 3:21; Rev. 19:8), as his being made our righteousness (1 Cor. 1:30;

2 Cor. 5:21), and as imputed (Rom. 4:6; Phil. 3:9). The Bible further describes our completeness as "in Christ" (Col. 2:10). Man, then, might well still bear the impress of his original goodness, in a personality now unhappily shattered by sin. His hope of experiencing the satisfaction which this structure urges on him must now come to reside in Christ. When this redemptive identification with the resurrected Christ becomes a part of his life, he has the possibility of experiencing failure and, paradoxically, faultlessness.

John expresses this paradox by saying, "If we say we have no sin, we deceive ourselves, and the truth is not in us" (1 John 1:8); "no one born of God commits sin; for God's nature abides in him . . ." (1 John 3:9). Paul, who candidly refers to himself as the "chief of sinners" (1 Tim. 1:15), describes his continuing shortfall from sinless righteousness:

> For I know that nothing good dwells within me, that is, in my flesh. I can will what is right, but I cannot do it. For I do not do the good I want, but the evil I do not want is what I do (Rom. 7:18–19).

He then continues this paradoxical thought: "There is therefore now no condemnation for those who are in Christ Jesus" (Rom. 8:1).

In the second place, the Bible affirms that the human ideal is the end point of a process and not a static reality, either contemporary or historical. The Greek word most commonly translated "perfect" in English, *teleios*, subsumes a concept for which we do not have a good English word. *Teleios* is also translated "mature"; it is an ideal which is ultimately experienced in its maturity. Like a flower, the end point determines the character and meaning of the entire budding and unfolding process. The writers of the New Testament see the sufferings of this present time as being part of a growth process which culminates in maturity (James 1:2–4). Christians here are pilgrims, wanderers, people of the Way, ambassadors, citizens of the heavenly kingdom, and children—all in the process of growth (Phil. 3:12–14; Heb. 5:12–14). Our identity is ultimately determined by the position we hold at maturity. As Christians, then, our *teleios* lies in our part of the flowering of God's purposes in Christ—the supreme event of the entire historical process which is variously described as a marriage (Rev. 19:7), as a gathering together of all things into one (Eph. 1:10), as a reunion of the Father and the Son, and so on.

The individual believer and the church as a whole are involved in this maturity or perfection, and the end point of both is described as oneness coming out of diversity. This dual nature of the identity of the believer leads to the third biblical principle: The ideal includes these two identities, that of the individual member and of the body. An individual is one with others, but retains his distinct individuality. He experiences this phenomenon psychologically—he is one with his mate, with his family, and with the various groups and communities in which he participates. In a spiritual mode, the same paradox is repeated. We are individual members, yet of one body—the body of the Lord himself—the church (Eph. 5:29–32). The *teleios* must be both an individual and community perfection.

With this concept before us, one might expect to find that the process of individual maturation occurs as a part of a whole as well. The goal of our contemporary culture—autonomy and the desire to be "whole" within ourselves—might not be a truly valid one.

Paul incorporates these principles in the theological view he gives us of himself in Philippians 3:5–21. Here Paul roots his ideal in Christ as opposed to his culture (vv. 8, 9). He views his righteousness as "of God," "through faith in Christ" (v. 9). His meaning now is to "gain Christ" and to be "found in him" (vv. 8, 9), to "know him" (v. 10). He views his identity as being in process (v. 12), with the end point, the determining character, variously expressed as "attain[ing] the resurrection" (v. 11), the "upward call of God in Christ Jesus" (v. 14). He describes this individual process as "press[ing] on to make it my own, because Christ Jesus has made me his own" (v. 12). Ultimately then, he envisions this in community (v. 16) and culminating in a transcendent historical experience on the basis of which his present life is enriched with hope (v. 21).

Discussion

What are some practical implications of this understanding for the treatment of Christians who are suffering from both the pressure and potential of the ideal?

In the first place, the ideal must not be destroyed, ignored, or depreciated. We must have confidence that God's creative purpose in building this image into man continues to exist even though man has fallen far from it. We must also confidently transmit the hope that this perfection is ours now in the sense that God is in the process of maturing us. The problems and trials of our lives become the means of this maturing. His power and authority assure us of our ultimate possession.

Many people tend to think that their growth is behind them by the time they are twenty-one, and that immaturity is in itself something to be guilty about. It is our task to convince our clients that God is not through with them yet. They frequently think of their failures and conflicts as detours on the way rather than as means of growth. Clients must recognize both their need to grow and the place of suffering in that process to be brought into ultimate conformity to the Lord.

However, this is usually not enough. Clients must also come to understand that their present problems are more than just problems of immaturity. Christ himself is involved in the conflict and pain that this divergence from the ideal presents to us and has eternal purposes in our struggles. The key is that his ideal is in the process of being perfected in the sense that it is being revealed in his involvement with us. This can come about even when we fall short.

Paul comes to see this in learning the meaning of his "thorn in the flesh." God's purpose is not to remove it but to indwell it so that his strength can be perfected in weakness (2 Cor. 12:9). Our mistake is to hope that we might find this perfection now, completely within ourselves, and apart from Christ. In contrast, the Book of Romans states that God's grace superabounds our sin (Rom. 5:20).

The sequence of thought in the Book of Romans leads us to a second practical consideration relevant to counseling. Our sins are real and as such need to be dealt with. For the redeemed, the consequences of sin are experienced in the normal sequence of cause and effect here on earth. What we sow we reap, and these fruits, along with our individual tendencies to continue to sin, must be lived out. The life core of sin was executed with Christ on the cross (Rom. 6:3), and our identification with him in his resurrection assures us that the ultimate consequence is eternal life (Rom. 6:5). Both death to sin and new life in Christ become increasingly real and more splendidly displayed as they are placed in apposition to our flawed lives. As Augustine said, there is the possibility for us to see that even our sin is a part of all those things which work together for our good (Rom. 8:28). Paul might have said, "His purity is perfected in my sinfulness."

This still leaves us with some other practical problems, though. What can we say about the person who has an extraordinary sensitivity to flaws, or the one who is overwhelmed by guilt? These can be most helpfully considered in the context of the community rather than of isolated individuals. Just as our gifts and callings are essentially given to the body and not to us as individuals, so our shortcomings and needs are, in a very real sense, community property. I cannot attend to the pain of my brother in the fullest sense without making it my own. Perhaps his sensitivity is designed for all of us rather than for himself alone. Maybe even hypersensitivity to disorder and sin is a reminder to the rest of us of the purity and cleanness which are Christ's. Without such a reminder, those of us less troubled by our consciences become blind to this quality of God's by our own callousness. By our sharing with our brother our adjustment to the reality of our faults, and our brother sharing with us his sensitivity, we can both benefit.

Conclusion

In summary, the ideal is a structure within man's personality, which brings him both pain and meaning. The secular thinking of our day would encourage us to hammer this lofty model down into the baser dimensions of our earthly lives and thus be relieved from its harsh, punitive condemnation. If one is successful in this, though, he has lost the transcendent meaning in his life, and an internal stimulus to growth.

The Christian needs to view this ideal as a property of God which becomes internalized in us in the form of the indwelling Christ. As such, it is community property. The ideal is expressed in experience as a growing process toward a consummation in which total perfection and complete oneness are both realized:

> But grace was given to each of us according to the measure of Christ's gift ... From whom the whole body, joined and knit together by every joint with which it is supplied, when each part is working properly, makes bodily growth and upbuilds itself in love (Eph. 4:7, 16).

References

Ausubel, D. P. Relationship between shame and guilt in the socializing process. *Psychological Review* 62(1955):378–90.

Flew, R. N. 1934. *The idea of perfection in Christian theology.* London: Oxford University.

Freud, S. [1914] 1955. *On narcissism: An introduction.* In *The standard edition of the complete psychological works of Sigmund Freud,* edited and translated by J. Strachey. Vol. 14. London: Hogarth.

_____. [1920] 1955. *Introductory lectures on psycho-analysis.* In *The standard edition of the complete psychological works of Sigmund Freud,* edited and translated by J. Strachey. Vols. 15 and 16. London: Hogarth.

_____. [1921] 1955. *Beyond the pleasure principle, group psychology and other writings.* In *The standard edition of the complete psychological works of Sigmund Freud,* edited and translated by J. Strachey. Vol. 18. London: Hogarth.

_____. [1923] 1955. *The ego and the id.* In *The standard edition of the complete psychological works of Sigmund Freud,* edited and translated by J. Strachey. Vol. 19. London: Hogarth.

_____. [1930] 1955. *The future of an illusion, civilization and its discontents.* In

The standard edition of the complete psychological works of Sigmund Freud, edited and translated by J. Strachey. Vol. 21. London: Hogarth.

————. [1933] 1955. *New introductory lectures on psycho-analysis and other works.* In *The standard edition of the complete psychological works of Sigmund Freud,* edited and translated by J. Strachey. Vol. 22. London: Hogarth.

————. [1938] 1955. *Moses and monotheism, an outline of psycho-analysis and other writings.* In *The standard edition of the complete psychological works of Sigmund Freud,* edited and translated by J. Strachey. Vol. 23. London: Hogarth.

Hartmann, H., E. Kris, and P. M. Lowenstein. Comments on the formation of psychic structure. *Psychoanalytic Study of the Child* 2 (1946):11–37.

Jones, E. The origin and structure of the superego. *International Journal of Psychoanalysis* 7(1926):303–11.

Kohut, H. The psychoanalytic treatment of narcissistic personality disorders. *Psychoanalytic Study of the Child* 23(1968):86–113.

Lampl-de Groot, J. The ego ideal and superego. *Psychoanalytic Study of the Child* 17(1962):94–106.

Mowrer, O. H., ed. 1953. *Psychotherapy, theory and research.* New York: Ronald Press.

————. 1960. *Learning theory and the symbiotic process.* New York: Wiley.

Novey, S. The role of the superego and the ego ideal in character formation. *International Journal of Psychoanalysis* 36(1955):254–59.

Piaget, J. n.d. Piaget's theory. In *Charmichael's manual of child psychology.* 3d ed., edited by P. H. Mussen. 2 vols. New York: Wiley.

Reich, A. Early identification as archaic elements in the superego. *Journal of the American Psychoanalytic Association* 2(1954):218–38.

Sandler, J. On the concept of the superego. *Psychoanalytic Study of the Child* 15(1960):128–62.

Sandler, J., A. Holder, and D. Meers. The ego ideal and the ideal self. *Psychoanalytic Study of the Child* 18(1968):139–58.

Sangster, W. E. 1954. *The path of perfection.* New York: Abingdon-Cokesbury.

Schafer, R. The loving and beloved superego in Freud's structural theory. *Psychoanalytic Study of the Child* 15(1960):163–88.

Spitz, R. A. On the genesis of superego components. *Psychoanalytic Study of the Child* 13(1958):375–404.

Part **2**

Specific Therapies and Techniques

7

Basic Biblical Counseling
Lawrence J. Crabb, Jr.

Christian counselors find themselves divided in their understanding of which approach to counseling is truly biblical. Christianized versions of transactional analysis (T.A.), gestalt therapy, rational-emotive therapy, psychoanalysis, and behavior modification continue to compete for the allegiance of evangelicals. For some, confusion has given way to clarity in Bill Gothard's Systematic Theology of Practical Christian Living. Others have responded to the nouthetic counselors' insistence that their approach is truly biblical. How does one determine what constitutes basic biblical counseling?

Integrating Psychology and Theology

The first step is to arrive at a broad position on the thorny and far from resolved problem of integrating psychology and Christianity. The problem facing evangelicals who are wrestling with integration is simple enough to describe. There is a body of revealed truth to which all true evangelicals are committed: the inerrant and inspired Word of God. There is another vast literature consisting of the diverse, sometimes contradictory, theories and observations which we can call "secular psychology." Let each be symbolized by a circle (see fig. 4). The circle of revealed truth revolves around the person and work of Jesus Christ. Secular psychology is built upon humanism, a belief system which fervently insists that man is the central being in the universe and that his individual welfare is supreme. What is the relationship between these two circles?

Figure 4

Dichotomy of Theology and Psychology

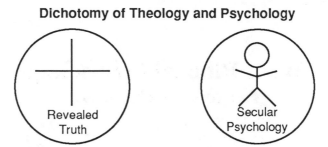

Evangelicals have generally adopted one of four positions. Some regard the two fields as separate but equal. If you have the flu, see a physician. If you want to design a building, talk with an architect. If you suffer from a psychological disorder, consult a psychologist or psychiatrist. The most critical issue in selecting a professional is competence, not religious beliefs. If your problems are spiritual however, check with your pastor. Figure 5 illustrates this position.

Figure 5

"Separate but Equal" Model

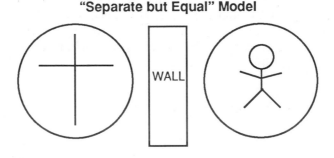

A second position tends to snatch a few relevant concepts from Scripture, mix them with helpful ideas from psychology, and serve up a tasty blend called Christian psychotherapy. The problem with this approach, which I call the "tossed salad" model, is that concepts with antagonistic presuppositions do not get along well over time. A definite tension exists which can be resolved either by discarding all but one set of presuppositions or by adopting a Hegelian view in which truth exists in the interplay between opposite positions.

This solution, which has crept into much of our thinking, is spiritual suicide. Rather than concerning ourselves with truth based on Scripture, we use whatever procedure seems right to us according to the pragmatic criterion, "Does it work?" We assume that truth represents that synthesis of all competing ideas which seems to best fit the current situation. The absolutes of Scripture become flexible limits which can be bent to accommodate our understanding of what appears most workable.

Biblical epistemology, however, is firmly rooted in the logical law of antithesis (if *A* is true, non-*A* is false) which absolutely refuses to accept concepts which are in any way inconsistent with each other regardless of their apparent value. When we treat this law casually, the authority of Scripture is lost and man's wisdom becomes supreme. There is a way that seems right to a man, but Scripture teaches that the long-term consequence of following it is spiritual death (Prov. 14:12). We must not only insist upon the authority of Scripture, but we must also go to great lengths to be sure that all of our concepts come under that authority. At the very least, that means that integrationists will need to be as familiar with Scripture as they are with psychology, and that whenever the findings of psychological research contradict Scripture, those findings will have to be discarded (see fig. 6).

Figure 6

"Tossed Salad" Model

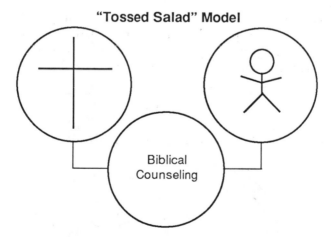

A third position has neatly solved the problem of integrating the two disciplines by eliminating one of them. Because its adherents insist that secular psychology, with its humanistic stain, has nothing to offer, I call them "nothing butterists": nothing but the Word, nothing but the Lord, nothing but faith (see fig. 7).

Figure 7

"Nothing Butterists" Model

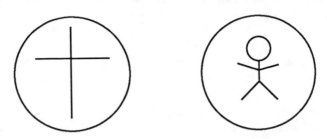

Many current popularizers of Christian psychology, especially those from the pastoral community, would fall into this category. I take issue with my "nothing-butterist" colleagues on at least two grounds. First, their insistence that psychology has nothing to offer is misguided. Much truth has been discovered which in no way violates the truth which God has propositionally revealed. Second, for some reason, "nothing butterists" seem to reduce counseling to a simplistic model of "identify sin and command change." A certain gentle sensitivity to emotional pain is often lost in their unwarranted assumption that all problems reflect willful sin.

I subscribe to a fourth position, which I call "spoiling the Egyptians." We leave Egypt in the strength of a redeeming God, absolutely depend upon his infinite resources, refuse any compromise with his commands, and gladly accept whatever help God provokes the Egyptians to offer. Figure 8 sketches this approach.

Figure 8

"Spoiling the Egyptians" Model

Discovered Truth

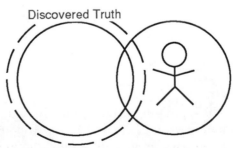

Secular psychology often stumbles onto a biblical concept, then develops it through research. Christians are free to profit from the thinking of secular psychologists but must carefully screen and reject those concepts which depend upon humanistic presuppositions and contradict Scripture. Whatever involves no departure from the character and Word of God is quite acceptable as sustenance on our difficult journey to the Promised Land.

Presuppositions

After choosing a position, the next step in developing a biblical model is to define the limits of what can be considered biblical, or put another way, to clearly articulate the presuppositions upon which one intends to build. We need to agree on a few essentials, broad enough to include every possible fragment of relevant truth but narrow enough to deserve the title *biblical*. A conservative theologian once said that the central presupposition of Christianity is Jesus Christ as the second Person of the sovereign triune God as presented in the Bible, his infallible Word. He adds that this presupposition is " . . . the central truth of the entire system of truth and reality in the universe, the truth so integrated with all other truth as to sustain it and be revealed in it." Everyone who accepts this belief and is fervently committed to working within its broad boundaries can rightly be called evangelical. Those who reject or question this position should not, in my judgment, call themselves evangelical.

I begin my model with the irreducible fact that an infinite, personal God really exists. He is infinite, but I am finite. I am therefore a contingent being. He is personal; I, too, am personal, made in his image. So I am a dependent, personal being. As a personal being, I have certain personal needs which must be met if I am to truly live as a person. As a contingent being, these needs must be met outside of myself. What are these personal needs? Paul's purpose in life was Christ; to honor him, please him, and serve him. Frankl insists that our lives require a meaning beyond ourselves. I am suggesting that our first personal need is significance, the compelling necessity to see our lives as fitting into and moving toward a logically meaningful goal.

The second essential ingredient required for effective personal living is security, the experience of being loved unconditionally by someone whole. Glasser stresses the need to be involved with at least one other person. Rogers builds his entire approach to counseling around this need for genuine, unconditional, nonpossessive acceptance. Paul basked in the thrilling knowledge of a personal God who loved him and gave himself for him. I am proposing, without taking further time to defend it, that as a personal being I basically need significance and security if I am to be truly whole.

As a contingent being, I require a source of meaning and love outside of myself. No finite point can serve as its own framework for integration. The finite depends for its existence and character on its infinite context. I am finite. So I turn to the infinite. If that something infinite is impersonal, then I am in trouble. Undesigned impersonality can provide nothing but random direction which is logically meaningless and brute impersonal matter incapable of love. If there is no personal God, or if I fail to make him the context of my life, then I can have neither significance nor security.

If the infinite is personal then there is meaning available in infinite design and direction. I become a truly significant being in a meaningfully ordered universe, a being who can actually shape the course of history by my choices. I can also enter into a relationship with a personal God. We are two persons who can care for each other. There is therefore love available through involvement with this infinite Person. Christians believe that the only valid source of significance, a life full of meaning and security, a persevering love which accepts me at my worst, is Christ.

However, our entire race has been separated from God by sin. Apart from God we are left to our own resources to meet our needs. And so we develop alternative strategies for finding significance and security, strategies which will sooner or later fail. The core of all psychopathology is the desperate but sinful attempt to meet needs apart from God, an attempt based on the satanically inspired belief that it can be done.

All of us have been programmed by Satan through a false world system to believe that in order to be significant and secure, we need _____. How we have learned to finish that sentence is the basic problem. We believe a lie and we organize our lives around it. Adler calls this a "guiding fiction." Perhaps we believe that our personal worth (our significance or security) depends upon financial success, flawless behavior, great achievement, consistent praise, the absence of all criticism, a loving spouse, a closely knit family, and so on.

Some of these beliefs are more realistic and achievable than others. As long as life provides what we believe we need, we function relatively well. But life apart from God guarantees nothing. Stephen Crane tells of the man who approached the universe and said, "Sir, I exist." To which the universe responded, "However, that fact creates in me no sense of obligation."

Whenever a problem arises which we unconsciously believe is a threat to our significance or security, we consciously evaluate that event as terrible and consequently feel personally threatened. We may try another behavioral approach to overcoming this obstacle to our significance and security, and if we are successful, we feel much better. But the real problem has not been solved. We are still depending on something other than God and what he chooses to provide to meet our needs.

Our modern thinking on marriage offers a classic example. Many books teaching women how to be Christian wives are really textbooks on how to more effectively manipulate husbands. The message seems to be: "You need your husband to love you or you can never be secure; here are a few feminine tricks to seduce your husband into meeting your needs." Now I have not the slightest objections when my wife follows the advice offered in these books. I love it. But I am concerned that a central problem remains untouched: spouses are regularly turning to each other to meet their personal needs. I call this a "tick-on-a-dog" relationship. The problem is that there are two ticks and no dog.

If we cannot manipulate our environment to provide for our needs, the natural response is to retreat to a position of safety. A wife decides, "If my husband cuts me down, I will establish distance between us so that his cuts won't hurt as much." Now what is the problem here? With her conscious mind, this woman evaluates her husband's criticism as terrible. She believes that she needs her husband's love if she is to exist as a secure, worthwhile person. To rebuke her withdrawal and, in the name of Scripture, to command submissive acceptance of her husband is to suggest that she put her neck on the chopping block. Before she will be able to willingly and rationally move toward her husband, she will have to change her mind about what she requires to be secure.

Mental Health and Psychopathology

Figures 9 and 10 detail my theory of mental health and psychopathology.

I need significance and security. I am motivated to meet those needs. I adopt a basic assumption which tells me which goal I must reach in or-

Figure 9

Mental Health Theory

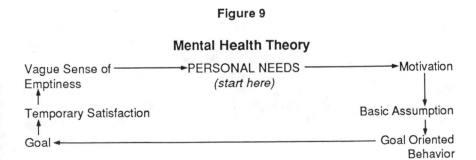

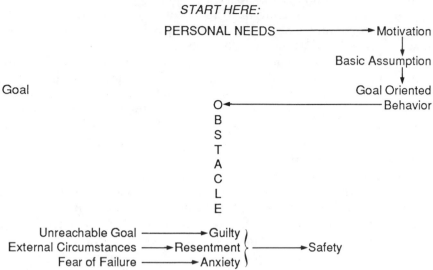

Figure 10

Psychopathology Theory

der to become significant and secure. I then engage in behavior designed to reach that goal. If my behavior is effective and I reach the goal, I feel good. But, because nothing apart from Christ truly satisfies, I sense a vague discontent and go back through the cycle again. I believe that most people today whom we would not call neurotic function in the way this model of mental health suggests.

If, however, I encounter an obstacle en route to meeting my goal, I become frustrated. Behavior therapists, reality therapists, nouthetic counselors, and others emphasize changing a person's behavior from inappropriate to appropriate, or from irresponsible to responsible, or from sinful to biblical. But the real problem is not the behavior. The person is headed toward a wrong goal determined by a false idea about what constitutes significance and security.

If the obstacle derives from an unreachable goal (e.g., I need to be perfect in order to be loved), the person will likely come down hard on himself for failing to reach the necessary goal and feel guilty. If the obstacle is an environmental circumstance (e.g., I need to win the promotion to be significant but the boss gave it to someone else), the likely consequence is resentment against whatever the client perceives as blocking his path to the goal. A third possible obstacle is a fear of failure (e.g., I need to have a man love me but I'm afraid to get married; my husband might reject me). In this case, the predictable psychological reaction is anxiety. Miller and

Dollard's classic conflict paradigm is helpful in understanding this particular disorder.

People who fail to reach their goals and who therefore feel insignificant and insecure tend to desire protection from further hurt. I agree with Adler that most neurotic symptoms are best understood as moving a person toward safety. If I am too depressed to work, I cannot fail on the job. If I suffer from a compulsive disorder, my husband's rejection will be a response to my problem, not to me. Neurotic symptoms often have a rather complex etiology but are most easily understood by a teleogical analysis. Toward what goals are the symptoms directed? What is achieved through the symptoms?

A woman once consulted me concerning severe, almost continuous headaches which apparently had no organic basis but which had plagued her for nearly two years. By studying the consequences of the headaches, it became clear that they were having definite effects. Her mother was displaying a great deal of interest and concern and was terribly inconvenienced and worried about them.

Further analysis suggested that my client's basic assumption involved the belief that she desperately needed her mother's love in order to be secure. She had encountered two obstacles en route to the goal: a fear of failure which created anxiety, and an environmental block (her mother, who had in some ways rejected her) which produced resentment. The headaches relieved her fear of rejection by eliciting attention and they also served as a safe expression of hostility toward her mother.

To openly discuss her relationship with her mother would have been too threatening and to verbally express her anger would have risked further rejection. The symptoms therefore moved her toward a safe but costly resolution of her problems. When my client understood the reason for her headaches, we then discussed her wrong belief that she needed her mother's love in order to be secure. As she slowly began to grasp the love of the Lord, she began to initiate the break in inappropriate dependency. Over a period of three months her headaches disappeared.

Skinner renews circumstances. Rogers renews feelings. Glasser renews behavior. Analysts renew the personality. Christ renews minds. The basis of all transformation is to think differently, to believe differently, to change basic assumptions. Significance and security as a contingent personal being depends exclusively on one's relationship to Christ.

The big problem of course, is grasping that biblical insight in a way that really transforms us. To tell a depressed person that "Jesus loves you" usually elicits about as much interest as informing someone who is starving that a balanced diet is important for health.

Biblical Counseling

How can we change the thinking of our clients and ourselves in a way that touches our deepest inward parts where it really counts? Let me illustrate. A woman consulted me concerning her habit of uncontrollably lashing out at people who in any way crossed her. Insisting that she control her behavior in accord with biblical standards had produced nothing but frustration. She was a sincere Christian who for years had been trying to behave more graciously but experienced constant defeat. She was at the point of wondering whether God really existed and, if he did, whether he cared about her at all.

My first concern was to communicate that I accepted her. Since my acceptance would be meaningless until she knew that I understood how she felt, I simply tried to empathize with her, to enter at least a bit into the emotional pain she felt. She began to share the hurt she experienced at the hands of her harshly rejecting mother. She then shared her deep fear of being rejected again. We discussed her present reactions to the experience of rejection, how perhaps, she was lashing out in a defensive attempt to protect herself whenever she felt threatened. At that point I began exploring her basic assumptions about what constituted security.

Profound rejection as a child had taught her that rejection hurt and it hurt badly. She came to approach life with the idea, the guiding fiction, that she could not exist as a secure person in the presence of any criticism or rejection. Her central problem was the false assumption, the belief that she was worthless unless she was totally loved by everyone. Any rejection rendered her hopelessly insecure. Because she unconsciously believed that her security rested on the absence of rejection, she evaluated any rejection as terrible, she felt angry toward those who were stripping her of her security, and she lashed out.

She understood that the Lord loved her but had never thought through the relevance of his love to her need for personal security. She was still chained to other people, depending on their love, and furious with them for letting her down so often. When I explained to her that security in Christ made her free from needing acceptance from everyone else, her response was, "But how do I stop getting mad?"

It is at this point that counseling cannot proceed without a commitment to believe what God says. Resistance often becomes a problem because the sinful nature is thoroughly committed to unbelief. This particular woman, however, did agree that Scripture was true and that she would cooperate to make it *experientially* true in her life. I then instructed her to write on a three-by-five card the sentence, "All I need to be secure is Jesus' love and I have it; therefore I have all that I need to respond in any situation as a secure woman." Whenever she felt angry, she was to picture her mind as a tape recorder and consciously thrust into the recorder a tape which played this sentence over and over. Then (and here is another critical point in therapy which often takes a while to work through) she was to deliberately choose by an act of her will to say something kind to her attacker, believing that she had all she needed within her to do so. She was to choose this behavior regardless of how she felt.

After the first week, she reported that she would say a few gracious things but only through gritted teeth. She still felt furious. After several weeks of religiously following the program, she burst into tears in my office and said, "For the first time in my life, I can really believe that Jesus loves me." Further therapy helped her come to the point where she could express her anger acceptably, without a bitter spirit, in an attempt to constructively deal with problem relationships. Figure 11 illustrates the entire process of such counseling in a simple, seven-stage model.

Figure 11

Biblical Counseling Model

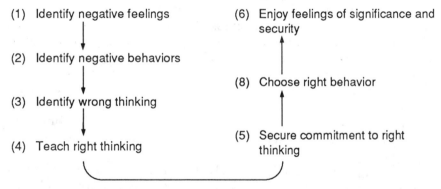

Such a model lays down a broad framework within which there is considerable room for freedom in technique and approach. Rogerian reflection is useful at stage 1. Adlerian life-style analysis is helpful at stage 2. Stage 3 can sometimes be facilitated by free association, dream analysis, and historical tracing. Cognitive restructuring, cognitive dissonance theory, and rational-emotive procedures are all appropriate at stage 4. Gestalt techniques, straightforward moral persuasion, and contractual agreement may help in stage 5. Behavior modification, psychoactive drugs, and hypnosis have a place in stage 6. And stage 7 is the Sabbath— sitting back and enjoying what has happened, resting in the wonderful feelings of realized significance and security.

The Place of the Local Church
in Biblical Counseling

Wouldn't it be nice if it all worked that smoothly? The truth of the matter is that counseling rarely does. One reason why our counseling efforts so often do not really reach the final stage is because we fail to use a major, God-given resource as effectively as we should. I am speaking of the local church.

If we agree that a person's basic personal needs are significance and security, it can be seen that the input of the local church becomes critical in promoting personal maturity. Significance comes from understanding that I belong to the God of the universe who is directing my life as a part of the most important project going on in the world today, the building of the church of Jesus Christ. I can really make a difference on my world for eternity. I can have impact. Pastors and congregations need to stop thinking of the pastor as the only one endowed with the gifts and responsibility to do the work of the church. Paul teaches us that pastors are to equip the saints for the work of the ministry, so that they too can enjoy the thrilling significance of contributing to God's eternal purposes (Eph. 4:11–13).

A man in my home church was utterly miserable a year ago. His marriage was on the rocks, he felt depressed, and he was losing his grasp on God. Although he was able to keep functioning and to pretend that he was a happy Christian, he felt alone, inadequate, and hopeless. In this past year he has come to see himself as a minister, building up other people, sharing with them what he knows of the Lord by leading a small-group Bible study, and helping his wife develop spiritually by loving her as Christ loved the church (Eph. 5:25). Today he is a vibrant, excited, whole Christian, still battling depression sometimes but growing stronger all the time.

A local church is not only uniquely designed to provide a vehicle for meeting significant needs, it is also a natural resource for developing Christian security. What a tragedy that in so many churches fellowship is reduced to sitting next to another believer for one hour a week, sharing a hymnbook, shaking his hand, and glibly commenting, "Nice sermon today, wasn't it?" God designed local bodies to experience close, open, deep relationships. Meaningful Christian fellowship—where I share a burden and you help me, where I bring you food when you're sick, where we get together during the week to encourage one another, to discuss problems with our kids and to seek God's wisdom, where I know you'll accept me no matter what I do—goes a long way toward meeting security needs.

There are three levels of counseling based on the seven-stage model already presented (see fig. 12):

Figure 12

Counseling Levels

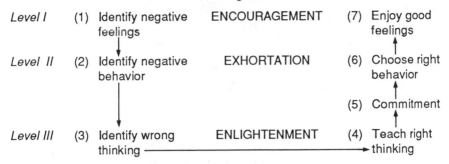

LEVEL I *Counseling by encouragement*
Every member of the body needs to be trained how to be more sensitive, how to listen, and how to communicate care.

LEVEL II *Counseling by exhortation*
A group of mature believers can be taught biblical principles for handling common problem areas and trained to help people approach difficulties biblically.

LEVEL III *Counseling by enlightenment*
A few selected Christians in each local church could be trained in perhaps six months to a year of weekly classes to handle the deeper, more stubborn problems which don't yield to encouragement or exhortation.

Counseling people who desperately need significance and security in an environment which potentially provides both is an exciting possibility. Counseling in that setting should help us to better grasp that Jesus Christ, the second Person of the sovereign, triune Godhead as revealed in the inerrant, infallible, objective Word of God, is the foundation of all counseling that is truly biblical because he alone can meet our deepest personal needs.

8

Assertiveness Training
Rodger K. Bufford

In the past decade assertiveness training has become increasingly widespread. Alberti and Emmon's book, *Your Perfect Right* (1978), has now gone through three editions with ten printings and more than a quarter of a million copies. It has been joined by a burgeoning group of related volumes, each purporting to teach assertive behavior and often oriented toward a special group such as nurses, women, or blacks (e.g., Dawley and Wennrich 1976; Herman 1978; Kelly and Winship 1979; Whitely and Flowers 1978). A review of an issue of the *Psychological Abstracts Index* (Vol. 61, Jan.–June 1979) revealed two full pages of entries under the topics of *assertiveness* and *assertiveness training*.

With assertiveness training workshops being offered throughout the country and the proliferating literature on assertiveness, it is not surprising that the Christian community has become increasingly interested in assertiveness as well; despite some initial misgivings, assertiveness is now widely accepted. This acceptance has been promoted in part by the work of a number of individuals who have suggested that assertiveness is illustrated by Jesus and others in Scripture and that there is clear biblical support for assertive behavior (e.g., Swenson, Brady and Edwards 1978).

Acceptance of assertiveness in the Christian community, however, has not been without some misgivings. Irwin (1978) suggests that Scripture contains a number of teachings which are not consistent with current conceptualizations of assertiveness. The present discussion focuses on three areas which need further consideration in developing a biblical perspective on assertiveness: theoretical conceptions of the nature of assertive behavior and its relationship to aggressive behavior; empirical data regarding the relationship of assertive and aggressive behavior; and biblical teachings which emphasize giving priority to the rights, desires, and needs of others.

Theoretical Conceptions

From the outset there has been ambiguity regarding the distinction between assertion and aggression. Wolpe (1958), one of the developers of assertiveness training, originally defined assertiveness to include "not only more or less aggressive behavior, but also the outward expression of friendly, affectionate and other nonanxious feelings" (114). In more recent writings, Wolpe has drawn a distinction between assertion and aggression (Wolpe 1973; Wolpe and Lazarus 1966).

Others who have confused assertion and aggression include Rathus and Ellis. The first item in the Rathus Assertiveness Scale (Rathus 1973), one of the more widely used assertiveness scales, reads: "Most people seem to be more aggressive and assertive than I am." In his 1973 presidential address to the American Psychological Association, Albert Ellis suggested that assertion is one form of aggression, perhaps the healthiest form. He discussed the ranges of behavior which might be called aggressive, and concluded: "Almost everything good that has been said about aggression can fairly easily be subsumed under the label of assertion" (cited in Dawley and Wennrich 1976, 24).

In a critical review of assertion, Galassi and Galassi (1978) suggest that there is confusion regarding the definition of assertion and the distinction between assertion and aggression. In an extensive discussion of this same issue, DeGiovanni and Epstein (1978) claim that clinical and research literature fails to distinguish assertion and aggression. They note that this confusion stems from several sources: confusion of assertion and aggression in early theoretical models; semantic confusion regarding distinctions between assertion and aggression (the dictionary gives "assertion" as a synonym of "aggression"), and differing value judgments among investigators regarding the appropriateness of specific behaviors. They claim that available self-report and behavioral measures of assertion confound assertion with aggression and also fail to provide for separate assessment of aggressive behavior. They conclude that adequate evidence of discriminant validity between assertion and aggression is lacking "for all measures reviewed."

Echoing the criticisms of DeGiovanni and Epstein, Mauger and his colleagues have developed the Interpersonal Behavior Survey (IBS) with the explicit purpose of assessing assertive and aggressive behaviors in a single inventory (Mauger and Adkinson 1979; Mauger, Adkinson and Simpson 1979). Results of research and scale construction hold promise of providing a clear distinction between assertion and aggression for the first time. Mauger and his colleagues have found that assertion and aggression as measured by the IBS are clearly independent behavioral dimensions. Not a single item in the test pool loads on both assertion and aggression scales; thus at both the item and correlational levels these two dimensions appear to be distinct. While we will note some problems and limitations later, Mauger's work holds real promise in helping to unscramble the confusion between assertion and aggression.

Empirical Data

At the theoretical level there appears to be confusion over the distinction between assertion and aggression. At the empirical level, DeGiovanni and Epstein (1978) report that measures of assertion are confounded with those of aggression. Mauger et al. (1978) report that scores on the Rathus Assertiveness Schedule correlated more highly with peer ratings of aggressiveness (.54) than with peer ratings of assertiveness (.34). Thus the behavioral correlates of the Rathus scale appear to be aggressive in nature.

Assertion and aggression are independent dimensions on the IBS. However, there appears to be one exception. Anderson (1979) used both male and female pairs in a structured interaction setting and measured the relationship between assertion and aggression using both the IBS and behavioral measures. He found that persons rated high on behavioral aggression were significantly higher on behavioral assertion than individuals low on aggression; the converse was not true. Thus highly aggressive persons seem to be assertive, while highly assertive persons are not necessarily aggressive.

In another study using the IBS, L'Herisson (1979) studied the effect of the sex composition of the assertiveness training team on acquisition of assertive behavior in women's groups, using the IBS as a dependent measure. Increases in aggression were observed in groups co-led by a male and a female trainer, while increases in assertion were observed in groups led by two female trainers.

In a study by Hull and Schroeder (1979) a confederate role-played a series of four assertiveness interactions with members of both sexes. The confederate role-played nonassertion, assertion, and aggression. Hull and Schroeder then assessed reactions to the confederate's behavior. In general, nonassertive behavior was ineffective but resulted in positive evaluations; assertive behavior was effective and resulted in generally positive evaluations; aggressive behavior was effective but produced negative evaluations. Hull and Schroeder, however, noted with some surprise that the assertive behavior of their confederate produced a fair degree of critical evaluation by the participants; the assertive confederate was perceived as dominant, aggressive, and unsympathetic. They caution that assertion may have more potentially adverse affects on social relationships than has been anticipated in the assertiveness literature.

Finally, Mauger et al. (1979) report that a fundamentalist group scored lower on several assertive measures than did a nonreligious university sample, while a group of Christian university students did not differ from the nonreligious sample. He interprets these results in terms of the presumed theology of the fundamentalist group. Another possible interpretation, based on Hull and Schroeder's findings, is that these groups may differ in their perceptions of possible consequences of assertive behavior due to different parental responses when they acted assertively.

In summarizing these studies we find that in some instances assertion training increases aggression, and that in some highly aggressive individuals assertiveness may also be high. We have also seen that assertion may sometimes produce adverse social consequences, and that such consequences may differ over groups. These findings raise some disturbing questions about the relationship between assertion and aggression at the empirical level.

Biblical Teachings

Because of its complexity and lack of clarity, we have left a definition of assertion to this point. It is the free expression of wishes, plans, desires, feelings, perceptions, impressions, thoughts, opinions, and beliefs, and the free initiation of desired courses of action while respecting the rights of others.

The rights of others is a problem area about which most authors have little to say. It is generally assumed that each person has rights, and that assertion is a legitimate method of affirming and seeking to acquire what is rightfully one's due. Alberti and Emmons cite the Universal Declaration of Human Rights adopted by the United Nations General Assembly. More simply, Kelly and Winship (1979) suggest that each person has three rights: the right to rectify a wrong or seek justice; the right to refuse; and the right to make requests of others. They suggest that the goal is open communication in which each individual has the right to make and refuse requests from others.

One of the problems with lists of rights is their source. The United Nations has no executive authority, and most authors probably do not accept governmental authority as the basis for their conception of rights in any case. Although not often acknowledged, consensual validation is probably the source of an author's view of personal rights. By contrast, from a biblical perspective, we recognize that all rights come from God. Most broadly stated, we have the right to choose our own course of action both in the natural world and in our relationships to other persons and to God. Paralleling these rights are the responsibilities of being called to account for our actions. We are responsible to the natural order; stepping out a high window without adequate provision results in coming down hard. Similarly, we are responsible socially to the government and to others with whom we interact. Ultimately we are responsible to God at the judgment.

A danger in present approaches to assertion is that they tend to foster or encourage rampant selfishness. The following discussion illustrates this problem:

> . . . There are three possible broad approaches to the conduct of interpersonal relationships. The first is to consider one's self only and ride roughshod over others. . . . The second . . . is always to put others before one's self. . . . The third approach is the golden mean. . . . The individual places himself first, but takes others into account. (Wolpe, cited in Alberti and Emmons, 1978, 9)

The difficulty is that it is very easy to shift from placing self first but taking others into account to placing self first. As we noted above, there is conceptual confusion between assertion and aggression and there is some empirical evidence which suggests that assertion and aggression may go together.

A biblical view gives a much more solid basis for assessing rights (and responsibilities), and also may help to resolve some of the sticky questions which are ignored by most discussions of assertiveness. For example, what happens when assertiveness fails? If A makes a request and B refuses, what then? If you attempt to rectify a wrong and are refused, what do you do next? If there is a disagreement about the facts, with the cleaner insisting that he returned your shirt, while you say he didn't, what happens next? It is here that the drift into aggressive modes of interaction seems most likely to occur. The danger with assertion as currently conceived is that it is sometimes promoted and sometimes perceived as a way of getting what one wants. Thus the limiting factor of the rights of others may be overlooked.

While there is not time to fully develop it, I would like to propose a fourth alternative to the three given by Wolpe, one which is more consistent with the biblical viewpoint. Briefly stated, the individual places others first, but also considers himself.

Putting others first but considering yourself is more consistent with the broad scope of biblical teaching regarding relationships to others: through love serve one another, turn the other cheek, consider others more important than yourself, show concern for the weaker brother, go the second mile, forgive 490 times, seek reconciliation when your brother is offended. Such an approach would be consistent with the basic command of Jesus to love God with your whole self and your neighbor as yourself.

I believe that assertiveness is consistent with biblical teachings if properly conceived. There is a place for rebuking your brother when he offends you, speaking the truth in love when a problem occurs, faithfully wounding a friend, continuing to ask, seek, knock, and so on. But we must be concerned when placing self first is advocated that selfishness may be subtly or blatantly encouraged. Let's place others first but consider ourselves.

References

Alberti, R. E., and M. L. Emmons. 1978. *Your perfect right*. 3d ed. San Luis Obispo, Calif.: Impact.

Dawley, H. T., and W. W. Wenrich. 1976. *Achieving assertive behavior: A guide to assertive training*. Monterey, Calif.: Brooks-Cole.

De Giovanni, I. S., and N. Epstein. Unbinding assertion and aggression in research and clinical practice. *Behavior Modification* 2(1978):173–92.

Galassi, M. D., and J. P. Galassi. Assertion: A critical review. *Psychotherapy Theory, Research and Practice* 15(1978):16–29.

Herman, S. J. 1978. *Becoming assertive: A guide for nurses*. New York: Van Nostrand.

Hernandez, S. K., and P. A. Mauger. n.d. Assertiveness, aggressiveness and Eysenck's personality variables.

Hull, D. B., and H. E. Schroeder. Some interpersonal effects of assertion, nonassertion and aggression. *Behavior Therapy* 10(1979):20–28.

Irwin, T. A theological study of assertion and assertiveness training. *CAPS Bulletin* 4(1978):8–14.

Kelly, J. D., and B. J. Winship. 1979. *I am worth it*. Chicago: Hall.

L'Herisson, L. A. Effects of the sex of group leaders on women participants in assertion training. *Dissertation Abstracts International* 39(1979):4041B.

Mauger, P. A., and D. Adkinson. The interpersonal behavior survey. *Assert 28*, October, 1979. P. O. Box 1094, San Luis Obispo, Calif. 93406.

Mauger, P. A., D. R. Adkinson, and D. G. Simpson. 1979. *The interpersonal behavior survey manual*. Atlanta: Georgia State University.

Mauger, P. A., S. K. Hernandez, G. Firestone, and J. D. Hook. Can assertiveness be distinguished from aggressiveness using self-report data? Paper presented at the Convention of the American Psychological Association, Toronto, August 1978.

Rathus, S. A. A 30-item schedule for assessing assertive behavior. *Behavior Therapy* 4(1973):398–406.

————. 1978. Assertiveness training: Rationales, procedures and controversies. In *Approaches to assertion training*, edited by J. M. Whiteley and J. V. Flowers. Monterey, Calif.: Brooks-Cole.

Swenson, G., T. Brady, and K. Edwards. The effects of attitude pretraining on assertion training with Christian college students. *CAPS Bulletin* 4(1978):14–17.

Whiteley, J. M., and J. V. Flowers, eds. 1978. *Approaches to assertion training*. Monterey, Calif.: Brooks-Cole.

Wolpe, J. 1958. *Psychotherapy by reciprocal inhibition*. Stanford: Stanford University.

————. 1973. *The practice of behavior therapy*. 2d ed. New York: Pergamon.

Wolpe, J., and A. A. Lazarus. 1966. *Behavior therapy techniques*. New York: Pergamon.

9

The Encounter
with the Family of Origin
Mary Vander Vennen

Family therapy as a perspective on human nature and behavior surfaced in the mid-1950s as the result of the work of a number of therapists in different locations who were unknown to each other at the time. Nathan Ackerman in Topeka and later New York, trained in psychoanalysis but influenced profoundly by social theory, began seeing whole families and looking at the interactions between family members rather than exclusively at the process within individuals (Ackerman 1966). On the west coast, Don Jackson, Virginia Satir, Jay Haley, and others began incorporating some of the concepts of cybernetics, communication, and systems theory into their thinking about clinical treatment (Jackson 1973; Haley 1976). In England, John Bell, John Howells, and Ronald D. Laing began seeing families as the unit of study and treatment (Laing and Esterson 1960). And in Washington, Murray Bowen began hospitalizing the families of schizophrenics (Bowen 1978).

These people were among the vanguard of those who were beginning to see that the old medical model (one patient with a single disease which had a specific etiology and diagnosis and which necessitated relatively standard methods of treatment) simply was not adequate to explain the phenomena of emotional dysfunction which they saw. In looking beyond the individual patient to the context in which that patient was embedded, they began to see a wholly different order of behavioral events, an order

111

in which the old diagnostic categories and the old doctor-patient treatment setting seemed obsolete. Probably no one who has interviewed a family with a schizophrenic member has escaped the conclusion that within that family context the patient's behavior, however bizarre, makes perfect sense. Then the question becomes, "*Who* is the patient?"

The whole notion of the etiology of symptoms changed as well. Linear causality (Event A in the past is causing Event B in the present), a kind of thinking dear to psychoanalysts, gave way to circular causality (Event A brings about Event B which in turn has an effect on Event A which may bring about a repetition of Event B or possibly Event C). In other words, there are identifiable and predictable sequences of interactions in families which produce symptomatic behavior. Further, the symptomatic behavior is not an end product but is actually part of the sequence and helps to maintain it. So rather than searching out first of all the origin of a symptom, therapists began asking a different question: "What purpose does the symptom serve for the family?" The particular sequence of interactions or events will vary from family to family, but the process seems to be a universal characteristic of family systems.

The confluence of several streams of thought (i.e., psychoanalysis, object-relations theory, behavioral models, and systems theory) has produced some interesting differences in the practice of family therapy. One of these differences lies in the question of the place of history (or of history taking) in the therapeutic process. Those therapists who emphasize a more purely systemic, strategic approach tend to feel that family or personal history per se is irrelevant (Haley 1976). The "here and now" is the arena where conflicts must be faced and fought out. On the other side are family therapists who always take a detailed family history covering at least three generations and more if it can be obtained (Boszormenyi-Nagy and Spark 1973). This longitudinal family history often yields rich fruit. Families begin to see that the problem which brings them to therapy has roots, that there are patterns of dealing with major events like separation and loss, patterns of marital choice, rules about how men and women relate to each other in the family, and patterns of childrearing which have been consistent over generations. Families often experience some relief at seeing this, at hearing that what seems at present so unexplainable and hard to deal with does in fact make sense in the context of their family history. As a therapist, I am often awestruck at the power and consistency of these patterns over generations. If I may paraphrase the Old Testament, the patterns of behavior of the fathers and mothers are indeed visited upon the children unto the third and fourth generation, and beyond.

Although I am, generally speaking, on the side of the family historians, I believe that simply recounting history may be a waste of time. I believe that the task of the therapist is to help clients encounter their history, and particularly, to encounter the significant figures of their past, usually their parents, in a new way. I want to describe in this chapter the concept of *differentiation* and my way of working with adults to help them achieve a greater level of differentiation within their family of origin by re-encountering their parents.*

The lifelong developmental task of human beings is that of differentiation. This task begins at conception and takes a leap at birth when a mother and her infant physically separate from each other. Emotional differentiation does not occur at birth. Emotionally the infant is in an almost completely reactive position, that is, the baby's emotional state is almost completely dependent on, and reactive to, the emotional state of those around him or her, especially the mother or mothering figure. If the mother is anxious, the infant will tend to be fussy and not eat and sleep contentedly. If the mother is relaxed and secure, the baby will tend to thrive physically and emotionally. Differentiation will usually then proceed to the point where the infant can identify the mother and other people in the environment as separate from the self, with whom interaction can take place.

Over a period of years and through successive developmental stages, the child moves toward an active adult position. The adult says, "This is who I am, this is who I am not; these are the values (spiritual, emotional, behavioral) I live by, these are values I reject; these are things I will commit myself to doing in order to make my life a closer approximation to what I believe and feel it should be, these are things I refuse to do because doing them will violate me and my sense of who I am." Less and less of the adult's behavior will be determined in the strict sense of that word by the behavior of others, and more will be internally generated.

We should not think of an absolutized ideal of differentiated adult which a person achieves at a certain age or stage of life. Differentiation is a process which goes on throughout a person's life unless the process "gets stuck" at some point. Getting stuck in differentiating lies at the heart of most problems which bring a family into therapy. It is minimally a two-generation problem, because it always involves the dialectic tension inherent in the parent-child relationship, the tension between holding on and letting go. It usually involves three generations and sometimes more, though for practical purposes more than three generations are not often directly available to the therapist. Children rarely move beyond their parents' level of differentiation from *their* parents unless some external circumstance or therapy nudges them along. At the

*For much of my thinking and practice in this area I am indebted to the work of Murray Bowen (cf. Bowen 1978).

heart of every symptom, in adult or child, from alcoholism to delinquency to schizophrenia, lies a struggle with or anxiety about differentiation. Moving on in the differentiation process involves encountering the significant figures in one's life in a new way. Usually that means going and talking with one's parents as an adult rather than as a child.

Relationships between adults and their parents tend to fall into a stereotyped pattern. If they live close to each other, there may be frequent contact by way of phone calls or visits. Contact tends to be initiated more by one than by the other, and though the receiver may be somewhat resentful of the contact, there is some anxiety if for some unknown reason it is not made. Conversation tends to be rather superficial: what the (grand)children are doing, social activities, gossip, and so on. There may be the ritualistic Sunday dinner with everybody gathered at the same place, invitation unspoken but carrying the force of a command, with penalties for "no shows." Conversation too tends to follow unwritten but very real rules. Certain subjects are taboo, or if not taboo, avoided because an argument will certainly follow. Certain ways of reacting or of behaving are not tolerated. Some or all of the people may be uncomfortable with the pattern, but nobody challenges it. The older adults want to do something to keep the family together and the younger ones say, "After all, Mom and Dad won't always be with us, and we had better keep it up while they're still here."

If there is a geographical distance, contact may be made by letter or perhaps by phone call. Visits take place on certain holidays, or there may be a lengthy summer visit during which people live in the same house. These contacts may be anticipated in various ways and to various degrees, but there is often a half-guilty but very real sigh of relief when they are over.

Sometimes younger adults cut themselves off completely from the older generation and proudly display the fact as proof of their adulthood and independence, as proof that they have no difficulties with their family of origin. ("I don't have any problems with my folks. We never see them. We leave each other alone.")

The characteristic common to all the situations I have described is that contact and communication are stereotyped, utterly predictable, and sterile. Everybody knows, though it is almost never explicit, what the rules are, and deviation from the pattern raises anxiety and is perceived as a threat to the closeness of family relationships.

When that situation occurs it is a sign that parents and their adult children have not learned to relate to each other on an adult-to-adult basis. The differentiation process has become stuck at some preadult level, a level which contains sore spots, unrecognized and/or unresolved conflict, and anxiety. If family members are aware of this, the feeling may be that peace at any price is preferable to the pain of opening up old wounds again, and relationships remain static. If there is little or no recognition of conflict, there may be a vague restlessness or depression around contacts with each other. Contacts are made at least partly out of a sense of duty, but there is very little if any satisfaction in them.

When I ask adults whether they think they can do something to change their relationship to their parents, I often hear, "They're getting old and I couldn't risk hurting them," or "What's the use? I couldn't possibly talk to my parents about what's bothering me. You don't know my parents! *Nobody* can talk to them! They'll never change!" Unfortunately, often these same adults are coming to me because of problems with their own children. In such cases, therapy becomes a three-generation effort.

We organize our therapeutic work around three questions: What do you want to say? What do you want to hear? What can you do to make the saying and hearing happen?

This work needs to be done with each parent individually. Attempting to talk with both at once re-establishes old triangles, and besides, the issues with each may be different. I often hear adults say they have never talked about anything personally significant with just one of their parents. For them to insist on a one-to-one contact is often in itself a big step toward establishment of an adult position.

"What do you want to say?" may require some work in therapy before encountering the parent. Empty chair gestalt work may be effective at this point. I sometimes ask less verbal clients to write a completely uncensored letter to the parent, bring it to a session, and read it aloud to me. Often this has a cathartic effect, with much anger and grief poured out. Then we begin looking at the client's role in making or keeping things stuck and at how to begin to take responsibility for the self. For example, "You make me feel/do" must be separated into "When you do . . . I feel/do . . . ," and the client needs to own responsibility for what "I feel/do" and look at some alternative responses. The objective in this work is not to ask or manipulate the parent to change. The objective is for the *client* to initiate change, leaving the parent with freedom of response.

Answers to the question "What do you want to hear?" are often touchingly simple. Many adults are longing for messages of love and acceptance, forgiveness, or acknowledgment on the part of the parent that certain actions were wrong or at least ill-advised. Sometimes they have questions which they have never asked but to which they suspect answers. "I have always felt you loved my sister more than you loved me. Is that true?" "Why didn't you trust me?" "Why did you have so many (or so few) children?" "How did it happen that . . . ?" "What were you like when you were my age?" "Why did you and Dad get married?" "How did you feel when I was born?"

The process and effect of this kind of work *with* the family of origin are different from going to a therapist and talking *about* the family of origin, though some of that may need to be done as a preliminary step. Furthermore, coming to know one's parents in a different way gives a person knowledge of origins, rootedness, and self. These are essential ingredients for responsible adulthood and responsible parenting of one's own children.

The actual difficulty of rebalancing relationships of course varies from family to family. Sometimes children are stunned to find that their parents are able and even eager to respond to the changes they initiate. Children may find that parents have been just as dissatisfied with the status quo. On the other hand, there are families which are extremely threatened by change and consequently resistant to it. It is possible that a mother and daughter can never have an intimate relationship. But if in trying to develop one, a daughter comes to understand her mother's problem with intimacy, comes to understand herself and the part she has played in their distance, and is able to grieve for what she will never have, she will be relieved of guilt and will have taken major steps toward adulthood and responsible parenting of her own children.

What if the parents are already dead? Often I see people who have had unresolved conflicts with their parents, with either a lack of mourning or perhaps excessive mourning for their deaths. The consequences show up in their own lives and/or in the lives of their children in various ways. There may be a gradual blockage of all types of feelings, an unhealthy overconcern for one's children, depression, or other symptoms. The parent introject may be alive and active long after the parent has died. Unresolved problems with parents can and need to be worked at even when the parents are already dead. This may be approached following Williamson's (1978) model or adapting other approaches to grief work.

Doing this work always creates anxiety in clients. In my experience, deep healing usually occurs, though I am careful not to hold that out as a promise. Occasionally, the reality that one's parents have not functioned as parents is brought home with new and painful clarity. But whether healing between the generations occurs or not, the person who has done the work will have moved on in the differentiation process. Such people will have gained more ability to stand in a generational line, able to relate more freely with both the preceding generation and the next one, with fewer distortions, projections, and fantasies. God blesses such efforts for the generations to come.

References

Ackerman, N. 1966. *Treating the troubled family*. New York: Basic Books.

Boszormenyi-Nagy, I., and G. Spark. 1973. *Invisible loyalties: Reciprocity in intergenerational family therapy*. New York: Harper and Row.

Bowen, M. 1978. *Family therapy in clinical practice*. New York: Aronson.

Framo, J. 1976. Family of origin as a therapeutic resource for adults in marital and family therapy: You can and should go home again. *Family Process* 51(2):193–210.

Gurman, A., and D. Kniskern, eds. 1981. *Handbook of family therapy*. New York: Brunner-Mazel.

Haley, J. 1976. *Problem solving therapy*. San Francisco: Jossey-Bass.

Jackson, D. 1973. *Therapy, communications and change*. Palo Alto: Science and Behavior Books.

Laing, R. D., and A. Esterson. 1960. *Sanity, madness and the family*. London: Penguin.

Stierlin, H. 1977. *Psychoanalysis and family therapy*. New York: Aronson.

Williamson, S. 1978. New life at the graveyard: A method for individuating from a dead former parent. *Journal of Marriage and Family Counseling* 4(1):93–101.

10

Hypnosis and Theology
H. Newton Malony

Meg Greenfield, editorial writer for *Newsweek*, recently reported two incidents which are apropos to our thinking. The first had to do with the period immediately after Pearl Harbor. Seattle, where she grew up, did its duty and mobilized its citizens in preparation for possible air attack. As a girl in her early teens she was assigned the role of junior air raid monitor in the neighborhood civil defense organization. One night there was an air raid drill. All the lights in the city were blacked out. She went to her room, donned her helmet, put on her arm band, got her pad and pencil, turned on her flashlight, and started out the front door into the night. Her mother stopped her. "Where do you think you're going?" "I'm going to the corner—to my post. I'm a junior air raid monitor, you know", she replied. Her mother answered, "You're not going anywhere—it's dark outside!" What a let down for an eager twelve-year-old girl!

This may be an admonition that is just as appropriate for adult hypnotists as for junior air raid monitors. "You're not going anywhere—it's dark outside. Stop and think before you run out." There is a night out there in hypnotism that needs to be considered. We have become so enamored with the technique that we need to stop before moving too quickly. Perhaps we could use someone at the door to stop us and say, "You are not going anywhere until you think through your method again and its meaning in light of your identity as a child of the Creator/Redeemer God. "So my inference from Meg Greenfield's first anecdote is to stop, look, and think about the theology of hypnosis before using this technique.

The second incident Greenfield reported was a humorous reflection on the aging process. On her birthday she mused over the benefits of aging, one of which was the revelation that she was now too old to be stoned to death for adultery in Muslim countries. While basking in this relief she noted that, according to Muslim law, the worst fate that could befall her—at her age—for such an offense was to have her face stained with black mud and, thus, to have to parade her evil before everyone who saw her.

There are, indeed, benefits to growing old but there are also pitfalls. This is especially true of counselors and psychotherapists. As research has shown, experience is one of the crucial ingredients of help that really helps. This is the benefit of growing old. We have been through a lot; there are few surprises. We have learned from experience and our clients benefit from that. We are no longer hesitant novices thrown hither and thither by the latest therapeutic dilemma. Yet, therein also lay the pitfalls. Experienced therapists, like older people, can become set in their ways. They become less reflective and more conservative; they enjoy the security of the status quo. They tend to question themselves less and to prejudge others more quickly. Research, while it shows experience to be a crucial factor in good counseling, also shows therapy can be "for better *or* worse"—that is, some counseling continues to be unhelpful even though the counselor grows older.

More pertinent to our consideration of hypnosis is the haunting possibility that we grow more active in our counseling methods the older we get. I have talked to a number of my friends, some of whom espouse client-centered methodologies, and we have all agreed that as the years have gone by we have become more active in the therapy process. Hypnosis is an example of a very active therapy—in fact, there may be no more active method. Could it be that a study would reveal that a more frequent use of hypnosis would correlate with increasing age of the counselor? If so, we may have a confounding of the tendency for the use of a therapeutic modality with a pitfall of the aging process—namely, an inclination to be more directive and less reflective.

Once again, therefore, the inference I would draw from Greenfield's anecdote about aging is the admonition to reconsider the use of this methodology in light of basic values. This is particularly important for those who claim to be religious. If there is one message that the Judeo-Christian faith espouses, it is that confidence and security come to the old, as well as the young, through trust in God—not overreliance on this world's knowledge. As Isaiah wrote when admonishing Israel to give up dependence on horses and armies, "For thus said the LORD God, the Holy One of Israel, 'In returning and rest you shall be saved: in quietness and in trust shall be your strength; and you would not" (30:15). Let this last phrase, "and you would not," not be said of us lest we confound more active therapeutic means, such as hypnosis, with the common tendency of aging persons to put too much trust in their own opinions and abilities.

These introductory comments on the importance of reflection about the foundations of hypnosis lead me to the more general question of whether hypnosis needs theology or vice versa. The answering of this requires some definitions of terms. (Dictionary definitions will suffice at this stage of our discussion.) *Hypnosis* is defined as a condition like sleep in which one loses consciousness and will say and do things at the suggestion of the person who has put him into this condition. *Theology* is defined as the systematic study of God or the relation of man and the universe to God. As the history of psychiatry will attest, James Baird coined the term *hypnosis* to describe the trance state into which persons could be induced by being asked to fix their gaze upon a single point for a short time. The history of the term *theology* is less clear, although it is apparent from the study of religions that for much of recorded history there have been those who presented what they believed to be the truth *(logos)* about God *(theos)*.

What need have these disciplines for each other? Initially the answer might be "none" in that they appear to be directed toward different objects of study; on the one hand human beings and on the other hand God. Yet, on closer examination this is not and cannot be true. The very definition of theology includes the statement ". . . the relation of man and the universe to God." The study of God is always God in relation to persons. Theology inevitably includes anthropology. Although the study of God in and of himself is of import, the prime concern of theology is, and always has been, the relationship of God to humans. In this relationship the nature of human being—how persons behave—is critical. Often, it is assumed that God relates to the will alone. It is here that the drama of sin and salvation occurs (cf. 1 John 1:1–10, esp. v. 9: "If we confess our sins, he is faithful and just and will forgive our sins and cleanse us from all unrighteousness"; also John 1:6–13, esp. v. 12: "But to all who received him, who believed in his name, he gave power to become children of God.")

Yet this assumption—that the will alone is important—is not borne out by a closer examination of Scripture. As the writer of Psalm 103 so beautifully states, "As a father pities his children, so the LORD pities those who fear him. For he knows our frame; he remembers that we are

dust" (vv. 13–14). Whatever the essence of the first persons was originally (we do not know what substance God used in his creation of man;
see Gen. 1:27), it appears that both man and woman were created from
materials of the earth because God said to Adam after the Garden of
Eden debacle, "In the sweat of your face you shall eat bread till you return to the ground, for out of it you were taken; you are dust, and to dust
you shall return" (Gen. 3:19). Although "flesh" comes to have a negative
or sinful connotation in some parts of Scripture (cf. Rom. 1–5), more often it refers to the basic human condition of finiteness—complete with
frailty, aging, memory loss, partial knowledge, and so on (cf. Ps. 145:21;
Joel 2:28; 2 Cor. 4:11). Thus, the earth-boundness of the human situation
is of concern to theology both in terms of the factual essence of the being
created by God, to whom God comes, as well as the proclivity of that
same creature to deny and disobey God. Hypnosis, the tendency to go
into a sleeplike state and to obey the commands of an authority, is part of
that creatureliness and therefore is of concern to theology.

There is another way in which theology, of necessity, relates to hypnosis. All theology is *apologia,* that is, it seeks to relate the truth about God
to the truths of the day in which it is written. This was true of the Gos-
pels, most clearly the Book of John, which was a direct attempt to relate
the Christian revelation to the wisdom of Greece. It was also true of
Paul's outreach to the Greek world as depicted in his message in the Are-
opagus (cf. Acts 17:22–31, esp. v. 23, "For as I passed along, and observed
the objects of your worship, I found also an altar with this inscription,
'To an unknown God'. What therefore you worship as unknown, this I
proclaim unto you."). It has been true down through the centuries from
Augustine, to Aquinas, to Pascal, to Luther, to Wesley, to Schleiermacher,
Ritshl, Rauschenbusch, Niebuhr, Tillich, and Barth. All have been
apologists.

Although human capacities and the nature of the influence process
have been a part of speculative philosophy for many centuries and although the proclivity of persons to become possessed has been of concern to physicians since the post-Inquisition time of Jacob Weyer, we
have seen a veritable explosion of new knowledge regarding these issues
in the past two centuries. As Auguste Comte predicted, the human sciences have come into their own and hold a more than respectable place
within the scholastic world.

In 1781 Mesmer received wide acclaim in Paris. He had a wooden tub
filled with ground glass, water, and iron fillings from which protruded
iron rods which persons could touch to afflicted areas of their body and
receive healing via a mysterious magnetic force which Mesmer believed
permeated the universe. Although he was declared a charlatan by both
the Viennese and Parisian medical societies, it is noteworthy that he was

not condemned by the church and that the common people flocked to him and even reported cures from "bottled" magnetism and from his pointed index finger. The cultural environment was changing and the era of the human sciences was beginning.

By the mid-1800s hypnotism was a part of the intellectual milieu. Respectable physicians such as Baird, Liebeault, Bernheim, Charcot, Binet, Freud, Hull, Hilgard, White, Sarbin, and Barber have brought hypnotism out of the esoteric realm and into the mainstream of psychology. The fact that "suggestibility," the human capacity which has come to substitute for Mesmer's "animal magnetism," is now thought to be normally distributed in the human being and the undeniable ability of some hypnotists to influence persons far beyond the effect of simple commands are such accepted truths that theology, if it would have an apologetic role in the modern world, cannot ignore them. It must enter into dialogue with hypnotism just as it does with anxiety, egotism, power, and a whole host of other basic human processes.

The early church father, Tertullian, asked, "What has Jerusalem to do with Athens?" By this he meant, "What has the truth about God (Jerusalem) to do with the truths of this world (Athens)?" The answer is "Everything!" Theology must take seriously its imperative to be apologetic. Theology not only needs hypnosis, it wants it. It intends to do dialogue with and probe the depth of behavioral science. It is like relating a surface to its depth, a cross section to its longitudinal perspective, function to structure, and the foreground to the background.

That brings me to the related question with which I began this section: "Does hypnosis need theology?" An answer might be, "It may not need it but it has it!" It cannot avoid it because there are theological presumptions behind all human knowledge. In this regard, a helpful distinction could be made between "felt" and "real" needs. Felt needs are those acknowledged and overtly accepted. Real needs are those unacknowledged but nevertheless present and active. Thus, hypnosis may have a real but not a felt need for theology. Perhaps it would be more correct to say that hypnosis has a theology whether it wants it or not, whether it knows it or not.

There are implicit theological assumptions in all human endeavors, especially those encompassed by the social/behavioral sciences and the healing arts. Thomas Oden has clearly demonstrated this for client-centered therapy. His proposal is that where the therapeutic conditions of empathy, congruence, and warmth are offered that there God in Christ is present because these are the essential ingredients of the incarnation. Some have wondered whether his construct of the *implicit Christ* is valid since religious language is never used. Yet this is the very issue when hypnosis is considered. While most hypnosis is undertaken without religious overtones of any kind, is it not possible, even probable, that God is uniquely present in many of the processes involved? Further, is it not highly likely that there are strategic theological assumptions underlying both the state of hypnosis and the procedures utilized which are operative whether they are admitted to be present at all or not?

It might be said in rebuttal that everything in the universe is related to everything else and in that sense hypnosis is related to theology—but, in a practical sense, theology has no impact on or meaning for hypnosis. This is probably the spirit in which most of the helping professions and much of behavioral/social science functions. Yet in answer to this contention, the distinction made by Tillich between "ultimate" and "penultimate" concerns is informative. This distinction is grounded in the difference between "basic" and "neurotic" anxiety which Tillich suggests is the type of insecurity we feel in relation to ultimate reality on the one hand and the uneasiness we experience in our relationships with people on the other. Penultimate issues are those everyday, interpersonal concerns we have about our place and status in the present moment. These are neurotic anxieties. Ultimate issues are those concerns we have about the meaning of life and our final security in the universe. These are basic anxieties. Tillich's contention is that, while a descriptive distinction can be made between the two, in the final analysis all neurotic anxieties (penultimate concerns) are grounded in basic anxieties (ultimate concerns). Once a person settles the issues of ultimate concern the matters of penultimate concern are experienced in a different context. So it is with hypnosis.

Certainly, the majority of the problems dealt with in therapeutic hypnosis are penultimate in nature (e.g., handicapping but forgotten memories, phobias, social inhibitions, problem habits). Yet, they, without a doubt, are grounded in penultimate or basic anxiety. Furthermore, the trust relationship that inevitably precedes good hypnotic inducement more than likely resembles Oden's therapeutic conditions for the incarnation. Finally, the processes involved in suggestions for change and promises of health are intricately bound up with hope for deliverance and salvation. As Ernest Becker has noted, one of the cruelest frauds perpetrated by mental health professionals is the implicit promise of the complete and final cure. Hypnotists are not immune to offering false promises. Becker notes that all cure is "for a time" and no one ever cheats death. Ultimate anxieties about death cannot be assuaged by the illusion of a cure that will not fade, although many clients will make this assumption.

The history of hypnosis is instructive in this regard. It will be remembered that the antipathy of psychoanalysis to hypnosis is based on the rejection of the method by Freud when he discovered that the symptoms often returned or that there was symptom substitution after hypnotic treatment. He preferred free association to suggestion and self-conscious, aware insight to semiconscious, unaware trance to prevent what he came to term *the return of the repressed*. Of course, there are many who suggest that his rejection of hypnosis was shortsighted and who question whether his preferred treatment is, in fact, more effective. However, this historical vignette must not be forgotten by contemporary hypnotists who run the risk of promising too much with the method and who either send clients away falsely confident they have settled ultimate issues or who leave disappointed and disillusioned, not knowing where to turn for final answers since the method they were led to trust failed.

In summary, it can be said that hypnosis is realistically and meaningfully related to theology whether this be known or not just as theology must consider hypnosis if it would have an apology to make to the modern world. It is appalling to note in a survey made of the literature from the late 1950s to the mid-1970s that no book or article was written relating hypnosis to theology or vice versa. Thus the attention of this chapter to these issues is needed and important.

Dimensions of Hypnosis and Theology

Hypnosis is an ability, a state, a process, and a method wherein persons, through talking with another individual, can do things they could not or would not usually do and wherein they unintentionally engage in acts they would or could do normally.

Hypnosis is an ability in the sense that some people are hypnotizable and some are not; among those who are, there are differences in the degree to which trance can be induced. In the general population, about 18 percent of the people have little or no susceptibility, about 64 percent have a moderate degree of it, and about 18 percent have a large degree. Although the underlying trait has been described by several names, the most commonly accepted one is *suggestibility*, which refers to the ability to entrust oneself to and to be influenced by another person. Those with marked ability in this regard are termed *hypersuggestible*. In spite of the fact that this ability or trait is sometimes deprecated in common conversation, it is used in a descriptive, valueless manner by social-behavioral scientists.

Second, hypnosis is a state. This refers to the widely accepted conclusion that when persons are hypnotized they are in an altered state of consciousness. Earlier it was thought that a person went to sleep during hypnosis but this has been rejected in favor of a state of hyperconcentration and confident entrustment in which an individual is open to and susceptible to heightened influence from another person. Although the spontaneity and awareness characteristic of the normal waking state are missing, individuals evidence control and responsiveness in hypnosis quite unlike that which they exhibit in sleep. In contrast to sleep, hypnosis is probably an exaggeration of awake behavior in which persons are responsive to each other and in which they seek and allow mutual influence to take place. The difference is most likely quantitative rather than qualitative. In hypnosis the individual is hypersuggestive, hypersensitive, and hyperopen to being obedient to the direction of another individual whom he trusts almost without question.

Third, hypnosis is a process. Earlier it was thought that individuals would go into a hypnotic state with the pointing of a finger or the giving of a simple command. Freud seemed to believe this. It is noteworthy that in the case of Emmy von M. he reported: "Her chief complaint referred today to a cold sensation and pains in her right leg which emanated from the back, above the crest of the ilium. I prescribed warm baths and massage twice daily. She was an excellent case for hypnosis. I held my finger before her and called out 'Sleep!' and she sank down with an expression of stuporfication and confusion. I suggested sound sleep and an improvement of all the symptoms." When he finally declared hypnosis a failure in the case of Lucie R. and abandoned the method, one gets the impression that it was due to his impatience with what has come to be known as the "necessary process" in the inducing of hypnosis. Freud was correct in suggesting that hypnosis involved a type of relationship between client and therapist that included transference-countertransference dimensions. It is a process of relating whereby the client comes to trust the therapist and in which the therapist assumes great responsibility for the client. However, what Freud wanted to avoid, hypnotists of today accept, cultivate, and use with respect, intuition, and great sensitivity. Hypnosis is a process that develops over time in a relationship between two people.

Finally, hypnosis is a method. The emphasis here is on the technique as practiced intentionally by persons trained in a set of skills. This takes hypnosis out of the realm of the esoteric. Much is known of the influence process in general and even more is known about the inducement of the hypnotic trance state in particular. Although the procedures are amazingly simple they are perpetrated by responsible persons to be used in a skilled and professional manner. Stage and clinical hypnosis utilize the same methodologies but general and ill-considered use of the skills is discouraged by most trained hypnotists. Nevertheless, hypnosis is a method whose skills can be learned and practiced by anyone with interpersonal sensitivity and intuition.

These four considerations—hypnosis as ability, state, process, and method—are basic for such dialogue as can be carried on with theology. They provide the basis for much thought about how the study of God and his relations with human beings interrelates with this exceptional phenomenon we term *hypnosis*.

Although there are theologies inherent in all of the world's great religions that might be appropriately related to hypnosis in that it is a universal human phenomenon, the discussion herein will be confined to theology as conceived in the Christian tradition. Thus, the dimensions of theology concerned with God as revealed through Jesus Christ will comprise the content of these remarks.

The doctrine of God has sometimes been termed the *cosmological component* of theology. It pertains to the basic understanding of the reality which transcends, supercedes, creates, sustains, and directs the universe in general and the world in particular. The doctrine of God in the Judeo-Christian tradition has included affirmations that there is One who brings the world into being; creates living things to live within it; calls persons to be his faithful servants; has a purpose for each person and all of history; steadfastly loves, guides, forgives, and empowers persons to live to his glory; reveals himself supremely in Jesus Christ; and who will come again at the end of history to complete his final will. Further, he is above us as well as within us. He is personal yet transcendent. Overall, the Christian faith is that there is a God and that "the earth is the LORD's and the fulness thereof, the world and those who dwell therein . . ." (Ps. 24:1).

The doctrine of man has sometimes been termed the *anthropological component* of theology. It pertains to the basic understanding of the human being as perceived in the light of the doctrine of God or cosmology which precedes it. This last comment regarding which component of theology has priority is crucial to note. The doctrine of man is not formulated inductively by surveying the acts of people and then making pragmatic statements or laws about human behavior. Theological anthropology is not the gathering together of facts into generalizations. Quite the contrary, the doctrine of man is that which is deduced from the doctrine of God. It is a statement of who persons are in light of who God is. This is the critical distinction between what theology says and what psychology says. Theology makes statements about the human being wherever and whenever he or she is found. Psychological statements are always contingent upon circumstances and averages. Psychology is descriptive while theology is prescriptive. The Judeo-Christian tradition has included such statements as: the human being is that being for whom Christ died; who was created by God to have dominion over the earth, to live in peace with other persons, and to obey God in all endeavors; who is corrupted by sin and willful disobedience; whose sins are forgiven; and who can live a new life by God's power. As has been said, these affirmations declare both the grandeur and the misery of man.

The doctrine of redemption is implicit in the above description of the doctrine of man. It is that set of affirmations which pertains to the process of human history as conceived under both the purpose and the intervention of almighty God. The Judeo-Christian faith affirms both an ultimate fulfillment of God's purposes in history apart from the help or hindrance of human beings as well as a fulfillment of God's will in those individuals who, by faith, confess their sins and turn to God for salvation. Christ declares the ultimate victory of God's love over all evil as well as offers forgiveness of sin and redemption to those who will accept his love for them. The Christian doctrine of redemption always holds these two themes in tension. It claims all the power for God and disallows any pleas based on human righteousness—yet calls each believer to live a good life based on God's will.

These components, therefore, are the rudiments of Christian theology: a doctrine of God, of man, and of redemption. Putting the emphasis on the human situation they could be summed up in the following four statements: Man—created by God, corrupted by sin, corrected by Christ, and completed by the Holy Spirit.

The Christian Hope and the Therapeutic Task

All therapy, especially hypnotism, needs to be placed within the context of Christian hope (cf. Matt. 25:31–46; John 14; Rev. 21:1–6). As always, the promise of God that he will come again is one that includes judgment and fulfillment. He brings his kingdom in through the work of his people but also on his own terms and by his own power. There is always the element of surprise in the final judgment. The parable of the master who hired laborers at all hours of the day in Matthew 20 typifies God's love and his demand. Evelyn Underhill held that persons are called to be faithful, not to be successful. The important thing for the therapist to remember is that while God is depending on him or her to do a good job, in an ultimate sense God is not dependent on any of our efforts.

Further, while all his energies are directed toward change in the client, the therapist should not forget that he, too, is being redeemed by God's action. In other words, the kingdom is coming in the life of the therapist as well as the life of the client. God is doing something in therapy with both parties. Therapy is a part of holy history just as much as is the history of nations. In a real sense, persons may get better in spite of us as well as because of us. This is obviously true in an empirical sense. But, more importantly, it is true in a theological sense. Therefore, let us, in such an active therapy as hypnosis, not cease our attempts to do a skillful job. But let us cease our perfectionistic expectations or overdependence on methodology. We can rest in the assurance that while God is working through us, he is also working over and beyond us for the ultimate good of those whom we counsel.

Christian Knowledge and the Therapeutic Relationship

Freud decried the transference-countertransference process that hypnosis involved. He felt it compromised the neutrality of the therapist. Further, it confounded the reflections of the client with feelings about the therapist. According to Freud, the best therapy occurred when the therapist was a passive catalyst for the working out of the repressed feelings of the client.

Hypnosis, at its best, involves a close relationship between hypnotist and client. As indicated earlier, research since the time of Freud has clearly indicated the importance of trust, empathy, and warmth in preparing people for trance inducement and in carrying them through hypnotic concentration and posthypnotic suggestions. Milton Kline, for example, includes in his book some poems written by young women who had been in hypnoanalysis. Some of these verses are as follows:

> Love is to be with you
> Soft voices taking me
> Outside where I have never been
> If ever the stiff straight wall
> Between me and man
> Might fall, it is when I
> Lose the little gain the much
> And lose the trembling flow
> Below me hidden for I dare
> Not know what reason
> In the voice the sensual
> Craving of a breast for hand
> Is half implicit. . . .
>
> Wherever the heart is, the eyes are looking
> And we have been so close
> To go now.
> Open your heart—I lost mine somewhere
> And I want to feel it as I did
> Before I knew you—
> What have I lost—
> What have I not gained (Kline 1958, 4).

These are obviously the words of a person in a close and deep relationship. They would be an affront to Freud.

This is not true of Christian understanding. The Hebrew meaning of the word *knowledge* is relationship. To know God is to have a personal encounter with him. If God is to be revealed through Christian persons, as I assume every religious hypnotist would affirm, then he is to be revealed through the relationship between therapist and client. Certainly most writing about psychotherapy since the time of Freud has asserted that equally as much healing occurs by modeling and identification as through insight. In fact, it is widely agreed that insight, by itself, does not heal. It may sound trite to say that God reveals himself through persons and that what people come to trust in life is other people. Thus, the very naive way in which most hypnotists promote dependency could be said to be Christian in the best sense of the word. It is no accident that the poems noted above have a quasi-sexual connotation because the best experiences between therapist and client do resemble sexual intimacy. Of course, there are dangers here but the important thing to remember is that closeness, dependency, and identification are not bad in and of themselves. In fact, they are integral to Christian witness (Ellens 1982).

Christian Devotion and the Hypnotic State

It is commonly assumed in hypnosis that the hypnotist cannot make the client do anything that the client does not want to do. Of course such a presumption is based on the thesis that all motivation is unconscious. It may well be, from this point of view, that a person would not be aware of wanting to do something and may in fact be resistant to it or find it difficult in a waking state. However, under hypnosis this same individual may be able to remember, do, or agree to undertake any number of actions which are in harmony with ultimate good health. Thus we assume that he wanted to do what the hypnotist told him to do deep within his subconscious mind.

Another common assumption is that in the hypersuggestible, single-concentrated state of hypnosis the individual is able to focus attention and to disregard distractions to the point where he or she is able to do that which posed great difficulty in the waking state. Thus, clients are able to direct their energies into a single channel and to keep themselves focused on tasks without giving way to other alluring or compelling alternatives. The final assumption is that the therapist, through intuition and skill, can be trusted to know what is best for persons and what they would truly like to do or be.

These assumptions have parallels in theology in terms of the nature of the ideal response to God as indicated in both Old and New Testaments. Joshua set the tone for the Old Testament when he posed for the children of Israel the alternative of worshiping the baals of the land or remaining faithful to Yahweh. In Joshua 24 he states: "Now therefore fear the LORD, and serve him in sincerity and in faithfulness; put away the gods which your fathers served beyond the River, and in Egypt, and serve the LORD. And if you be unwilling to serve the LORD, choose this day whom you will serve . . . but as for me and my house, we will serve the LORD" (v. 15). Deuteronomy 6:5 asserts this same theme: ". . . you shall love the LORD your God with all your heart, and with all your soul, and with all your might."

In the Sermon on the Mount Jesus calls for a style of life that is no less focused and single-minded. After a series of admonitions to love one's neighbor and to forgive one's enemies, Jesus sums it up with these words: "You, therefore, must be perfect, as your heavenly Father is perfect" (Matt. 5:48).

The ideal Christian response to God has consistently been pictured as single-minded devotion in which one puts aside the distractions of the world. If hypnotists help persons achieve this skill they are well within the spectrum of what true life is all about. If one assumes that the optimal state of mind would be that in which persons know what they want and pursue it without distraction, then the hypnotic state would be the norm rather than the waking state in which persons either deny their true selves or are unable to focus their attention because of many distractions.

Of course, such thoughts as these presume that deep inside what persons want is what God wants for them. This is problematic. It may be that original sin has clouded not only the mind but the heart so that even desires beneath the conscious level will not be in accord with persons' true being as conceived by God who created them. This problem was addressed by Kant with his distinction between practical and pure reason as well as by Barth who thought that persons could not be trusted to know what was best for them in a faith sense. Thus from this latter point of view there would need to be revelation from outside the hypnosis relationship for the client and the hypnotist to know what to induce in the trance because neither individual could be counted on to supercede original sin. The alternative to this point of view is to say that the heart of man has not been touched by the fall and that what hypnotism does is to assist persons in getting in touch with who they truly are in a faith sense. Thus, the hypnotist could be trusted to know what was best for the person and the person could be trusted to know it was good down in the subconscious mind.

Single-mindedness is at the heart of the ideal response demanded by

God to the good news of the gospel. Christian hypnotists can take heart in knowing that when they delimit the effect of distracting influences and assist persons in concentrating on a single task they are potentially helping persons to be who God intended them to be. As Jesus said, " . . . do not be anxious. . . . But seek first his kingdom and his righteousness, and all these things shall be yours as well" (Matt. 6:31, 33).

References

Becker, E. 1973. *The denial of death.* New York: Free Press.

Ellens, J. H. 1982. *God's grace and human health.* Nashville: Abingdon. (See particularly the final chapter.)

Kline, M. V. 1958. *Freud and hypnosis.* New York: Julian Press.

Oden, T. 1966. *Kerygma and counseling.* Philadelphia: Westminster.

Tillich, P. 1951. *The courage to be.* New Haven: Yale University.

11

Meditation and Altered States of Consciousness
Bill Zika

During the past decade, a great deal of attention has been focused on the application of meditation, hypnosis, and other consciousness-altering techniques to psychotherapeutic outcomes. Laboratory and applied research as well as case-study reports have documented the beneficial effects of these techniques in terms of affective change, improved cognitive and perceptual ability, and reductions in pathological personality factors (Bandler and Grinder 1979, 1981; Barber, Spanos and Chavez 1974; Erickson, Rossi and Rossi 1976; Orme-Johnson and Farrow 1977).

Earlier research, particularly into transcendental meditation (TM), appeared to validate the claims of its proponents that the technique led to improved psychophysiological functioning and elicited a fourth major state of consciousness separate from waking, sleeping, or dreaming (Wallace 1970). It may be noted that dramatic improvement in psychophysiological functioning has also been reported with the use of other consciousness-altering techniques such as hypnosis and dates back at least to Mesmer in the eighteenth century (Shor and Orne 1965).

In both meditation research and research into hypnotic phenomenon later findings have indicated that a degree of caution is necessary with respect to such claims. In hypnosis research a number of paradigms have been developed to explain the effects reported with the use of hypnosis (Edmonston 1977). In meditation, the recent research into the variables leading to beneficial effects have failed to identify clear causal factors in results (Morse et al. 1977; Pagano et al. 1976; Smith 1975). Therefore, there are important questions remaining about the usefulness of meditation and altered states of consciousness in achieving psychotherapeutic effects. The dynamics leading to these outcomes need to be more fully explored and possible detrimental effects deserve attention. This point is underscored by the conclusion that positive expectancies and involvement in imaginings may be responsible for the reported results achieved with these techniques (Smith 1975, 1978; Spanos and Barber 1974).

The questions of the psychodynamics involved in the application of consciousness-altering techniques as well as the use and abuse of these techniques by their practitioners deserve the attention of the psychologist and the theologian. This is relevant to both fields since the therapist and pastoral counselor may decide to apply consciousness-altering techniques in their work with clients seeking psychological or spiritual wholeness. While the psychotherapeutic process itself may involve a change in consciousness (Watts 1961), the therapist may also choose to enlist such adjuncts to the therapeutic process as meditation, hypnosis, and neurolinguistic programming techniques in a more formal manner in order to facilitate a more satisfying set of responses and subjective experiences for his or her client.

Important questions facing the clinician with respect to the appropriateness of these methods are: Can these techniques be used to promote personal growth and positive behavioral changes from a secular point of view? Can they be used to encourage spiritual awareness from the theistic point of view? Can these disciplines be abused and in the long run result in detrimental effects for the individual?

The purpose of this chapter is to consider these basic questions from the point of view of the psychodynamics involved. This dynamic interpretation draws essentially from three schools of thought. The first relates to the conscious and unconscious components of motivation, behavior, and identity within an analytical framework. The second relates to cognitive organization and strategies of mapping and responding to the territory in which we live. The third relates to the proposition put forth by Krishnamurti (Holroyd 1980) that it is the ego and the images supporting it which create separatism and conflict, both internally and externally. This conditioning of the psychological structure establishes the nature of the psychodynamics and the way in which cognitive mapping takes place. Direct appreciation is then lost and images of reality rather than "choiceless awareness" (Holroyd 1980) motivate behavioral reactions.

The use of meditation and consciousness-altering techniques can be therapeutic and enhance spiritual growth when unconscious resources are engaged (Barnett 1980; Bandler and Grinder 1979). This engagement allows for a reorganization of the cognitive mapping to a better representation of the reality of the territory. From this reorganization new behavior is unconsciously generated toward positive outcomes. Finally, this unconscious resource in conjunction with the conscious motivation, intent, and awareness may be able to re-establish a wholistic, direct appreciation of reality where action is the result of sensitive and caring choiceless awareness.

Meditation and consciousness-altering techniques may be abused by promoting images which reinforce existing subconscious dynamics as well as moving the cognitive mapping of the territory further away from reality. This may also act as a negative resource, alleviating symptoms in conjunction with the motivation and intent of the conscious mind. In other words, these techniques may establish a compensatory response by exchanging one set of images for another. The defenses of the conscious mind would contribute to the abuse of techniques.

The use and abuse of meditation and altered states of consciousness, therefore, may relate to the motivation or interest of the client as importantly as the technique itself. Motivation to experience the reality of the internal and external territory may encourage unconscious resources to respond to that territory in constructive ways. On the other hand, motivation to relieve symptoms or feel better may lead to the cognitive mapping becoming incongruent with the internal and external territory and encourage subconscious ego complexes to develop strategies which are either destructive or have short-term advantages (Barnett 1980).

An attempt will be made to demonstrate the dynamics of the ego in relation to two parts of the unconscious. One part is a resource for creative, productive understanding and wholistic experience of the territory. The other is a subconscious ego complex of maladaptive behavior patterns based upon early critical experiences which shaped the cognitive mapping inappropriately. This latter part is fragmented into various complexes involving id and superego reactions and supports a defense of seemingly necessary beliefs toward the world. The images and fragmentation are incompatible with the creative part and result in conflict. Meditation and other altered states have been advanced as ways of dealing with this conflict and its behavioral correlates. As a dilemma in both the psychological and spiritual sense, the motivation and intent of the client become key variables for the psychologist and pastoral counselor to consider.

There are various therapeutic approaches involving consciousness alteration and communication with unconscious resources as a means of changing behavior, including meditation, analytical hypnotherapy, Ericksonian hypnosis, and neurolinguistic programming (Bloomfield and Korry 1976; Barnett 1980; Erickson and Rossi 1976; Bandler and Grinder 1979, 1980). The most persuasive explanation put forth by the proponents of these approaches for the detrimental results, ineffectiveness, or partial success in some cases is that either the technique was not applied or adhered to correctly or that the part of the subconscious sustaining the behavior could not accept the alternatives presented by the creative part of the subconscious. The argument presented here, alternatively, is that the creative part of the unconscious may only respond when the intent or motive of the conscious mind is to re-establish contact with internal or external reality so that the map and the territory are congruent and positive responses are an expression of this choiceless awareness. Conversely, inappropriate solutions, delusions, or ineffectiveness may result when the intent or motive of the conscious mind is to avoid contact with reality. Therefore, one set of images sustained by a maladaptive part of the subconscious is replaced by another set of images while leaving the motives based upon past experience as well as the subconscious ego complex substantially unchanged.

Psychodynamics of the Ego Struggle

Various therapeutic models have proposed that the ego moves away from a direct experience with reality to a fragmented representation or mapping of the territory based upon subconscious complexes (Barnett 1980; Janov 1970; Lowen 1972). Cognitive belief systems and structures are then established to either control urges according to a set of rein forced roles (superego) or to rebel and attempt to express these urges in order to satisfy the needs according to the belief system of the id. While these psychoanalytic terms are not always referred to, a closer look at therapeutic models encouraging a movement toward direct experience of the territory reveals a rejection of the fragmented way in which the ego structure has established these images.

For example, gestalt therapy, primal therapy, and bioenergetics represent a movement away from fragmentation and images toward direct experience through an unconditioning process whereby a shift in consciousness to present-centered reality allows a behavioral change to take place (Janov 1970; Lowen 1972; Perls et al. 1972). The gestalt model states: ". . . we consider the self as the function of contacting the actual transient present . . . we explain the various neurotic configurations as various inhibitions of the process of contacting the present" (Perls et al. 1972, 371). A number of therapeutic models which make use of meditation and hypnotic techniques have also attempted to explain therapeutic changes in a psychodynamic manner. Goleman (1971) proposed that the practice of transcendental meditation leads to psychotherapeutic un-stressing by integrating unconscious processes through a derepressive and calming effect of the mantra. Bandler and Grinder (1979) and Lankton (1980) propose a neurolinguistic model which concentrates on the subconscious organization of representational systems into patterns of behavioral responses. Their psychotherapeutic techniques, such as re-framing, make use of the concept of unconscious mechanisms mediating maladaptive patterns of behavior. They encourage the client to change behavior in the direction of more positive outcomes by using dissocia-tion in trance to allow the conscious mind to step away and generate new choices from the creative part of the subconscious.

A review of Erickson's work with trance utilization (Erickson, Rossi and Rossi 1976) also suggests the importance of an integrative ability by the unconscious to make substantial changes in behavior as well as iden-tity. In Erickson's work, the unconscious mind relates more closely to the wholistic creative mind rather than the analytic concept of the un-conscious as an accumulation of repressed experiences.

Both concepts of the unconscious are accurate. The unconscious may comprise creative, wholistic potential which promotes choiceless aware-ness leading to the mapping becoming more congruent with the terri-tory. It may also comprise subconscious ego complexes reflecting the images and fragmentation which promote maladaptive behavior; this represents an incongruence of the map with the territory.

Psychodynamically, conflict seems to be the outcome of fragmenta-tion based upon the images created by the subconscious ego complexes. The past unresolved experiences and needs of the id, or child part of the subconscious, lead to a set of behavioral patterns which often conflict with the limits imposed by the judgments and conditioning of the super-ego or parent part of the subconscious. Even when these complexes are in balance there is a conflict based upon an experience of the world (ter-ritory) which is the product of conditioned images. The images are not present-centered and therefore conflict with the wholistic unconscious which attempts to integrate the map with the territory in a direct appre-ciation of and response to reality.

In the analytic model, the ego, or adult part of the subconscious, may attempt to mediate between the id and superego to change neurotic suf-fering into normal human misery as Freud expressed it (Freeman 1980). However, this only leads to greater conflict, since it relies on a stronger ego effort often resulting in further suppression. In addition it is based on prior self-knowledge, experience, and images which are themselves in conflict with the wholistic unconscious.

Meditation and Consciousness-Altering Techniques: Restructuring Images or a Resolution of Conflict?

The central questions relevant to this chapter may now be examined, since a framework of the psychodynamics has been advanced. These questions are as follows: Can meditation and consciousness-altering techniques be used to promote personal growth from a secular point of view? Can they be used to promote spiritual awareness? Can they be abused and result in detrimental effects to the individual? The question of use and abuse will be explored by contrasting the potential of meditation and consciousness-altering techniques for restructuring the images, with their potential for facilitating choiceless awareness, leading to the direct experience of the wholistic unconscious.

From a secular point of view, the psychotherapeutic potential of consciousness-altering techniques in resolving psychological conflicts and initiating positive behavioral outcomes is attractive. This avenue of personal growth has been promoted through meditation techniques (Bloomfield and Kory 1976), analytical hypnotherapy (Barnett 1980), neurolinguistic programming (Bandler and Grinder 1981), and rational-emotive therapy (Ellis 1973). The evidence from the reported use of these techniques suggests that the cognitive restructuring which eventuates, produces a substantial therapeutic change in behavior. From the framework proposed in this chapter, it is possible that this therapeutic change is the result of superimposing one set of images (positive outcomes) over another set of images (negative outcomes). If these former images are initiated by the conscious mind or subconscious ego complex, there is a danger that the newly structured image and consequent behavior is a superficial treatment of the problem leaving the motive which is based upon past experience unchanged. The image is still not congruent with the territory. This may be likened to the relief of a symptom in psychosomatic medicine which leaves the cause unchanged.

In terms of spiritual awareness, the ability to restructure the images of the ego may also provide a feeling of spirituality by identifying with the faith or deity in which one believes. However, the danger to spiritual growth appears to be that the subconscious ego complex becomes the source of these spiritual feelings. It is therefore a facsimile of contact with the sacred rather than a real experience of the wholistic unconscious. The map is still incongruent with the territory and various defenses are often constructed to avoid these inconsistencies. For example, an individual's claims of religious adherence to beliefs and spiritual values may be in conflict with indirect expressions of hostility, prejudice, and other forms of destructive behavior.

The final question of whether consciousness-altering techniques can be abused and in the long run lead to detrimental effects for the individual is important. Due to the aforementioned secular and spiritual factors, the potential for detrimental effects upon behavior, self-awareness, and spiritual growth appears likely.

Some cases where detrimental effects are possible have been reported by Bandler and Grinder (1979). They comment that in applying a meditative approach to all problem solving, a key difficulty arises in some situations where a relaxed, passive response is inappropriate. For instance, if an emergency requires quick, spontaneous action to avert danger, the relaxed, passive response may result in hesitation.

In another study by Williams (1978), evidence is reported which supports these claims. In this investigation, TM practitioners performed less effectively than nonmeditators on a perceptual motor task requiring accurate motor response to external stimuli. He suggests that the inner reflection and passive nature of the technique may be inappropriate for this task. French, Schmid and Ingalls (1975) report a case involving a young woman who experienced an acute schizophrenic episode after meditating excessively over a period of three months.

On the other hand, there are enough reports of success in the use of meditation and consciousness-altering techniques to resolve psychological conflicts to suggest that this outcome is also possible. The use of these techniques to dissociate the conscious ego and contact the wholistic, creative part of the unconscious offers a cognitive restructuring by creating solutions which affect the subconscious aspect of the ego without the suggestion of imposition of external images. This change appears to allow a present-centered response to situations free from subconscious ego complexes and provides a congruence between the map and the territory. The behavioral outcomes are therefore positive and spiritual awareness and growth proceed without inconsistencies between beliefs, values, and behavior. Defenses are unnecessary and the experience is validated by the wholistic unconscious.

The use of meditation and consciousness-altering techniques in this manner contrasts markedly with the abuse of these techniques in the willingness of the individual to observe and experience the problems related to subconscious ego conflicts rather than impose solutions to deal with the symptoms of these conflicts. The solution may actually lie within the problem itself, since by observing and experiencing the images and conflicts of the subconscious ego complexes there is a rapport established with the wholistic unconscious which supplies an effortless solution.

Intentionality and the Use and Abuse of Meditation and Consciousness-Altering Techniques

Meditation and altered states of consciousness are capable of being used to alter or dissociate the ego or conscious mind from subconscious ego complexes and encourage the creative, wholistic unconscious to integrate changes in maladaptive patterns of behavior.

The intentionality of the practitioner of these techniques may be the key element determining whether meditation or consciousness-altering techniques are used or abused. The techniques themselves appear to be amoral, but the choice made by the individual may be moral or immoral. The thin line between use and abuse may be mediated by the intentions of the practitioner, since the only role of the ego in bringing about constructive and substantial change in this framework is in the positive expression of volition to experience the problem, establish rapport with the creative part of the wholistic unconscious, and allow the solution to be created by the unconscious. In both the secular area of the psychodynamics of behavior and the spiritual area of the existential source of meaning, the map can become congruent with the territory.

Discussion

The psychodynamics presented here in relation to the use and abuse of meditation and altered states of consciousness have important implications for the fields of psychology and theology. This is particularly evident for the psychotherapist who holds either a secular or theistic point of view and who chooses to use self-regulation techniques such as meditation, hypnosis, relaxation, contemplation, or reflective prayer as an adjunct to therapy. There is room for integration of these seemingly exclusive models of secular and theistic psychology by recognizing common psychodynamic elements of ego and subconscious functioning which are related to either psychological and spiritual wholeness or disintegration and conflict. On the other hand, and perhaps more importantly, the possibility is raised that through these adjuncts to psychotherapy the therapist operating from either a secular or spiritual paradigm may facilitate an integration and resolution of conflict leading to a greater freedom of choiceless awareness which determines behavior in a creative manner. Conversely, he or she may facilitate a set of restructured images which are false resolutions of conflict resulting in a reinforcement of maladaptive behavior patterns. Cognizance of the importance of the intentionality of the client in using these self-regulation techniques in the former manner may provide control of a critical variable for the therapist in leading to a psychotherapeutic outcome which is also a movement toward spiritual wholeness.

References

Bandler, R., and J. Grindel. 1979. *Frogs into princes: Neurolinguistic programming*. Moab, Utah: Real People Press.

————. 1981. *Trance-formations: Neurolinguistic programming and the structure of hypnosis*. Moab, Utah: Real People Press.

Barber, T. X., N. P. Spanos, and J. F. Chaves. 1974. *Hypnotism—imagination and human potentialities*. New York: Pergamon.

Barnett, E. 1980. *Analytical hypnotherapy: Principles and practice*. Toronto: Junica.

Bloomfield, H. H., and R. B. Kory. 1976. *Happiness: The TM program, psychiatry and enlightenment*. New York: Simon and Schuster.

Carrington, P. 1977. *Freedom in meditation*. New York: Doubleday.

Davidson, R. T., and D. T. Goleman. 1977. The role of attention in meditation and hypnosis: A psychobiological perspective on transformations of consciousness. *International Journal of Clinical and Experimental Hypnosis* 25(4):291–308.

Edmonston, W. E., Jr., ed. 1977. *Conceptual and investigative approaches to hypnosis and hypnotic phenomena*. New York: Academy of Sciences.

Ellis, A. 1973. *Humanistic psychotherapy: The rational-emotive approach*. New York: Julian Press.

Erickson, M. H., E. Rossi, and S. Rossi. 1976. *Hypnotic realities*. New York: Irvington.

Ferguson, P. C., and J. C. Gowan. 1977. Psychological findings on transcendental meditation. In *Scientific research on the transcendental meditation program: Collected papers*, edited by D. Orme-Johnson, and J. Farrow. Vol. 1. New York: Maharishi European University.

Fischer, R. A cartography of the ecstatic and meditative state: The experimental and experiential features of a perception–hallucination continuum are considered. *Science* 174(1971):897–904.

Freeman, L. 1980. *Freud rediscovered*. New York: Arbor.

French, A., A. Schmid, and E. Ingalls. 1975. Transcendental meditation, altered reality testing and behaviour change: A case report. *Journal of Nervous and Mental Disease*. July 161(1):54–58.

Gill, M. M., and M. Brenman. 1959. *Hypnosis and related states: Psychoanalytic studies in regression*. New York: International Universities Press.

Goleman, D. Meditation as meta-therapy, hypothesis toward a proposed fifth state of consciousness. *Journal of Transpersonal Psychology* 3(1971):1–25.

Hartland, J. 1971. *Medical and dental hypnosis and its clinical applications.* London: Baillere Tindall.

Holroyd, S. 1980. *The quest for the quiet mind.* North Hamptonshire: Aquarian.

Janov, A. 1970. *The primal scream.* New York: Dell.

Jung, C. G. 1959. *The archetypes and the collective unconscious.* Pantheon Bollinger Series, vol. 9. London: Routledge and Kegan Paul.

Kent, I., and W. I. Nichols. 1972. *Amness: The discovery of the self beyond the ego.* New York: Bobbs-Merrill.

Krishnamurti, J. 1953. *Education and the significance of life.* New York: Harper and Row.

————. 1975. *Beginnings of learning.* New York: Harper and Row.

Lankton, S. 1980. *Practical magic.* Cupertino: Meta.

Lowen, A. 1972. *Depression and the body.* New York: Coward, McCann and Geoghegan.

Masters, R. 1975. *How to control your emotions.* Los Angeles: Foundation.

Maupin, E. W. Individual differences in response to a zen meditation exercise. *Journal of Consulting Psychology* 29(1965):139–45.

Morse, D., J. Martin, L. Merrick, and L. Dubin. 1977. A physiological and subjective evaluation of meditation, hypnosis and relaxation. *Psychosomatic Medicine* 39(5):304–24.

Orme-Johnson, D. W., and J. T. Farrow, eds. 1977. *Scientific research on the transcendental meditation program: Collected papers.* Vol. 1. New York: Maharishi European University.

Pagano, R. R., et al. Sleep during TM. *Science* 191(1976):308–10.

Perls, F., R. Hefferline, and P. Goodman. 1972. *Gestalt therapy: Excitement and growth in the human personality.* London: Souvenir.

Rosen, H. 1953. *Hypnotherapy in clinical psychiatry.* New York: Julian Press.

Shapiro, D. H., and S. Zifferblatt. Zen meditation and behavioral self-control. *American Psychologist* 31(1976):519–32.

Shor, R., and M. Orne, eds. 1965. *The nature of hypnosis.* New York: Holt, Rinehart and Winston.

Smith, J. C. Meditation as psychotherapy: A review of the literature. *Psychological Bulletin* 82(1975):558–64.

————. 1978. Personality correlates of continuation and outcome in meditation and erect sitting control treatments. *Journal of Consulting and Clinical Psychology* 46(2):272–79.

Spanos, N., and T. X. Barber. Towards a convergence in hypnosis research. *American Psychologist* 29(1974):500–11.

Tart, C. T. A psychologist's experience with TM. *Journal of Transpersonal Psychology* 2(1971):135–40.

————. 1972. Transpersonal potentialities of deep hypnosis. In *The highest state of consciousness,* edited by J. White. New York: Doubleday.

Wallace, R. K. Physiological effects of transcendental meditation. *Science* 167(1970):1751–54.

Watts, A. 1961. *Psychotherapy east and west.* New York: Ballantine.

White, J. 1976. *Everything you want to know about TM including how to do it.* New York: Pocket Books.

Williams, L. R. 1978. Transcendental meditation and mirror-tracing skills. *Perceptual and Motor Skills* 46(2):371–78.

Wolberg, L. R. 1960. *Hypnoanalysis.* New York: Grove Press.

12

Preventing and Reversing Marital Burnout
David R. Leaman

An intriguing challenge for a counselor is to work with a married couple in distress stemming from prolonged, unfulfilled expectations. The person who tries to cope in a relationship in which the expectations are unclear and the rewards are minimal, eventually experiences burnout (Freudenberger and Richardson 1980). The burnout symptoms in marriage are similar to those in the work setting. They include decreased motivation, lack of gratification, pervasive apathy and anger, lowered productivity, and decreased ability to deal effectively with others (Carroll and White 1981). Consequently, the emotional needs of the partners are unmet. When these symptoms are prolonged in a marriage, unresolved conflicts lead to emotional or actual divorce.

Marital Burnout

The process in which a marital relationship deteriorates to a burnout point may take many years, depending upon the tenacity of each person's unrealistic expectations. This process can be viewed as occurring in gradual phases ending in divorce, unless the couple's expectations can be clearly identified and realistically adjusted.

The marital burnout process has been divided into four stages by

143

Baum-Bricker and DeTorres (1982). The process is initially characterized by partners who hold high expectations of what the relationship should be and how each spouse should fulfill the other's needs. The couple, in this stage, tend to adhere to unrealistic ideas about marriage based on childhood perceptions. They have fixed concepts about roles and often exhibit inflexible attitudes with tunnel vision. They deny evidence that their expectations need to be challenged and they resist change.

The second phase emerges as each partner attempts to make the other conform to his or her expectations. Much energy is invested in manipulating one's spouse to function according to preconceived notions about marital happiness. Since the desired results are not obtained, the partners react negatively with critical and condemning interactions. This phase is usually volatile and intense as each spouse continues to believe that the partner can and must be changed. Each person may feel unappreciated and misunderstood as disillusionment emerges.

Eventually, after repeated and unsuccessful efforts to make the relationship conform to their expectations, the partners avoid each other or withdraw. This is the third phase marked by hostility, detachment, and a gnawing sense of futility. The couple has minimal motivation to resolve their conflicts. Therefore, there is a marked decrease in rewarding interactions. Since their expectations and needs are unfulfilled, they become disillusioned.

The final stage of burnout is characterized by a deep sense of hopelessness and fatigue. The couple experiences such disillusionment that apathy often pervades other areas of life. They resist suggestions to improve because they are convinced that nothing can help their marriage. In despair, they either experience emotional divorce and feel trapped while staying together, or conclude that actual divorce would be less painful. Many couples delay seeking professional assistance until the second or third stages, when their disillusionment is highest.

Needs Assessment

The process of marital burnout is not irreversible. Couples can learn methods by clarifying their needs and mutually fulfilling them. The focus of this chapter is to delineate a specific technique that can accomplish that goal. The needs assessment technique is not a panacea but it can be an effective tool to reverse the process of marital burnout and enable couples to experience a mutually rewarding relationship.

Two conditions are necessary in order for the technique to be employed in the therapeutic setting: (1) the couple must express a desire to improve their marital interactions; and (2) the individuals have learned, or are learning, the basic communication skills of active listening.

The procedures of needs assessment can be utilized in both group settings and marital therapy. Several sessions will be necessary. After therapeutic rapport has been established and the necessary social history acquired, the couple can be introduced to the concept of unfulfilled expectations and be led to recognize their efforts to change each other. The therapist can encourage the couple to consider that a rewarding marital relationship is possible by identifying and sharing their needs openly and contracting to meet one specific need of the spouse on a trial basis. The following practical definition of love may help the couple develop a readiness for needs assessment: "Love is the accurate estimate of the other person's needs and a commitment to try to meet those needs" (Foth 1974).

Prior to initiating the needs assessment technique, several inhibiting attitudes might have to be explored and challenged. Some examples include:

1. My spouse should know my needs, so why should I tell him or her?
2. If I share my needs honestly, my spouse will exploit my vulnerability and use it as a weapon against me.
3. If I give on one item, my spouse will take advantage of me and expect more than I can give.
4. If I meet his or her need, and my spouse doesn't try to meet mine, I'll look like a fool and be hurt.
5. If I give now, I have the right to demand later.
6. I'm afraid I can't meet any of my spouse's expectations to his or her satisfaction no matter how hard I try.

These representative beliefs and others can be identified and discussed. Their exploration provides insightful information regarding marital interactions. These concerns are common and the participants can be reassured that it is risky to self-disclose, but essential for the growth of the marriage. Also, both spouses have the same potential to be helped by the technique. The contract in needs assessment is reciprocal so that each partner expects to give something and receive something meaningful in exchange. The therapist should emphasize that the needs assessment procedure is to be experienced on a trial basis.

Procedures for Needs Assessment Fulfillment

The therapist assists the couple in completing the following procedures, especially coaching in active listening and identifying specific behavioral needs. The first three skills should be covered during one therapeutic session. The fourth should be completed in another session.

Listing Your Needs

Think about your needs in the marriage. What are the things you would like to experience more in the relationship? What do you need from your spouse, or what do you desire your spouse to do more often? Be specific. Try to avoid using general statements such as, "I need to be happy" or "I want to be loved." Write down both little and big needs (at least three). Do not be concerned that your spouse may have more needs than you. Be honest in identifying what you need and listing your requests. Write what you need, *not* what you want your spouse to stop doing.

Sharing Your Needs

Take turns sharing your needs. Sit face to face so that you can comfortably touch each other. Try to look at your spouse as you share.

1. Begin by saying, "I need from you . . . " or "One thing I want in this relationship is. . . . " State only one need at a time. You may want to share why you need it or explain your request more completely.
2. Your partner listens in silence until you have stated your first need clearly. Then your partner paraphrases it without further comment; there should be no attempt to answer, justify, complain, or accuse. Your partner simply listens carefully and repeats it.
3. You continue in this manner until you have shared all your listed needs.
4. Now switch roles. Your partner states a need as described above and you listen. In listening, try to "tune in" as accurately as you can. Attend to the verbal message and to nonverbal body messages.
5. Your partner continues sharing and you listen until all listed needs have been identified. The lists are to be kept for future exercises.

Selecting the Need You Are Willing to Meet

1. Take a few minutes to reflect carefully on your spouse's needs. Ask yourself, "Which need am I capable of meeting if I really try?" or "Which of my spouse's needs am I willing to make a special effort to fulfill during the next week?" *Select only one need.* Changes come in small but definite steps. You cannot meet all of your spouse's needs at one time. Consider your limitations as well as your capabilities.
2. Share with your spouse the one request that you have chosen. Remember that in marriage both persons' needs must be met and

that each person must be willing to give sincerely in order to receive the benefits of love. You may want to share why you have selected that particular need, especially if you also have the same need.

It is not appropriate to remind your spouse that she or he has not met that need in the past. No grounds for accusations and criticism exist since both have unfulfilled needs. Only honest listening and genuine concern are appropriate.

After completing this session, the participants are encouraged to think of how each would meet the need of the spouse through specific actions. The couple may be given a week to think about it without contracting to change any behaviors. If the couple is Christian, a homework assignment such as reading Colossians 3:12–15 together and sharing their thoughts on it could be given. Also, the couple could be challenged to think of one fun activity to do together during the next two weeks.

Making a Contract to Fulfill Your Partner's Request

1. Flip a coin to decide which person's request will be considered first. Then discuss how you plan to meet that one need. Identify what will be done, when it will be done (or how often), where, and how. Do this for each partner.

   These specifics are important since they involve a careful consideration of your commitment and a clear description of what each will do to improve the relationship regarding this need area. This exercise may seem somewhat mechanical but it helps to clearly establish the goal and saves a lot of arguing later on. Both persons discuss the need and how both will know when the need is met. Again, active listening is essential.

2. Discuss your plan of action and establish an agreement. Describe the specific changes you intend to make in terms of each request. Then write the agreed plan of action on paper and sign it with your partner. (The Need: _____; Action: I will _____.) You may want to include a bonus or special reward clause for keeping the commitment. The contract should specify the length of time.

   The therapist must assist the clients in clearly defining how needs will be met through specific behaviors. The more specific in terms of what, when and how often, the easier it is to evaluate fulfillment. Again, emphasize that this is an experiment in learning to meet each other's needs. Some clients will object to the approach because it seems mechanical and they want their spouse to spontaneously perceive and meet their needs. This is a method for teaching spouses how to respond to mutual needs, and spontaneous giving will eventually result.

3. Pray together, either silently or aloud, that God will help you keep this commitment contract with your spouse and do it without begrudging. Agree to pray together regularly for each other. Especially ask God to help you meet your spouse's requests. Prayer is a great unifier. The more a husband and wife make friends together with God, the greater he makes their friendship for each other. Prayer increases the motivation to meet a spouse's needs.*

Celebrating the Fulfillment of Each Need

1. Affirm one another by expressing gratitude for the efforts your spouse has made. Let your spouse know that you appreciate the change in his or her behavior. By complimenting the small steps, you motivate bigger ones.
2. Celebrate your success by doing a fun activity together. The activity does not have to be costly, but should be something enjoyable that you don't usually do. An alternative is to reward your spouse by doing something special for him or her.
3. Share your contract and the positive outcomes with at least one other couple or individual (besides the therapist). Such sharing can strengthen your unity and increase your motivation to meet your spouse's other needs.
4. An optional activity could be to start a "marriage" diary in which you keep a record of ongoing progress in your relationship.
5. Give thanks to God for your partner and the efforts your partner has exerted.

The procedures described above enable the spouses to identify and clarify realistic needs. The context provides an opportunity for them to share in a supportive atmosphere with sufficient structure so that each can understand clearly the needs of the other. Contracting to meet each other's needs is a practical method for exercising commitment. Since the behavioral changes are observable and measurable, the results are mutually rewarding. It is a practical way to actualize the "golden rule" concept in marriage. The needs assessment procedures provide a workable framework to help couples develop marital satisfaction and thus prevent burnout.

Freudenberger, H. J., and G. Richelson. 1980. *Burn out*. New York: Bantam.

*If the couple is non-Christian this step may be eliminated, but it is an essential element in reconciling Christian spouses.

Limitations of Needs Assessment

Although this technique is beneficial in helping many couples, not everyone can use it effectively. Some individuals may be psychologically unable to meet the needs of others. Due to intrapsychic factors from early development, a person may be emotionally inhibited, even though he or she may desire to fulfill the partner's needs. In such cases, more intensive individual therapy may be necessary.

Also, in particular marital relationships, one or both persons may attempt to sabotage the growth of the other by prohibiting successful achievement of the marital goals. Such psychopathological interactions would become visible during the use of the needs assessment technique. Therefore, the technique may have to be suspended or discarded until those psychodynamic factors are explored.

The needs assessment technique is limited to the individual's ability to recognize and verbalize his or her needs. Those needs must be in conscious awareness. However, sometimes important needs are beyond immediate awareness and are unconscious, but have a significant influence on the marital relationship. Internal conflicting needs may obscure a person's ability to clearly identify them, especially when the person is highly ambivalent about the marriage. In such instances, further individual therapy is necessary before the technique can be useful.

A final observation is that no human being can totally fulfill the needs of someone else. Certain needs can only be met partially, and every person will have some areas of unfulfillment; but that is the existential condition of humanity. The needs assessment technique is not intended to provide complete satisfaction or resolve every conflict, but it can be a useful tool in therapeutic encounters with couples.

References

Baum-Bricker, C., and C. DeTorres. Marital burnout model. Paper presented at psychological workshop, Philadelphia, June 1982.

Carroll, J., and W. White. Understanding burnout: Integrating individual and environmental factors within an ecological framework. In *Proceedings of the first national conference on burnout*. Edited by W. C. Paine. Philadelphia, 1981, 127–56.

Foth, R. Speech presented at the Faith at Work Conference, Indianapolis, March 1974.

Part **3**

Case Studies

13

A Terrible, Swift Sword: Christ Imagery in Therapy
William G. Bixler

The "healing of memories" has become a well-known spiritual-psychological exercise popularized by individuals within the charismatic movement such as Agnes Sanford and Francis MacNutt. While there are no doubt numerous variations to the technique, a basic approach involves having the patient imagine a traumatic scene from the past and, instead of reliving the painful experience as it happened, imagining Jesus Christ entering the scene and intervening to prevent the debilitating experience from occurring.

Reports from counselors and patients who have utilized this exercise suggest that it can be extremely effective for a number of persons in mitigating or eliminating symptomatology associated with the patients' original traumatic events.

This chapter will present a case study in which Christ imagery was used to help a patient deal with traumatic memory and affect. The specific content of the imagery differs somewhat from the stereotypic healing-of-memories exercise mentioned above. Following presentation of the case itself we will discuss the imagery content and present suggestions as to why this particular exercise may be psychologically and spiritually efficacious. Lastly, we will raise some questions and concerns about this procedure which cannot be addressed directly in this chapter due to constraints of space. However, it is hoped that the presentation of such questions will stimulate the reader to further investigation into this fascinating subject.

Case Presentation

April Anne was a twenty-three-year-old single female from western Canada attending a Bible school in the Midwest. She was a senior majoring in Christian education and had hopes of eventually teaching in a Christian elementary school. The school guidance counselor referred her for psychotherapy after she had been discovered burning her forearms with a cigarette lighter.

The patient was the second of four children. She had a younger brother and sister, and an older brother. Her parents were nominal church goers while April Anne described herself as a "born-again" Christian. She stated that she had made a faith commitment as a small child in Sunday school.

The first few sessions April Anne denied any developmental or family history which would explain her self-mutilating behavior. She did disclose, however, that she was given to vomiting and black-out episodes as well as a compulsion, to which she often yielded, to insert sharp objects into her vagina such as scissors and bent coat-hangers.

She began to hint about sexual events in her past which apparently were too anxiety provoking to discuss. Attempts to gain further information from her about these events resulted in dissociative episodes in which she would become disoriented as to place, time, and her therapist's identity. These episodes increased in frequency, length, and intensity during the course of treatment. The vaginal self-mutilation also increased to the point that inpatient hospitalization was deemed necessary. The hospitalization allowed us to see April Anne more frequently for therapy while also providing hospital staff to prevent her self-mutilation as well as to support her during periods of prolonged dissociation.

Through the use of supportive therapy and hypnosis April Anne was able to describe what she was psychologically reliving during her dissociative episodes. During a period from thirteen to eighteen years of age the patient had been the victim of sexual abuse at the hands of her older brother. Several times a month he would engage in some form of sexually sadistic behavior including forced intercourse, oral sex, bestiality, and the insertion of sharp objects into April Anne's vagina. While engaging in the sexual torture, her brother would verbally abuse her by telling her that she was an animal and that she would never stop belonging to him.

On several occasions during a dissociative episode April Anne would speak as if she were her brother. She would use the third person grammatically when speaking of herself and would confront me (as therapist), saying such things as, "You'll never get her away from me; she's mine and will always stay mine." (It should be noted that on these occasions the patient's voice characteristics did not alter, nor were there any bizarre facial or bodily behaviors that one would associate with persons who are described as being "possessed.")

This led us to hypothesize that the verbalizations of the "brother" were reflective of basic, deep self-assumptions drilled into the patient's mind while under the duress of the sexually torturous experiences. In effect she was brainwashed in the manner of a prisoner of war.

While April Anne could admit a great fear for her brother and experienced terror during the dissociations, she had difficulty allowing herself to feel any anger toward him. Through a long, laborious therapy process she began to give herself permission to admit that she did, in fact, have some anger. However, this admission was not accompanied by congruent emotional expression. The lack of congruent expression caused her to continue to internalize her rage via self-mutilating behavior.

Imagery Exercise

In order to help April Anne deal with her suppressed rage as well as the terror she felt toward her brother, we decided to use an imagery exercise which had been suggested to us by a pastoral counseling intern. The following is a description of the exercise (the origin of which is not known to the author). While we placed April Anne in a light hypnotic trance prior to commencing, we feel this is not essential to the procedure itself.

April Anne, now that your eyes are closed, and you're comfortable and in this safe place, I'd like you to imagine a scene for me.

You're in a room at home. You look around and you become afraid because your brother is there with you.

He starts to come toward you with that awful grin on his face . . . you know what he wants.

He keeps coming closer.

But wait. Look down at your feet. What is it? Look closely. It's a sword. A long sword.

You pick it up.

It's large, but not heavy like you thought it would be.

You wave it back and forth in front of you and the air whistles.

Now look up at your brother . . . he's still coming toward you.

You're still afraid, but I want you to do something.

I want you to strike him with the sword.

Stop him from hurting you.

I want you to kill him.

Strike him with the sword again and again, everywhere.

Again.

Again.

Until there's nothing left.

Keep going . . . again . . . don't stop until there's nothing left of him . . . until he's dead.

[*Pause*]

As you look at the remains of your brother you become aware that someone is entering the room.

You look up . . . you recognize him immediately.

It's Jesus.

He walks slowly toward you . . . you keep your eyes fixed on his face.

You see that he's looking at you and you notice that he's neither smiling nor frowning . . . just looking.

He comes toward you . . . he holds out his hands . . . you give him the sword.

He kneels down beside what remains of your brother. He reaches down in front of you and touches these broken pieces that were your brother.

What you see now you can hardly believe. At Jesus' touch your brother is becoming whole again.

He is coming together . . . he is coming back to life.

Jesus raises him up and your brother stands in front of you.

But he never looks at you . . . he keeps his eyes on Jesus.

He walks toward Jesus . . . walks right up to him . . . right into him . . . and he disappears.

You're alone with Jesus. He turns and looks at you with a smile and a deep love for you on his face.

You and Jesus walk toward the door together with his strong arm around you.

You watch him go . . . but you don't feel alone or afraid anymore.

The imagery exercise produced very positive results for April Anne. The brother's "voice" that talked through her ceased. The terror she had felt also disappeared. While she did not completely stop the dissociative episodes, she no longer experienced them with the same degree of fear and panic that she had previously.

This did not provide an instant cure for April Anne and, of course, was not intended for that purpose. However, this exercise did mitigate some of her symptoms and certainly seemed to ease some of her internal torment.

Discussion

Victims of sexual abuse are often left in the wake of the devastating experience feeling completely helpless. The sense of personal autonomy and power—the sense that one can protect and defend oneself in the face of danger—is often stripped from an abused person. Until recently the experience of helplessness was exacerbated by a legal system which often humiliated the abused while wrist-slapping the perpetrator.

The image of the sword and the directive to the patient to wield it may help to overcome the sense of helplessness and powerlessness. The sword is an archetypal symbol calling forth images of knights in armor, swashbuckling pirates, dashing musketeers, and the Jedi knights of *Star Wars*. The patient may form an unconscious identification with these sword bearing heroes who epitomize personal power and fearlessness.

This does not, however, exhaust the possible meanings that the sword may have for patients, especially those with strong religious commitments and experience. For the Christian the sword is a biblically sanctioned symbol of both human and divine power. The Old and New Testaments are replete with literal and figurative descriptions of swords being used in the service of the Lord. From Genesis to Revelation the sword is used to overcome evil. Thus the Christian patient who undergoes this imagery experience may also be unconsciously tapping into the numerous religious and spiritual connotations associated with the sword.

The imagined slaying of the abuser continues the theme of overturning the helpless orientation of the victim, albeit in a radical way. Almost all victims of this type of abuse have some homicidal thoughts about the perpetrator. Not all are comfortable admitting this, and some feel terribly guilty that such thoughts would even occur to them. Others, such as April Anne, suppress their rage and then internalize it in the form of self-mutilation.

The therapist, whom the patient has come to know and trust, implicitly sanctions the expression of rage by suggesting the slaying of the perpetrator. The graphic nature and description of the slaying allows for a cathartic expression of rage.

The slaying scene could meet an even deeper need than the expression of rage, that is, the need for justice. The notion of a universal, God-given sense of justice and fairness has many defenders among philosophers, theologians, and social scientists. If there is validity to this concept, then the slaying or execution scene could be looked at as helping the patient overcome some frustrations regarding unfairness and injustice, especially if the perpetrator goes unpunished.

If the imagery exercise were to end at this point a number of questions and objections might be raised in regard to whether revenge is an appropriate theme to promote emotional and spiritual healing. The imagery does not ignore the issue of justice, but takes the patient beyond that via the healing and resurrection scene. This is the most dramatic and often the most emotionally powerful part of the exercise. Several possible interpretations of the healing and resurrection come to mind.

From a psychological standpoint the raising of the perpetrator could assuage the guilt the patient has for being the executioner. Despite the rage and the aforementioned need for justice it is unlikely that many persons can look back on the killing scene without some ambivalence. This ambivalence could well be mitigated by the death not being final. It is a reversal of the irreversible.

This theme—the reversal of the irreversible—pervades the entire exercise, but is consummated in the resurrection. The patient may see the resurrected perpetrator as somehow purged by the sword and brought to life as a "new creature." The justice theme also could be served by connecting the raising with the notion of the resurrection of the righteous and the unrighteous to face judgment on the last day.

The absorption or disappearance of the abuser into Christ can be viewed similarly as a transformation of evil into good, or of the defeat and swallowing of evil by Christ. Whichever interpretation the patient might adopt would not alter the larger and greater theme, that is, that Christ is greater than any evil and that one's focus should be on him alone. This is the significance of the patient being left alone with Jesus. Not only the perpetrator, but the rage, fear, and humiliation of the patient cannot continue to exist in Christ's presence. It is this great reversal which, I believe, explains the power and efficacy of this imagery exercise.

Questions and Concerns

Given the violent content of the imagery caution should be exercised in the use of this technique. There are a number of situations in which the use of this type of exercise could be contraindicated. For example, it would probably be unwise to have a patient undergo this experience if he or she is still denying any anger toward the abuser. In such a case the slaying scene could mobilize more resistance to dealing with the personal rage rather than providing opportunity for it to be expressed.

Persons with poor reality testing and/or poor impulse control might have trouble separating the fantasy from real life situations. In such a case the therapist-directed imagery could be mistakenly understood as implicit endorsement of acting out.

Those patients who come from a religious tradition of pacifism and nonviolence may very well be offended by the suggestion that they take up the sword against anyone. This difficulty could possibly be dealt with by explaining to such persons the exact nature and function of the exercise, including the resurrection scene, prior to actually beginning the procedure. However, the therapist needs to be sensitive to these and other issues which might call for the use of a different imagery exercise or the reshaping of the one presented here.

Finally, we will offer some questions to the reader without comment as a stimulus for further investigation into this area.

1. What criteria, either psychological or spiritual, would one use to determine if and when this type of exercise would be beneficial?
2. What part might the placebo effect play in helping to effect change via this method?
3. How ought one to view this method in relation to purely secular imagery techniques?
4. Would the depth of spiritual experience of both therapist and patient differentially affect treatment outcome?
5. What part do prayer and the Holy Spirit play in this type of exercise?

14

Treatment of
Multiple Personality
Vance L. Shepperson

The treatment of multiple personality disorder has become increasingly popularized in the literature since the early 1970s. What was thought to be a rare disorder is now being seen as much more prevalent. The following chapter is devoted to examining the etiology, symptoms, and treatment of a prototypical multiple personality who comes from an evangelical religious background. Throughout this work the multiple personality is viewed primarily as a subtype of the borderline personality disorder (see Benner and Joselyn 1984). Techniques of object-relational, marital, and family therapies were used within a Jungian theoretical context, hypnotic modality, and an evangelical Judeo-Christian religious framework. This case is presented with the awareness, consent, and response of the patient.

Etiology

Ruth was the youngest of four children. Her mother was eminently gracious if not passive. She was unpredictably prone toward being emotionally absent to her husband and children. Ruth's father was a crusty, sadistic alcoholic who expressed his anger both by withholding and being aggressive. Days and weeks of moody silence would alternate with outrageous physical tantrums. Ruth's mother would assuage her own fears by holding the children close. Clinging, regressive behavior was rewarded in the children; signs of individuation and mastery were subtly discouraged (see Masterson 1981, for a further discussion of this dynamic).

Ruth was molested sexually as a young girl (from ages six to eight), as is so often the case with multiples. Her father would send her down the block to his friend's house to borrow tools. When she would tell him that Stokie was frightening and hurting her, Ruth's father would tell her she was imagining things; in the same breath, though, he told her not to tell her mother.

The emotional residual of these childhood experiences was that Ruth's mother was idealized and unattainable; her father was villainized but seen as being a closer representation of the true self. The two could never meet—either in the parents' marriage or in their introjected representations. A dissociative barrier separated the two selves effectively. On the outside Ruth was warm and hospitable to others; on the inside she was simmering with hostility. In this fashion she remained loyal to both mother and father. However, this inside world of anger, this loyalty to the hated father, was unacceptable to the conscious self. As a result, this self was split off and began to form its own identity separate from the conscious self. As Rock, an alter ego, later put it, "Ruth gives me her shit and everybody else her sugar."

Symptomatology

Once this protective mechanism of dissociation was created within the self other ego states, both masculine and feminine, were subsequently born. In each case Ruth's object was to wall off unacceptable feelings which didn't fit conscious identification with her mother. This walling off of selves was sometimes semipermeable and sometimes not: some ego states would know of the others' existences but not vice versa. Only one or two ego states knew the whole scope of affairs.

Ruth, age thirty-nine, served efficiently in a middle management position for a large financial institution. She functioned well as long as she was able to isolate her other selves out of consciousness. She was married to Marty, age fifty-seven. Marty was an angry, rigid individual on the inside and a hearty, cheerful fellow outside. He pastored a fundamentalistic church. This was Ruth's second marriage; her teen-age daughter, Marie, lived with them. Ruth's presenting problems at the beginning of therapy included severe clinical depression mixed with suicidal ideation.

Most of Ruth's energy was invested in her other ego states; as a result, she tended to be a depleted shell and felt exhausted most of the time. Most of her available energy was spent being pleasant and keeping a mask of congeniality in place.

Rock, the *persecutor self* mentioned earlier, would war against Ruth in various ways. He would carry out his sadistic assaults by mutilating her with razors (particularly on the breasts and navel); feeding her prescription drugs until she was semicomatose; fueling self-destructive intentions of driving her car off a cliff; and so on.

Esther, a *rescuer self,* epitomized the less acceptable aspects of Ruth's mother. Her intentions were golden; her delivery, erratic. Her role was to mend the damage Rock did after the fact. She saw herself as being ugly and misshapen, but the best mother available for Tammie.

Tammie, an *infant self,* represented the victimized part of Ruth. She was totally naive and powerless; often her very existence was precarious. She was bonded tightly to Esther and persecuted by Rock.

Gorgeous One (G.O.) represented Ruth's hopeful, pure, and *sexual self.* She was kept by Rock in a glass cage that seemed to be hermetically sealed. She was dressed in white and utterly pure. Her close proximity to Rock in effect recreated the marriage of Ruth's parents in which Rock represented the sadistic father and G.O., the mother. Rock zealously protected her from exposure to anything outside the cage. He refused to believe that when he mutilated Ruth he also cut G.O. When I had her walk up to him, bare her breasts and show him the wounds, he still would not believe he had done it. Such is the power of the dissociated belief system.

During the third year of therapy G.O. left Rock after I persuaded him that it was very important to give her a choice. Rock never forgave me for this. Most recently, during a crisis in which Rock was threatening to "cut Ruth's heart out" if he didn't get her back, Gorgeous One chose to return to him. This felt like a death to her, an exchange of her life for that of "the family." The resulting depression precipitated hospitalization (February 1985).

Michael, the *internal self helper (ISH),* was the core self. This was the self that knew all the others, served as an expert chronicler of Ruth's history, and often was quite wise. Unfortunately, the ISH's wisdom is often inversely proportional to his potency to effect change; thus far this has proved to be the case for Michael.

Other selves are also worth mentioning briefly as being prototypical of many one may find in a multiple personality. *The Roar* represented the unbridled rage deep within the self, less socialized than that of Rock. *Secret Keeper's* name epitomized his function; he was formed when Ruth was a teen and was asked by her mother to help safeguard the knowledge of a secret relationship that she was having with another man. *Jim and his family* represented an earthy, practical part of the self that lived close to nature. *New Man* represented a transformed part of the Roar and can best be viewed as being conceived in the therapy process.

The internal typography was as follows: Rock sat up on a lifeguard's chair scanning the ocean for approaching storms. Underneath him was a little box, "the coffin," in which he kept Tammie. Esther alternately circled the chair and implored Rock for Tammie's life, then retreated into the dunes or "over the hill" for indeterminate periods of time. Gorgeous One was slightly off the beach and at the edge of the woods in her box. Secret Keeper circulated around the beach area. The Roar lived on a nearby mountain; no one had ever seen him—they just heard his thunderings. The rest of the ego states lived "over the hill" in their own village. Ruth lived outside both scenarios and knew nothing of them.

Treatment Issues

Initially the most crucial issue with Ruth, as with most multiples, pertained to accurate diagnosis. We had passed through eighteen months of object relational therapy before her multiplicity was uncovered in a hypnotic session. Prior to that time I had thought of her as either being severely depressed or suffering from a borderline personality disorder. A key diagnostic pointer in the treatment was when Ruth mentioned she tended to "lose" periods of time during the day.

The course of treatment tended to be in a spiral direction, deeper into self and further along toward a differentiation and integration of self. Ruth would make some gains toward our stated goal of having the many selves work together collaboratively as a team. This growth would typically involve a lifting of her dissociative walls so that she and the other ego states could feel one another's emotions; simultaneously she would become more assertive with her husband and work associates.

Ruth was quite afraid of being abandoned (by me, Marty, and/or her mother) as a result of her growth. It was important at these times for me to keep in mind that Ruth's mother had abandoned her emotionally when she showed signs of individuation as a child. Another predictable "falling apart" occurred when I left the area on vacations twice a year: Ruth, like most multiples, had never resolved her own anxiety over the physical loss of her mother's (or therapist's) presence.

Ruth's fear of abandonment would be defended against, typically, by rageful behavior or clinging ingratiation. I would intervene to counter these defenses with a combination of tactics: limit setting; a fluid blend of empathy and confrontation; orchestration of different coalitions within the internal family to combat violence or ingratiation; protective hospitalizations; enlisting the aid of Marty, Marie, Ruth's mother, and others; and so on. Overall, structuring and confrontation (i.e., asking each ego state to be responsible for its own actions) tended to work better than interpretation. As a result of these varied interventions, more growth would occur and the cycle would repeat itself, this time a bit further along toward individuation of an integrated self, separate from the family of origin.

Spiritual Integration Interventions

The religious background. Ruth was overtly "Christian" in her behavior. She sang in the church choir, taught Sunday school, organized visitation programs for her husband, and smiled a lot. Inside, consciously, she didn't believe at all. Her show of religion was a felt sham. Her only intense convictions were that she was damned to hell and headed straight for it. She also tended to take complete responsibility for the dwindling attendance at her husband's church. Neither Rock nor The Roar were believers. This "coalition block" was the most powerful one in the family of self: such was the power of Ruth's introjection of her rageful, nonbelieving father. Internally, other parts of the self had varying degrees of faith. However, this "voting block" was relatively impotent to effect change in the face of the more malevolent coalition.

The crisis. At about the three-year point in treatment we were once again heading for a crisis. Rock and The Roar were acting independently to cut Ruth with razors on her left breast and navel, as well as on the arm and neck. Ruth was terrified and losing quite a bit of blood; often she would change the absorbent padding in her bra four and five times a day. One gash in her breast, according to Michael, was four inches deep. When a client such as this is out of control the therapist needs to function as a sort of auxiliary ego.

I asked Ruth and Michael if it was okay to enlist the aid of another therapist, Earl Henslin, for a marathon session. This session, which turned out to be about five hours long, involved Earl and I dealing directly with The Roar for the first time. The session began, as usual, with Ruth quickly establishing a deep hypnotic state. At this point I asked to speak with The Roar. Ruth began quivering and shaking with tension. Low gutteral sounds, clenched fists, and reddened face accompanied The Roar's initial entry to consciousness. This gave way to screaming, pounding, clawing at her face, attempts to ram her head (and mine) into the sharp edges of a nearby bookcase and so on. During this interval it was all that Earl and I could do to physically contain The Roar's destructive rage.

During this time it became apparent that much of Ruth's rage originated from the continual sexual molestation that she had experienced from ages six to eight by the "friend" of the family. Earl and I verbally prodded The Roar to channel his rage toward the molester as well as toward Ruth's father.

After several hours The Roar became more able to talk instead of roar. He told us he was Rock's father, and that Rock hated him intensely. Then The Roar, as we had known him, began to die. He shuddered and left, leaving a new personality in his place. New Man, as we came to call him, was weak but a viable new identity within the family of self. I told him that in order for him to survive he was going to need outside help from the sovereign Lord. I told him that I was a vassal for this Lord, as was Earl. I described in detail to New Man the strong and warm fathering functions of God the Father. I also included a portrait of the loving, nurturing, and maternal holding functions of the Holy Spirit.

New Man listened intently. Together we went with Michael and Esther to meet with the sovereign Lord and ask him for protection and strength to keep New Man alive. First I talked with the Lord and then I asked New Man to talk with the Lord. He did so, haltingly and fearfully, but with the implicit trust of a young child. Subsequent to this session the cutting was discontinued for a substantial length of time.

Sequelae

Issues with the father. In future sessions I kept checking on New Man. He told me that he was visiting the Lord daily and talking with him in his cave outside the village. I asked what he looked like and New Man described to me a "wise old man." The primary subject which he discussed regularly with the sovereign Lord was how to handle his son, Rock.

Apparently Rock was not accepting his father's claim to a conversion experience. He was still fuming and skeptical, unable to forgive the years of abuse in one stroke. Herein is contained a particularly interesting phenomenon: the father-child dynamics of Ruth's childhood were rippling through all the different parts of the self—trust issues between Ruth-father spread to The Roar-Rock relationship. When unresolved there, these issues were transferred to the sovereign Lord-New Man relationship. Further, all of these struggles were encased within the context of my "fathering" Ruth in the therapeutic relationship.

Issues with the mother. A major difficulty which remains to be resolved at this writing (February 1985) pertains to Ruth's relationship with her mother. I once told Ruth that the platform she has placed her mother upon is the coffin she keeps Tammie in. My meaning was clear to the two of us: her mother's idealization prevents Ruth's identification with her and condemns young life within her to be frozen.

In my initial description to New Man of the sovereign Lord I detailed many aspects of "mothering" as being integral to the Lord's character: feeding, comforting, holding, and so on. These internal functions are sorely missing for Ruth. She has not been able to "take in" (or identify with) her mother's good qualities; instead, she sees those qualities as being "other than self" or too good for her. In the same fashion as Ruth's mother has been idealized as being an impossible act to follow, so also are most others. Subsequently she walls herself off from contact with figures in the outside and inside world much as a leper would be kept outside the city walls in biblical times.

The work that remains is to use the therapeutic relationship as a maternal holding environment while associating the sovereign Lord's maternal qualities with my own supplies of affection, warmth, and so on. This holding without sadistic, inconsistent withholding in the midst of life's vicissitudes is essential for growth. Another approach in this regard is to associate Esther's increasingly steady mothering capabilities toward Tammie with the sovereign Lord's consistent mothering toward Ruth. As I continue to demonstrate both the warm, accepting mothering and firm, limit-setting fathering capabilities of the sovereign Lord to the many selves within this talented individual, she will eventually come to the place of integrating his life into her own.

This is a long-term venture. The average length of treatment of most multiple personalities is seven years. Currently we are well into our fourth year of treatment.

Epilogue: Ruth's Reaction Statement

I would like to take this opportunity to share in retrospect some of my thoughts and feelings of the last four years, as well as reactions to Dr. S. As the reader might discern, we have different points of view. His view is from outside and mine from inside.

I began therapy at the urging of my husband. I spent the first few months sharing parts of my childhood which I felt were safe. Those were long and tedious sessions for myself as well as Dr. S. I needed to establish a bond of proven trust with an individual for the first time in my life. After this period came months and months of exploration with no apparent result or purpose. I had periods of depression offset with a moderate amount of coping. However, I could not understand why my extreme mood swings continued without any sense of my controlling them.

I appreciated my sessions with Dr. S. because he was kind and placed no pressure on me that I could not handle. However, by this time I had reached a point at which we were not making any progress. At this point hypnotherapy began, and a whole new vista emerged for me through this method of inquiry. My feelings about this strange, internal world were dramatic.

The first personality that I became aware of was Rock. He was and is to this day extremely angry and hostile. When he comes forth in a session or at other times I am very exhausted and tight. I have suffered for years with headaches which I believe to be a result of Rock. The other personalities are less consciously felt but also vital.

My view of several of the personalities was through videotape recordings of my sessions. I had always been careful to be pleasant. Therefore, when I first saw Rock, the emotion was sheer shock. I didn't know I could act in such a way. Rock was a bitter, malignant, spiteful, and cutting person who was also loud and repugnant. On the other hand, Esther was a warm, caring person very much like my mother. After sessions in which she talked with Dr. S., I felt serene.

I do not remember if I ever saw Gorgeous One; I do understand she was beautiful and not at all as I view myself. My only remembrance of Michael was his first appearance. He was silhouetted on the videotape and I could only hear his voice. Odd as it might seem, the voice made something inside me jump. It was from a depth I do not know. He felt strong, supportive, and stable. The other personalities are also important but not vital at this point.

One very important experience I wish to address is the five-hour marathon with Earl. My preparatory work for the session concentrated on trusting Dr. S.; dealing with a stranger was frightening. When I arrived for the session I was full of fear and expectancy. When I left I must have been numb—I do not remember the session or coming home at all. The days which followed were emotional chaos: hours of tears, hours of torment, and lost time. The following couple of sessions I became hysterical and could not be consoled.

Since that time Dr. S. and I have worked hard. Without his strength and support my fear and weakness would have consumed me. At this point of my therapy it is Dr. S. who holds the hope for a better future. I look at the scars and cuts on my body and see the deeper ones within and I lose hope. Dr. S. has never promised it would be easy or without pain but he does say we can be integrated and have meaningful lives.

I could not end this response without expressing my thanks to both Dr. S. and my family. It has been important for them to stay with me when I have tried so hard to push them away.

References

Benner, D. G., and B. Joscelyne. 1984. Multiple personality as a borderline disorder. *Journal of Nervous and Mental Disease* 172(2):98–104.

Masterson, J. 1981. *The narcissistic and borderline disorders: An integrated developmental approach.* New York: Brunner-Mazel.

15

Developmental Pacing of Theology in Therapeutic Process
Clark E. Barshinger and Lojan E. LaRowe

Client Profile

Susan was a white woman in her thirties, who had been raised in an unhappy and dysfunctional home. Susan was sexually and physically abused throughout her childhood and adolescence. The few moments of love and tenderness shown to her were during sexual contacts with her father. She reached adulthood with a low self-concept, pathological self-consciousness, and greatly impaired personal functioning. As a young adult Susan served on the mission field, but, unhappily, a senior missionary took advantage of her vulnerability and impaired self-esteem and sexually abused her. Susan became increasingly fearful, regressed, and phobic toward men. She gained weight and developed numerous nervous habits.

Therapy Overview

Susan had a very spotty recall of the past experiences that were contributing to her unhappiness. The therapy process began slowly with simple rapport building and establishing deeper and deeper trust in her therapists as surrogate parents. The focus was often on day-to-day difficulties and Susan's crippling fear and low self-esteem. During the first year of therapy, she began to retrieve repressed memories of extensive childhood abuse. Over the following months she began to feel safe enough to enter our monthly group therapy retreat and to share her painful journey with others. She slowly began to build rapport with men in the group. It took many months before she would allow Clark to "touch" her with one finger on the shoulder. Later she could accept her first hug.

The recovery of memories was often accompanied by traumatic abreaction in which Susan would regress to early life states of mind and would need to be held and nurtured as she relived painful childhood experiences. Gradually she was able to risk accepting hugs from a few men in the group and to begin a limited intimacy with them. As her strength grew, she was able to accept her body, which motivated her to lose weight and maintain a regular exercise program at a health club. As her personal integration continued, she was more able to be self-caring and assertive in life and at work, although the resolution of past pain was not yet complete. She became respected as a model of courage and growth within the group.

Key Techniques Used

Apart from ongoing verbal therapy, which stressed an integration of behavioral management and client-centered approaches, Susan was introduced to regular homework assignments (often with suggested readings), written notes from her sessions for her notebook or refrigerator door, primal-regressive work, inner healing prayer, and naturalistic integration of theological lessons (and metaphors) as she progressed in her readiness to utilize them for healing. Susan also kept a daily record of her dreams, insights, and struggles to grow and change.

Primal-regressive work was done via a connected breathing technique (catalytic breathing, sometimes called "primal integration") which facilitates by-passing of the normal, conscious defenses of the ego and allows a more direct experience of the deep-seated emotions and primal issues locked in the neuromuscular defenses of the body. The primal work was done at first with just her therapist and later in a small group setting. Susan found this part of her therapy, within the safety, structure, and "logos" (cognitive information and insight integration) of the broader therapy context, a very powerful source of expression, release, and healing. Her body began to unfreeze, open, and soften.

Inner healing prayer was simple intercessory prayer for the areas of her life which needed Christ's redemptive touch. The experience of prayer during the sessions not only called forth the power of the Comforter, it also provided quiet, deep security by triggering the unconscious power of Susan's deep faith. It was often experienced as a break from the more catalytic moments of therapy.

Important Theological Considerations During Therapy

There were a number of theological issues in Susan's case which are common in psychotherapy. For one, she had to come to realize that it was not a sin to be angry at people who had done her harm. She knew it was normal to be angry, but the prolonged anger, and sometimes rage, that characterizes certain stages of therapy is hard to deal with as a Christian. Susan had to face the criticism of other Christians that she did not have strong enough faith to just forgive these people and turn it over to God.

Just as it is hard to turn over to God what you do not know about yourself, it is hard to forgive before honest hurt and anger are consciously faced. A key that we have found is the concept of *release*. Therapeutically, it is important to release the blocks to healing. Just as we must forgive in order to be forgiven, so we must release the burden of rage to be willing to forgive the abuser. Sometimes healing comes in releasing the resistance to facing anger and dealing with it. Sometimes the ability to release comes through an explosion, and sometimes it comes through a quiet, timely "letting go."

Another theological issue that Susan faced was anger at God for causing, or allowing, the pain to happen. This form of anger in therapy tends to come and go. We treat it as understandable and explain (sometimes) the transference behind it and encourage the client to move through and not get sidetracked on those feelings. This anger usually evaporates in the face of joy and freedom later in therapy, and in the relief of a renewed walk in freedom with God.

Like most victims of childhood sexual abuse, Susan was unable to conceive of God the Father in a nurturing or even a neutral way. The concept of a nurturing as opposed to an abusive parent had to be painstakingly built theologically from the bottom up. Jesus as friend and brother was a more accessible concept so that is where we began. Using sex-neutral images for God (such as a rock, a hiding place, the vine) was helpful to Susan.

Susan, like many of our clients, found it very helpful when we explained to her that her true parent was God and that her earthly parents were but temporary custodians to help her toward adulthood and the mission God had waiting for her in life. We referred to Christ's telling his earthly parents that they should not be shocked that he had to be about his Father's business (Luke 2:49). In a deep, prayerful state Susan was asked by her therapist to visualize agreeing to God's wish that she be born, that she say "yes" to this life, and at each turn, see herself accompanied by Christ as her true friend-brother-physician.

Susan was encouraged to remember that her true identity and worth did not depend on how well her earthly custodians cared for and regarded her, but flowed instead from the love of her heavenly source, God. Her true identity was as a daughter of the King of Kings. Acceptance of this reality allowed Susan to reassess her God-given femininity as a beautiful gift. Susan became more feminine and began to enjoy it. She began to experiment with clothes, hair styles, and make up. Formerly, she had associated femininity with sexual exploitation and vulnerability; she now began to view it as God-given, beautiful, and powerful.

The Developmental Pacing of Theology in Therapy

Progressive redemption proceeds from an individual's self-esteem back to personal history and then moves forward to the (as yet) unlived future. In other words, the individual forgives himself for living out the implications (unconscious habits, behaviors, destructive patterns, etc.) of the sins committed against him, and begins instead to actively accept the love of Christ via the Christian therapist and then to proceed progressively backwards to forgive those whose sins were so damaging. Finally, the individual moves forward in life as his increasing maturity (and the redeemed negative experiences of the past) allow a wiser, more wholistic perspective on his trauma. A personal commitment to Christ usually is renewed at this point.

Therefore, throughout the therapy process there should be a progressive (or developmental) ability on the part of clients to realize God's Word for and in them. There is a blissful, warming shower of God's love always available, but due to individual traumas, those who have not experienced parental love need time to risk taking that shower. They need time to prepare to put even one small part of themselves under that shower.

Thus, persons in therapy are in the process of recreating themselves by the grace of God and through the power of the Holy Spirit. It is a vivid and dramatic process of becoming a new creation in Christ. One is literally cancelling out old scars of trauma and creating a new heart attitude of openness to God's revelation. This process is not an instantaneous result of cognitive conclusions or of will power. Usually our clients are theologically ahead of their feelings. They know what they *want* to feel and what they are *supposed* to feel, but they simply are not there yet. That is why it is important in Christian counseling to remember that with God time is more wholistic and contextual than our short, linear time spans (" . . . with the Lord one day is as a thousand years, and a thousand years as one day", 2 Peter 3:8). We believe God accepts that it takes us time to get from the understanding to the realization of a spiritual principle in our lives. We work out our salvation with fear and trembling (Phil. 2:12). Sometimes, like with Susan, it takes years of seeking out the personal integration of God's healing. But all of us are in a continual process of becoming more perfectly conformed to Christ.

For that reason, we have found it to be important in Christian counseling to "pace" the use of theological input. In early work with an individual, it is usually unsafe to use an authoritarian approach to almost any theological point, except assurance of God's love, support, and permission to explore feelings and painful memories. Preaching does have its place, but later. When a Christian is developmentally a babe, he or she will not be able to handle the meat of spiritual maturity. Clients cannot run before they walk spiritually or psychologically, any more than they can physically. Primal nurture and a good conceptual map are often necessary to allow the client to understand and integrate the developmental issues in his spiritual life. That is why some Christian clients are overwhelmed by demands that they forgive and forget before the counselor has paced their level of personal redemption. Susan was often confronted by well-meaning Christian friends and counselors with biblical injunctions to let go of bad feelings and to be "happy in the Lord."

There come those times in therapy in which growth requires more than accepting unconditional love. C. S. Lewis has said that love is something much more stern and splendid than mere kindness. Growth is a challenge to risk and to develop inner strength on the way to deeper personal freedom and spiritual discipline. It is a process of becoming free. This process begins with the courage to honestly face one's self, hidden fears, unmet and unresolved memories, self-rejection, and immaturity. As this process develops, redemption unfolds and one becomes stronger, more able to courageously step under that shower of God's love, and to thereby accept the challenge of obedience to God and a healthy interdependence with others.

16

Anger, Denial, and the Healing of Memories
Arlo Compaan

In therapy involving a Christian therapist and a Christian client, religious issues frequently arise. The following case focuses on one such issue and explores its personal, therapeutic, and religious dynamics. Some suggested questions for further research and study are raised regarding the "healing-of-memories" experience.

Grace was a thirty-five-year-old, single, white female with a five-year-old son. She was a middle child, with an older sister and a younger brother. Her father was an alcoholic who physically abused her and her mother. He died from the effects of alcoholism. Grace was working full-time in a Christian ministry. Her decision to become a Christian and her continuing spiritual life were important to her.

A crisis in her faith occurred when she discovered that her son was being sexually abused by a teen-age boy (Bill) whom Grace had befriended some seven years earlier. She considered this relationship to be both a response to her deep desire to provide a better parenting relationship than she had as a child and a Christian commitment to be Bill's long-term substitute parent. This commitment she saw as modeled on God's commitment to "never forsake us" and was made in the awareness that Bill's parents had abandoned him to a variety of short-term substitute parents. Thus she saw a more permanent commitment as important for his development.

174

Reluctantly and with very mixed emotions Grace terminated the relationship with Bill and reported the abuse to the proper authorities. Subsequently Grace explored the relationship between her blindness to what was happening to her son (over which she felt considerable guilt and failure) and the experiences of her own childhood. She recognized that she had been sexually abused by a friend of her father, with his knowledge and seeming encouragement. The recall and acknowledgement of these memories were accompanied by strong feelings of anger toward her father.

This intense anger was the immediate cause of the crisis in her faith. Some months earlier Grace had willingly participated in two healing-of-memories experiences whose explicit aim was to remove her anger. The absence of anger she saw as the outward symbol of a healed memory.

The first experience was with a friend and involved considerable prayer, Bible reading, and meditation. Grace reported it was of little help and created some problems in their relationship because she felt judged and condemned during the attempted healing experience.

The second experience was with a group of people in a church where healing had been practiced for some time. She found these people to be very supportive and caring. When she left them, she acknowledged feeling much better toward her father. She no longer felt angry and truly believed she had been finally healed.

In therapy she recalled some additional trauma from her childhood and a flood of angry feelings returned, especially as she recognized that her blindness to what was happening to her son may have been enhanced by her own blindness to her own childhood trauma. She also felt considerable anger toward God, whom she felt had deceived her into believing that her relationship with her father was totally healed following the corporate healing experience. Thus she wondered about the validity of the previous healing experience and even questioned her Christian faith which affirmed that God is beneficent and heals.

Grace also reported a significant loss of hope. She wondered, "Will this never end? Can I ever get over what happened to me with my parents? Will I continue to have painful experiences as repercussions from my childhood trauma? What good is my faith?" The hope which was engendered as a result of the healing-of-memories experiences was clearly shattered by the new discovery of more anger and that her life was still being affected by her childhood experiences.

From the information about Grace's history, it was apparent that both her parents were poor care givers. The alcoholic father would be at times warm and seemingly supportive, only to become unpredictably cold, rejecting, and physically abusive. Her mother was domineering and distant, though most of the children's basic needs were met.

Object-relations theory suggested that Grace's search for a caring, loving, beneficent God was a compensation for the rejecting, cold, physically abusive parents of her early years. The positive and negative objects were split for her. Her father was totally bad. God was marvelously good, until she felt abandoned by God. Then God was also seen as all bad. Grace's thanksgiving was often for the wonderful things that God had done for her, usually in seemingly unexpected and dramatic ways. She had a need to have a God whom she believed was very caring for her—a caring which was nearly miraculous and came through unexpected, unusual events. Over the period of her years as a Christian, having this perception of God enabled her to see herself as being more cared for than during childhood. This perception of God changed her view of herself and increased her ability to be giving and caring to others.

Her view of God was also limited by her childhood experiences. The normal loving and caring behaviors of God shown through people were usually not recognized or paled in significance to the outstanding, unusual, nearly miraculous caring acts of God. Emotionally this meant great highs and dark valleys since the miraculous acts were not frequent enough to sustain daily life. The experience of God as an ongoing presence, caring and supportive throughout the difficulties of life, though not always acting to remove the pain, was an important addition to her experience.

In terms of Grace's development, her perceptions of God paralleled the childhood perception of parents as all powerful and very good, while the self is more often seen as powerless and not so good, sometimes even very bad. Usually that view of parents collapses in the adolescent years when the child sees more clearly the faults of the parents and recognizes they cannot always heal life's hurts, though they do stand alongside and care. However, for Grace such parents were absent. She only experienced actively rejecting parents and consequently was inhibited in her development.

The two perceptions of God as one who dramatically delivers from pain and one who stands with a person in the midst of pain parallel the Old Testament view of God the Father as miraculous deliverer and the New Testament view of God the Son as fellow sufferer, one like us who knows our condition. Grace's predominant perception and consequent experience of God fit the first view. The crisis of her faith was precipitated by the shattering of what she had believed to be a miraculous or near miraculous healing which was to remove from her all anger toward her father. This experience was traumatic partially because of the absence of an experience with parental figures who stood with her in the ongoing painful experiences of life. It meant feeling abandoned totally by God, a feeling reminiscent of her childhood. Had she experienced parents standing with her in pain they would have empowered and enlivened the reality of God, the Son, who is always with us. One of the therapeutic and church tasks is to provide such an object experience.

Grace's experience of the "healing of memories" raises three questions for consideration and further research. First, it seems that the expectations and perceptions of God held by other participants in the healing experience (authoritative leaders and church community) paralleled Grace's. All tended to see God as a miraculous, beneficent God who intervenes to dramatically and completely remove pain. Absent is the view of God as a "sufferer with" who does not always remove pain. Yet for Grace, it was the latter experience which was more significantly needed. How can this view of God be made real and powerful in the midst of healing-of-memories experiences?

A second issue for consideration has to do with the expectation of Grace and the church leaders for final, complete healing of her feelings toward her father. It seems in this case that the healing was limited to the healing of conscious memories. The memory of her abuse had been denied. Recalling it understandably brought back real feelings of anger. If Grace had been so advised, the recovery of the memory and the anger very likely would not have led her to doubt both her faith and God's healing and would have mitigated somewhat her feelings of being abandoned.

A third concern has to do with the expectations regarding anger that seemed to be present in the healing experiences. All seemed to believe that the absence of anger was the indication of the presence of forgiveness and healing. Thus when Grace found herself even more angry at her father and mother as she explored the full dynamics of the family situation, she wrestled with whether this meant she really had not forgiven and was not healed. Grace wanted to be without anger and wanted to meet the ideal envisioned by the Christian community. The question is whether this ideal, hope, and aim are realistic.

Certainly anger can turn into hostility and resentment and can so contaminate a person's life that he is unable to live effectively. In fact hostile, resentful living usually only creates additional difficulties. For Grace, repressing the events of her childhood and the attending emotion meant that they continued unwittingly to affect her and her relationships. No release was possible until the memories were recovered. When they were and the anger was expressed, significant changes occurred in the way she related to others. She wanted to be with her son more, to be caring and affectionate, and to feel greater freedom to care for herself. She saw herself not as bad and undeserving but as worthy and legitimately needing. She more actively cared for herself. Release from self-destructive internalization of anger came through the recovery of the memory and a directing of the anger to her father and significant other males who abused her. The recognition of this appropriate anger became a significant aid to her recognition of abusive situations, including Bill's abuse of her as he acted out with her son. Remaining in contact with her anger was important in order to protect herself from other abusive situations and people.

To expect to have no feelings of anger whenever thoughts and memories of abuse occur is not good. Anger prevents further abuse. Paradoxically being open to anger and being able to appropriately manage it enables us to be caring and loving, not resentful and depressed. Clearly the realistic question must be how anger is being managed. Realistic expectations need to focus on the healthy use of a God-given emotion. Resentment and internalized anger injure self and others. But also seeking to be without anger leads to repression and denial, steppingstones to other inappropriate manifestations of anger.

17

Hal and Gena: Theological Reflections on a Clinical Case
C. Markham Berry

Case Presentation

Hal and Gena came to my office because of a marital conflict. Actually, they had been sent to me by the board of the church in which Hal was pastor because the conflict had become public. The board members felt the impact on the church was serious enough for them to tell Hal that either this conflict would be resolved or the couple would have to leave the church.

Gena began almost immediately and blurted out her side of the story. In a nutshell, she didn't trust her husband in some of the relationships that he had in his church work, and he had refused to modify his behavior enough to relieve her anxiety. She told a long story which began with an episode that had occurred some twenty years earlier, not long after they were married, when Hal was in seminary. At that time Hal had a brief but meaningful homosexual experience with a young man in the church where he was serving as interim pastor. Some months after it had occurred, Hal had confessed the whole thing to his wife. It had been a crushing shock to her, and she had become so depressed that she was admitted to a psychiatric hospital. She improved greatly there, and afterwards their marriage seemed idyllic. They had raised two daughters and had a successful church career together. It was only during the past year that a series of suggestive incidents had reminded Gena of their earlier experience and she had become anxious and depressed again. Her concern was not only for herself but for the children, the integrity of the marriage, and the ministry of the church.

Gena accused Hal of being careless about being alone with young men at Bible studies on a nearby university campus and in driving students back and forth to church meetings. One or two students seemed to have particular affection for Hal and behaved, she thought, in ways which were provocative. Hal had not, to her knowledge, openly responded to them. But neither had he gone out of his way to divert their overtures and maintain a safe distance. She had suggested that transportation could be handled by others and the Bible class could be held in the church when she was present. Hal had ignored these suggestions.

Gena felt justified in bringing the conflict out in the open and discussing it with several friends because Hal had recently begun demonstrating a violent temper and though he had never actually hit her, she felt unsafe with him at times.

Hal openly admitted his previous sin and stated that he had confessed it at the time with a great deal of remorse, not only to his wife, but to the Lord. Since then, whereas he was aware of some ongoing homosexual inclinations at times, his behavior had been impeccable, and he had been faithful to his wife. It was his feeling that as bad as the incident had been, it was closed and she should forgive and forget as he was sure the Lord had.

He described an intense jealousy which had been building up in Gena over a period of a year. She had become absurd in her imaginations and accusations. He had chosen to stand his ground and fight back when he felt his ministry was challenged. He needed to have reasonable freedom of action, and he had finally drawn the line on her controlling his work with university students. This ministry had been going on for some years, involved both men and women, and had been uniquely blessed. He admitted to his angry outbursts and confessed that he had on several occasions had to refrain from hitting Gena.

Hal remembered the years prior to this last one also as happy ones and had always considered theirs a model marriage. He blamed Gena's recent anxiety on a recurrence of her mental illness and stated that she "needed another hospital admission."

Their arguments often involved quoting Scripture. Since both of them were Bible students, they could defend their separate positions with many proof texts. Gena felt that the Bible admonished people in Hal's circumstances to "abstain from every form of evil" (1 Thess. 5:22). The recent breakdown of their sexual life, she felt, placed him in special danger, "lest Satan tempt you through lack of self-control" (1 Cor. 7:5).

Hal said that Gena was committing the biblical sin of judging, which Christians are frequently warned against. He was convinced that his ministry was essentially a matter between himself and the Lord and that his wife was intruding offensively.

In spite of the heat and animosity of their conflict, Hal and Gena both wanted to continue their life together. They both, in fact, at one level, realized that there must be some way in which even this could "work together for good" (Rom. 8:28). The church board shared this opinion, and it was with this in mind that they had been sent to me.

A little deeper investigation of the two personalities involved and the events leading up to the crisis revealed the following:

Hal's homosexual involvement was deeper than he admitted and though his behavior was proper, he held this part of himself in an isolated compartment from which his wife was excluded. On Gena's part there was also a divergence. As she moved into menopause and the children began leaving home, she had become more actively involved in church life. Her Pollyanna sweetness and her tendency to be somewhat pushy and always right had turned off the college group and offended many others in the church. The beginning of the present crisis had coincided with a week of special meetings during which an emphasis had been placed on the subservience of the woman in the home and church. When it became apparent to her that several in the church felt this lesson was primarily directed to her, she was hurt and angry. The crowning blow was when she realized that her husband shared this opinion to some extent and did not defend her.

Ideal, Adamic Man and the Garden of Eden

Gena held a dreamy ideal of marriage, goodness, and purity which was shattered by her husband's sin. After the initial shock, she was able to effectively renew the ideal by denying the event and living as though it had not happened. Her fantasy life was romantic and somewhat childish. She was, in fact, writing a romantic novel in which the hero and heroine were perfect. In the current conflict her defense and fantasy broke down because of Hal's behavior.

Hal had cast Gena into the role of a submissive, subservient little helpmeet and found it difficult to deal with her restlessness in this role. His fantasy life was also romantic but unequivocally homosexual. Both of them felt restricted by the other's ideal and frustrated in seeking their own.

The board had been greatly upset when Gena told them the whole story. They were struggling with the question, "How can a man like Hal be the pastor of a church?"

It has been my observation in dealing with patients that a construct of
the ideal is involved in most of their thinking. The question I would like
to raise is where this comes from and what its meaning in our lives is.
Even though man has never experienced perfection since the fall, he still
carries with him the ideal of consummate order, beauty, truth, love, and
holiness. Philosophers have long struggled with this ideal. Freudians
have identified its traces deep within the unconscious life of the patients
they see (the ego ideal). They generally trace this to a combination of the
early symbiotic experiences of the infant with the mother and a somewhat later oedipal identification with the father. They usually conceive
of it in a structural conjunction with the superego and appreciate the
part it plays in the judgmental role of the latter.

Even though the role of the ideal in the human personality is doubt-
less a mixed one, I believe that we can use it constructively in several
ways. The first is to use Adam as a model for man. God, at the point of
creation, declared man to be "very good." He bore in some way the
image of God himself. Individual man has fallen away from the Edenic
model in an infinite variety of ways, but in a real sense, Adam as the head
of mankind, encompassed all of us in himself in perfection.

A second advantage of identifying this Edenic genetic root of man lies
in the fact that it reveals a little more of God's own personality. It was
from his constructive, expressive movement as the Word that the universe was created. As the crown of his creation, Adam bears the thumb-
print of the Creator himself. In Scripture our attention is repeatedly
drawn to characteristics of God which are seen in his creation by the discerning eye.

There are two dangers in any emphasis on the ideal, however. It can be
a means of denial. Man has a tendency to flee in fantasy to this refuge
from the pain and frustration of his flawed life. As such, it can be destructive as it was in the case of Hal and Gena. In addition, the constant moni-
toring of the Garden ideal over our sinful lives acts as an omnipresent
judge and adds a peculiar edge to the guilt and suffering which fallen
man experiences. Somehow, we need to understand this reality in our
personalities in a manner which is constructive and not destructive. To
do this it, helps to understand how God dealt with man after the ideal
was fractured.

Fallen Man and the Law

The overwhelming weight of evidence testifies that natural man is far
from perfect. My knowledge of myself and those I know, even those I love

dearly, bears witness to this. In fact, the only people I have ever suspected of being perfect were those I didn't know very well.

Secular psychologists, unencumbered with the burden of being wit-
nesses to a flawless Lord and the idea of man's being created in his
image, find it easy to deal with man's defects. They see them not as sin
but as expressions of man's animal forebears. At best, secular psychologists proffer us the vague hope that if we survive another billion years,
we might be better.

The biblical revelation reverses this pattern, and demonstrates a historical movement which is downward, away from perfection. Most of the
change which has taken place occurred in a single catastrophic event
when man chose to be disobedient to God. It is clear that his fall was, in
some sense, fatal. As such, it is unequivocally irreversible. We are given
no reason to expect or even hope that fallen man's Edenic perfection will
ever be restored to him.

A major effect of this disaster has been that each man has, to one degree or another, major structural defects in his psyche. Although these
differ from one person to another and can be remedied to some extent,
each of us suffers from some significant defect which cannot be attributed merely to circumstances. Gena's fragile narcissism and Hal's fragmented bisexuality are manifestations of these structural flaws. Before
any real resolution of their conflicts could take place, Hal would have to
deal with the incompatibility of his bisexuality and his concept of a Vic-
torian marriage. To work through to a new level of experience in marriage, he would have to face the realities of a psychological union formed
between two imperfect people.

Gena, too, would need to lay aside her romantic froth and plunge into
the fearful quest for her own vulnerable identity. She, too, would have to
come to the experience of a marriage to a husband who has the real capa-
bility to sin.

The board, on its part, also would have to face the reality that they and
all their church members share this imperfection. The church is made
up of redeemed sinners who still have major problems. A perfect pastor
would in many ways be useless to a congregation of people who are
searching for identity and meaning in personalities which long ago have
seen broken ideals. Had this not been so, at this point of crisis, Hal's
church would probably have turned to their elders rather than a psychiatrist. I suspect that they felt my secular training better enabled me to
deal with real problems of real people than those whose training is more
spiritual.

The fall, though, involves more than a static structural disorder in
man. Man became involved at that time with Satan himself as an active

agent of evil. With Hal and Gena, the circumstances, their misunder-standing, the "strange" coincidences, the flare-ups of fury seemed to have been designed to destroy a marriage, a family, a church fellowship, and a vital spiritual ministry just at a moment when they all seemed strongest. Satan's influence must be considered or therapy will floun-der.

We should not be discouraged at this point, however, since God has preceded us on our path. From the moment of the disobedience in Eden, God began a long series of merciful acts to make man's fallen plight more tolerable. Beginning with the protective move of separating Adam from the tree of life, to his covering the now exposed man and woman, moving on through the intricate details of the ceremonial exercises and laws given to Moses, God was active. From the mysterious utterances of the prophets all the way to the clothing of Christ himself in the flesh as the Son of Man born under the law, God moved mercifully in response to man's fallen dilemma.

The law has three functions which are of great value. For one thing, it provides protection and direction to us as vulnerable, confused, blind, lonely, stumbling creatures. At the same time, the law in all of its charac-teristics typically pointed forward to the ultimate fulfillment of man's vast need in a solution which lay ahead. Essentially every move was a type of Christ's redemption. Simultaneously and perhaps more impor-tant than either of these functions was God's further revelation of him-self. Though he worked largely through mediators, the great motifs of his personality are eloquently revealed in the pages of the Old Testament his-tory and prophecy.

If both Gena and Hal had been willing to abide by the admonitions of Scripture, the conflict would have largely subsided. There is little ques-tion that Hal's unwillingness to sacrifice a treasured measure of free-dom and his lack of caution in avoiding temptation did indeed aggravate Gena's anxiety. On the other hand, if Gena had been willing to turn judg-ment over to God, who was in every sense Hal's master, the issue might well have been dealt with by God in his time. Either way a good deal of tension would have been lifted from the turmoil.

It would not have been difficult for the therapist to think of many other scriptural principles which might have been helpful in this con-flict, both in reference to the problems which stemmed from personality flaws as well as from those which had their origin in the action of Satan.

To completely restrict our intervention to legalistic maneuvers, how-ever, seems to me to be committing us to some of the intrinsic limitations of the law. As helpful and as godly as it obviously is, the law is not the ultimate answer to man's dilemma. At the very best, it is a crutch, a weak reed, a schoolmaster. The law serves to graphically illuminate the full reality of our fall from the ideal. Ultimately, it should lead us to full re-demption in the Son himself, the Lord Jesus Christ.

We have a tendency at this point to fall into the error of spiritualizing the ideal and relegating it to the hereafter in somewhat the same way we have left the more concrete elements of the ideal in the remote past. The overwhelming burden of scriptural teaching, however, is that we are full participants in the heavenly kingdom while still being in the flesh. The full impact of both of these realms puts us, as believers, in a gigantic paradox of being both human and divine, both sinners and saints.

Redeemed, Christ-Indwelt Man and the Heavenlies

Scripture has many comforting things to say about the status of twice-born men as citizens of the heavenly kingdom. The sin-weary pilgrim hears with relief that he is forgiven, that his old life has passed away, and that all things have become new. His new life is described to him as one of peace, joy, and victory. Like Hal and Gena, though, he does not experi-ence it as conflict-free and without stress. His status as a saint has not relieved him of the responsibility of dealing with his difficult personality and painful relationships.

How, then, does this exalted status apply to working through one's prob-lems?

To answer this question in detail is beyond the scope of this chapter, but I would like to outline some of the aspects which apply to the distinc-tions between this area of the Christian's existence and others.

Fallen (and even the ideal) man is an earthbound creature, limited in time and space. Redeemed man inhabits eternity. His new existence is a new life. Its meaning and vitality come from Christ who indwells him. This new man and his problems can now only be fully understood in terms of the will and purpose which Christ has in his life. It is herein that our difficulty and our hope lay. It is difficult for Christ's purposes seem to differ from ours, and we cannot fully understand them. Certainly, we cannot predict what he is going to do in any given situation. We would like for him to heal broken fellowship, but he is apparently doing some-thing else. He has not come just to restore the ideal. His goal is far be-yond Eden and takes the redeemed ultimately out of time and space into eternal union with the Father. It is in this that our hope lies.

The biblical themes of the glory of God, the knowledge of God, the revelation of the Son, and the ministry of the Holy Spirit in illuminating Christ all focus our attention on Christ's existence in time and space as an unfolding of the character and nature of God. Of course, as we have mentioned, the earlier ways of God in the world had the same intent. But with the fuller revelation of the Son, man became a heavenly creature himself, and the scope widens. In this third mode, the center of the stage has moved to eternity and we cannot expect that it will continue to make the same kind of sense to us as men that it did before. We must now look at man's creation, his fall, and God's participation in both from a new, heavenly viewpoint.

God may or may not heal relationships. His intent is not that clients or therapists will be glorified. It is that something about himself will be exposed to those who are living through conflicts. We cannot even be sure that we understand what is going on, since some experiences might be designed more for a demonstration to the ages to come or the angels and principalities above than to us. What we can be sure of is that God is involved, that the conflict is permitted, and that both sides of redeemed man's paradox have critical roles in what God is doing. The gap that exists between the ideal and the reality of our fallen state is changed from a source of dejection to a dramatic focus in which both Christ and the nature of sin and rebellion are brought into opposition, each casting light, so to speak, on the other. It is not a contest to see which one will be the victor. The victory was accomplished in the slaying of the Lamb before the foundations of the world were laid. It is an exposition of sin and grace.

Hal and Gena came three or four times but were unable to come to grips with their problems. They seemed to polarize rather than draw together. They left the church and moved away. Should our consideration only be on them and their therapist we would be forced to consider this a failure.

Should we look at the same series of events as an apposition of sin and the Lord, we will see it differently. The first thing which strikes us is the disruption of the union between a man and his wife. As such, we are seeing played out another variation on the biblical theme that God's intent, in love, is the formation of a fitting, creative union between unlike elements. The effect of sin is to separate, disrupt union, and displace harmony with conflict. The theme is further developed when we see, in Hal's homosexual urges, a distortion of the creative dynamic which sex has in this unique fusion of man and woman, especially the frustration of its reproductive intent.

On her side, Gena's narcissism demonstrates some of the aspects of the problem Adam had when he left a life which was governed from outside of himself by God and became self-centered.

How does this become practical in the therapeutic situation? Each Christian who does therapy will answer this in a different way. Speaking for myself, I feel that much of my work is to do the best job I can to help people in an ordinary human way. For the most part, this approach might not differ much from a therapist's who has no interest in the spiritual. I would hope, though, that my confidence in the ultimate outcome as having meaning, and my sensitivity to these larger issues would make me more effective. More than this, though, I believe insights from the third realm of man's existence would make me more hopeful, more loving, and more closely identified with a troubled couple.

In working through problems, we come to know Christ more fully and understand more profoundly what sin is and how devastating its impact has been on a creation which was otherwise "very good." When the whole story is told, we will all know a great deal more.

This latter view "from the heavenlies," so to speak, brings into focus and integrates the other two realms which man inhabits. The central motif which ties them together is the same which helps us understand Christ's latest redemptive thrust into his creation. His unwavering purpose is to glorify the Father.

Conclusion

Both we and our patients, then, find ourselves involved in three different worlds, all at the same time. The Garden of Eden, though long gone in experience, is still with us. In fantasy, it creates the impossible dream that haunts us. At the same time, as a measuring rod of perfection, it identifies everything we do as "short of the mark."

We also are natural, fallen men and as such dwell in the realm of the law. We can find some relief from our fragmentation by compulsively organizing around the law, but all the while we are taunted by the knowledge that at best it only represents a splint—it does not in itself really heal.

Above and beyond both of these, we are citizens of the heavenlies. If we were only given clear vision, we could see that this citizenship overarches both Eden and the law. The ultimate solution, for example, to problems is not to hitch back time before a conflict, not to patch up a fight with a series of rules, but to somehow see that both of these elements, full strength, fuse together and eventuate in some new experience of righteousness and truth. The complex and conflict-ridden interaction of these three realms seems to be a tapestry on which a revelation of God himself and his full person is revealed.

18

The Dream of the Magician: A Case of Parataxic Distortion
Leigh C. Bishop

Freud introduced the term *transference* to describe how patients would typically attribute to the psychoanalyst characteristics of one or both parents. These attributes were felt to be derived typically from the odeipal phase of the patient's psychosexual development. The term later came to have a broader meaning among many psychotherapists. It was understood to include any characteristic attributed by the patient to the therapist based on the patient's previous experience with others. Sullivan used the term *parataxic distortion* to encompass this broader meaning. Parataxic distortion occurs not only in the therapeutic relationship but potentially in any interpersonal relationship. By extending this idea, one might readily guess that such distortion could also occur in the patient's relationship with God.

Case Presentation

A twenty-nine-year-old single female graduate student was in individual psychotherapy for complaints of recurrent episodes of depression and feelings of doubt about her chosen field of study. She was considering leaving graduate school. Her history included a series of unsatisfactory relationships with men. In her fifteenth hour of therapy, she began to talk about her father in some detail for the first time. He was an animal control officer for a small city in the Midwest. He was very good at his work, and the patient admired the compassion which he felt and demonstrated for the animals with which he had to deal. Nevertheless, she had never felt very close to him. As an only child, she had spent most of her time with her mother and maternal aunt while the father was working late hours and weekends at additional jobs.

Her father was a very religious man and attended mass faithfully. While she had attended church regularly in her childhood, she no longer did so and professed that while she believed that God did exist, she did not know what his nature was. However, she did not believe that God resembled any of the gods of traditional religion. Each time she visited home, her father would ask her if she was remembering to say her prayers daily. Although she no longer prayed at all, she always replied that she was doing so. She felt that while her father's religious life might be meaningful to him, she could see nothing about it that was attractive to her. She had a vivid childhood memory of her father talking with a priest wearing a black cassock and of feeling somewhat frightened of the priest in his vestments.

Two sessions later, she reported the following dream: "I was walking along a deserted beach and came upon a magician dressed in black evening dress, as magicians often are. He was doing magic tricks and bowing as though to applause after each one, though I don't recall there being any people around to applaud. He had with him some trained animals— a dog, a cat, a rabbit— that he would call by name and they would jump through a hoop. The names of the animals were all biblical names—such as Moses, Isaac, Joseph."

In association with the dream, she recalled that she had seen a magician on the cover of a magazine in the waiting room prior to the previous session. She also recalled a statement that she had made to the therapist a few sessions earlier in which she had expressed frustration that she continued to be depressed and that therapy had been of little benefit to her so far. Perhaps, she said, she should simply find a beach where she could sit alone for a long time and contemplate the possible solutions to her problem. A third association was that of seeing a small dog injured by the side of the road on the day before the dream. Though the animal was seriously injured, other drivers ignored it. She stopped and attempted to seek help for the animal at a nearby house, but by the time she returned it was dead. She recalled feeling intense anger at the drivers who had ignored the animal.

Discussion

The dream of the magician and the patient's associations with its content brought together many crucial elements. The figure of the magician combined features associated with several people in the patient's life: the therapist, the patient's father, the frightening priest. Clearly the patient was ambivalent toward each of these figures. Her experience of her father was that he was usually absent. Although she had spent a great deal of time in childhood in the company of her mother, she had difficulty describing the mother's personality. It emerged in therapy that the mother often had been emotionally inaccessible to her daughter. Her associations with the injured dog and her angry feelings at passing motorists suggested an identification with the wounded animal in its pain and in its being ignored. While she identified with her father in his care of animals, at the same time she was like a wounded animal that he ignored. She gladly would have received the care that he gave to the animals on the street. Yet he did not completely ignore her. He wanted her to be religious in the way that he himself was religious. There were hints that in childhood, God had been very real to her. She recalled thinking of him being stern and exacting—to please him one must always say one's prayers "properly." As she grew older, she replaced her early conceptions of God with a somewhat vague, impersonal one derived largely from readings of modern, existential literature.

The dream suggested that her intellectual concept of God did not match a more primitive, more emotionally-charged picture of him. He was like the magician, frightening yet somehow silly. Those who believed in him and served him (Moses, Isaac, Joseph) were like trained animals, thoughtlessly performing oft-repeated rituals. Clearly, the dream brought together in the dreamer's mind elements associated with her father, the therapist, and God. The dream can be understood on one level to be an attempt to portray the therapist, whom she knew a little, and God, whom she thought she knew, in terms of her father whom she knew well. Perhaps more importantly it revealed her actual, if mistaken, concept of God. It was a concept based on her relationship and experience with her earthly father.

Commentary

In most insight-oriented therapies, dreams provide helpful material in understanding the patient's psychodynamics. Frequently, they may be helpful in understanding the patient from a spiritual viewpoint. More specifically, the patient's concept of God may become clearer to the therapist through consideration of the dream material. In the absence of a more mature spirituality, that concept is often rooted in the child's experience of the parent. Heinrichs has explored how the individual's image of God can be distorted by a disturbed relationship between parent and child (Heinrichs 1982). Jesus implicitly commented on the possibility of such distortions. Comparing earthly fathers' care of their children to the care of God for his children, Jesus said, "If you then, who are evil, know how to give good gifts to your children, *how much more* will the heavenly Father give the Holy Spirit to those who ask him!" (Luke 11:13, emphasis added).

The capacity for object relations has to do with the individual's ability to form mutually satisfying emotional ties with others. A developmental disturbance in the capacity for object-relatedness is likely to affect not only the individual's ability to relate to other people but the ability to relate to God as well. The child who has not experienced a trust-based, loving relationship with a parental figure is likely to have difficulty conceiving of such a relationship with God. A similar problem may occur in the development of object-constancy, or the ability to tolerate inconstancy in one's interpersonal environment. If the child has never established adequate object-constancy with regard to a parental figure, he or she may have considerable difficulty in forming a concept of the invisible God in later life. He may be thought of as distant, absent, vague, cold, or uncaring. Such a concept of God may be present in spite of the individual's professed belief in him as personal, present and all-loving. That is, there may be incongruence between an intellectual or cognitive concept of God and the individual's affective experience in relation to God.

Clinically, the patient's tendency toward parataxic distortion is seen in the many ways in which the patient's image of the therapist departs from reality (Sullivan 1956). The patient's distortions of the therapist and the therapeutic relationship will be quite similar or identical to (and therefore predictive of) the distortions present in the patient's image of God. Dream material is often reflective of these distortions.

While a complete discussion of religious dream symbolism is beyond the scope of this chapter, a few comments are in order. God may be represented in dream material in a wide variety of ways. People, animals, or objects may be symbols of God. The presence of pastoral or priestly figures, biblical names, biblical symbols (e.g., cross, dove, fishes, wine, bread, wheat, clay), or images from the patient's church experience should alert the therapist. Dream symbols are virtually always overdetermined. As in the case presented, understanding the condensed nature of a dream symbol for God may provide the therapist with valuable information.

The clinical use of such dream material by the Christian therapist may vary widely according to his or her particular therapeutic method. Interpretation of the dream to the patient may be in order. In working with patients who are not Christians or who have not already expressed an interest in exploring spiritual issues in therapy, one must decide how best to introduce the possibility of such exploration. Recontracting with the patient to examine spiritual issues may be indicated.

In many cases, the therapist may best approach the patient's distorted God-image by first interpreting the patient's parataxic distortions of the therapist. Once these are recognized by the patient, distortion in the image of God may be more effectively addressed. Frequently, addressing the parataxic distortion of the patient's God-image will result in the patient becoming open to exploring anew the nature and character of God.

References

Heinrichs, D. Our Father which art in heaven: Parataxic distortions in the image of God. *Journal of Psychology and Theology* 10 (1982):120–29.

Sullivan, H. 1956. *Clinical studies in psychiatry.* New York: Norton.

19

Psychoanalysis and Religious Experience
William Edkins

James Grotstein, a noted psychoanalytic theoretician and writer, has stated that just like in a foxhole, so on the back wards of a psychiatric hospital, there are no atheists. He quickly adds that this is *not* because religion is the cause of psychopathology but because it best expresses human psychology in its most fundamental form. The Christian therapist is in a unique place to understand his or her patient's religious communications because he or she has the potential of hearing patients on both the psychological and spiritual levels. On the one hand, the Christian therapist believes that there is a personal reality behind religious experience. On the other hand, he or she knows that there is a dynamic level, a level of unconscious, personal meanings, which definitely influences a patient's communications regarding his beliefs and religious experiences.

Case Presentation

The patient was a thirty-five-year-old man, married with three children, and employed as a researcher in a large marketing company. He came in to treatment due to struggles he was having regarding intimacy with his wife and children, as well as a general unhappiness with his

193

social and spiritual life. His family was from the Middle East, and he was the youngest of two sons. They were of middle-class socioeconomic status. Other than a couple of brief hospitalizations for pneumonia and a car accident, his childhood was without any major trauma such as abuse or divorce.

His parents were evangelical Christians and he was raised in an evangelical Christian church. For almost as far back as he could remember, he had experienced God as a harsh judge who wanted him to "deny himself." He acted out his feelings toward this "god" when he was around eleven years old by taking the picture of God in Michaelangelo's "The Creation of Adam," stabbing it repeatedly with a knife, and then locking the mutilated picture in his desk drawer. Once he was old enough, he decided to stop going to church and got involved in a life-style which expressed his anger at God, including heavy drug usage. For a short time after he graduated from college, he attempted to commit his life entirely to Christ, but he looked back on that time as a complete denial of his real feelings and self, a vain attempt to do everything right. His solution to his difficulties in carrying out his commitment was to leave the church entirely. It was shortly after this that he started psychotherapy knowing his therapist was a Christian and in his own way asking for help with his spiritual struggles as well as with his psychological ones.

The patient was seen for two years in psychoanalytic psychotherapy, twice a week. The following session was selected for discussion because it especially illustrates how one's internal state does, in fact, dominate his understanding of God.

The Session

In the session before the one under consideration, the client talked of confronting a most difficult family situation involving inheritance property. He also stated that before the next session the whole family would get together at his request to confront an uncle who he felt was treating him very unfairly. He was quite distraught about the possible outcome of the meeting, whether his uncle would listen or if he would even insist on the patient being disinherited. He came to the next session stating that the meeting had gone remarkably well. "My uncle was actually reasonable about it. We even laughed." In fact, the patient felt so different regarding his uncle that when the uncle asked for help on a project which was unrelated to their meeting, the patient volunteered! The patient noted how surprised he was with the positive response of his uncle. "I expected this to be like all the other hard times I've had with teachers, bosses, and my parents."

For the past few months we had been analyzing his own harsh super-ego and it became clear to me as I listened to him that, although his uncle, certain teachers, and his parents probably were unreasonable and insensitive, he was also projecting this aspect of *himself* onto them. I pointed out to him, "Yes, why the negative, unreasonable response from your uncle would have felt so much more familiar is that you're talking about what's inside you, the side of you that you often find so unreasonable and critical, that can't humor yourself, your 'uncle' inside of you."

He went on to say that there was one point in the meeting where he was feeling angry at his uncle, "but then I couldn't think. I was talking but I didn't know what I was saying." He had this experience before even in our sessions, especially in the first year of therapy, where he would become very critical of anything he might be thinking and then freeze and become intellectually incapacitated. This was obviously an anxiety reaction but it was crucial for him to see from where the anxiety was coming.

It occurred to me that this experience was a perfect example of the internal situation I had interpreted to him just a couple of minutes be-fore. After I had pointed out the critical uncle inside of him, his associa-tion was to recall his anger at his uncle. In this he was telling me how angry he was at his own insensitive, cruel superego, which was exter-nally represented by his uncle. However, his critical superego was also clearly demonstrated in his response to his angry feelings. He responded to his anger by an immediate attack on himself so that he became so in-timidated that he could not even think.

The point is, this was not true signal anxiety, which has to do with the threat of a forbidden impulse overwhelming the ego. His anxiety was more persecutory in nature. It had to do with being psychologically at-tacked and beaten up by an internal object, that is, the "uncle" inside of him.

I said, "There it is, that's what we were just talking about! On the one hand you are fed up with this critical 'uncle' in you and you were experi-encing how angry you are for a moment while talking with your uncle, but then it changed to where you were again the harsh, critical uncle at-tacking yourself."

Then I recalled "the man." It was not until after about a year-and-a-half of treatment that he told me about "him." Each time he would go through these anxiety experiences, in which he would be talking without knowing what he was saying, besides feeling immobilized by criticism he perceived was coming from whomever he was with, there really was an-other conversation going on inside of him. "Someone," whom he labeled a long time ago, "the man," would be telling him how stupid he was and that he was not making any sense. (In reality, he was almost always lucid at these points.) Also, this experience of being criticized, feeling humiliated and stupid, would trigger a host of memories such as his teacher scolding him because he soiled his pants in kindergarten or when he had forgotten his lines in front of the whole church during a Sunday school play.

At this point I reminded him of "the man." "We're really talking about 'the man.' The side of you that says your thoughts are stupid." At first his face flushed and then he broke out into a big smile. Then, in a very curious way, after his projection onto his uncle was interpreted, he started to take in and identify with his critical superego. Now he was actually speaking for this aspect of himself instead of seeing others as disqualifying him for his feelings. He said, "I wonder if real Christians would ever make problems in their families like this? If I was really acting like a Christian I would have never complained."

Here is where I felt I could point out to him how his theology was influenced by his internal conflict. His critical, rejecting self not only was transferred onto his uncle, bosses, teachers, and myself, but also onto God, so that he saw God as thinking his feelings and thoughts were stupid and bad. My next association was to the time, at age eleven, when he had tried to destroy this "god" by stabbing the picture. I realized that this fusing of God and "the man" had been at the bottom of his rage toward God. Then I said, "So now you're seeing God as also rejecting your thoughts and feelings. You give that critical side of yourself to him too so that 'the man' actually becomes your 'god.' At the same time, that's what you hate about Christianity, how you feel God gives you no room at all to be yourself."

From this point in the session there was an interesting succession of responses in which the patient's deep ambivalence about God surfaced. At first he protested the interpretation and defended his projection. "But it all fits! 'Deny yourself.' 'Don't be selfish.' " He then explored his dilemma, "When I used to be into Christianity someone would ask a favor of me and even though I might want to say 'no,' I'd never know if it might be God wanting me to do it. This would happen to my cousin all the time. The youth pastor would ask to use their summer house. Something would get broken and my cousin would just say, 'No problem, praise the Lord.' " Eventually in this sequence the patient rejected his "god" as fostering an unlivable existence. "I'd be going nowhere in my life, being a fool for everyone, if I had stayed with the church."

I confronted his feelings about "the man." "So this all really does leave you in a nowhere, no-win situation. In a way you see 'the man' as your god and you want to submit to and become part of him but by doing that you rule out any possibility of being comfortable with yourself."

Up until this point in the session, as well as in his life, he had played out an internal drama involving a harsh "god" who criticizes and rejects an inadequate, weak self. What was also evident in the session was that he would split these two internal representations and identify with one and project the other. For example, he might split off his critical super-ego and project it onto God. Then he identified with his attacked, abused self and rose up in rage and rebellion against the inhuman treatment he got from "God." Or, he could split off his attacked, depleted self, project it onto his friends, wife, or children and then identify with his judgmental superego. In this scenario he became the rejecting judge of others who now were spoiled by his projection of his unwanted, weak self onto them. Now *they* were boring, a waste. *He* had now become the rejecting one.

Nevertheless, after we looked at his splitting and projections something different happened. He became anxious and depressed. "It's like I don't want to admit that I've been seeing 'the man' as God. I feel like I'm losing something." Here, with some owning of the projections, his anxiety changed from a persecutory nature to anxiety and depression over losing something. Developmentally this was more advanced and mature. It also shed light on the nature and purpose of the god-like "man" inside. Its function was to defend against and avoid these very feelings of needing someone and facing inevitable disappointment and loss. This was accomplished by idealizing an aspect of self, even though it was a critical one at that, in order to put him above the great vulnerability and inadequacy he felt in relating to others.

In light of this defensive function I responded to his statement of feeling lost without 'the man' with, "Yes, seeing 'the man' as God is your wish to have God as part of you all the time." Again, he smiled and said, "I'm glad you understand that. It's been a secret all my life."

Broader Theoretical and Theological Implications

The language of object-relations theory, which comes out of contemporary psychoanalysis, is very helpful in understanding the psychology of our patients' religious language. Instead of being based on instinct and an impersonal mental apparatus as is classical psychoanalysis, contemporary psychoanalysis emphasizes the role of internal representations of significant others, that is, *objects*, and the composite representations of the self. Guntrip's (1961) ideas on the superego utilize this object-relations approach. He understands what Freud (1923) called the "superego" to be a much more complex yet interpersonal representation involving a composite of intense rejecting and unfulfilling aspects of the parental representations, that is, the "rejecting object," and aspects of the self, that is, the "antilibidinal ego," which identifies with these rejecting aspects of the object against their own needy self. In normal development these representations are not overly intense and are modified with more loving aspects of the parents. They are then combined further with more advanced moral training to form a more healthy superego which can be a helpful guide in being able to evaluate one's behavior.

Clearly in this patient there was a primary, harsh superego. Guntrip has pointed out that one possible outcome for the individual who has failed to attain a mature superego is that he can actually form an admiration for the strong, internal rejector or saboteur. This is the case with this patient where he saw his "rejecting object," which he called "the man," as God.

In terms of integration, this is a curious psychological re-enactment of Genesis 3. Instead of experiencing all that is meant to relate as a creature, the irresistible, universal temptation is to "be like God" (Gen. 3:5). Specifically, this patient attempted to dispose of his childlike, needy self and instead become his own omnipotent, omniscient judge. Theologically, the kenosis passage in Philippians 2 is enlightening here. Christ, as the second or new Adam, did not count equality with God a thing to be grasped (v. 6). This is usually taken to refer to his choice before the incarnation. However, it seems even more plausible that this is referring to his life here on earth. Rather than grasping at being equal to God, as the first Adam did, the second Adam poured out his life to death as the Suffering Servant (Isa. 53:12).

The psychological implications of this aspect of the incarnation are astounding. Rather than sinfully avoiding all the frailty, neediness and weakness of mankind as creature, Jesus, *as a man*, refused to put himself above his Father but rather learned obedience (Heb. 5:8). He thus allowed himself to experience all the pain, vulnerability, and weakness that the rest of Adam's race has continually sought to avoid. Because of this he is able to truly understand and empathize with our weaknesses (Heb. 4:15).

Conclusion

The goal for treatment in a case like this is to help the patient experience and face what it means to relate to others as a human, a creature, without becoming an omnipotent, wrathful god who must do away with his weak and needy self by hating and attacking it. The therapy relationship is an arena for the actual experiencing of this, in which the patient can truly face his childlike self with all its vulnerability and limitations.

As he does this the goal is that he will experience greater freedom in seeing God beyond his projections and be able to come as a child to his heavenly Father to receive his saving grace.

References

Freud, S. [1923] 1961. *Ego and the id*. In *The standard edition of the complete psychological works of Sigmund Freud*, edited and translated by J. Strachey. Vol. 19. London: Hogarth.

Guntrip, H. 1961. *Personality structure and human interaction*. New York: International Universities Press.

20

Working Through Resistance by Prayer and the Gift of Knowledge
John McDonagh

Case Presentation

Lucy was referred to me for psychotherapy by her spiritual advisor. The reason for the referral was not clear in Lucy's mind; she was incensed that anyone would tell her that she needed to see a psychologist. It soon became apparent, however, that Lucy was filled with overwhelming rage, and that this rage was ruining her life. In particular, she felt betrayed by nearly every person with whom she was intimate. Most of this rage was being directed against her husband. Lucy believed that it was he, and not she, who "needed to be straightened out," and then her life would be fine. It did not occur to her that her intense anger pushed people away from her, because she did not see that she was angry. The therapist's reflection that she was very angry was met with a surprised expression of disbelief.

After many weeks of therapy, Lucy came to the painful awareness that she was angry. Only much later would she be able to see that it was rage and not simple anger. It was easy for her to project her anger onto others; there were people in her life who gave her cause to be provoked. Some were verbally abusive or disdainful of her, and she was indignant.

Lucy was a devout Christian, and believed that she needed to forgive those who had hurt her, but admitted that she could not do so. She

200

needed to hold on to her anger, almost as if her psychological survival depended on it. Only gradually did she come to see that this same anger was ruining her social relationships, and was creating a ripple effect throughout her whole family. It was wearing her out as well. Even when a relative called her several times to apologize and ask her forgiveness, Lucy refused. The therapist discussed with her how perhaps she needed to hold on to her anger as a defense against depression, feelings of power- lessness, and worthlessness. Elements of all these factors permeated her childhood and adolescent years. She had become a "professional vic- tim," who could maintain a position of equality or even moral superiori- ty by refusing to forgive. By so doing, she could prove that she was just as good or even better than those who were so unkind. To put it another way, pride was playing a role in preventing forgiveness. One could also say that this anger-pride combination was helping Lucy avoid psychological annihilation. In other words, she could avoid facing the fear that she was a "nothing."

Gradually, however, through contemplative prayer as well as dreams, Lucy began to have images of spiritual symbolism that confirmed some of these interpretations in varying degrees. While in prayer, a mental image of a cluster of grapes came to her. Each of these grapes repre- sented a deep wound she had suffered. During this time of prayer, she felt that a great burden of anger had been lifted from her, though much still remained. Her awareness of her own anger became more real to her. The associations with the image of the grapes included "the grapes of wrath," as well as wine, which in turn, was associated with the cup of suffering to which Jesus referred as he prayed in the Garden of Gethsemane. Frequently when in contemplative prayer, Lucy meditated spontaneously on Jesus praying in Gethsemane, as if she were stuck there because she could not deal with the next step—betrayal. Betrayal by those whom she had loved deeply was a recurring theme in her life, and the greater part of her hurts could be traced to feelings of betrayal. But the associations to grapes were secondary, because a lifting of much anger had occurred in prayer before any conscious associations were made. A healing was beginning. After this experience of anger being lifted from her, she said, "I am beginning something new." She was no- ticeably less depressed.

Not long after this experience, she was again hurt by an act of betrayal by a friend. When the friend asked to be forgiven, Lucy refused. Clearly, there was an obstacle. She was still stuck. A couple of events followed which further loosened the grip that rage had upon this client.

She had a dream in which it was shown to her that pride was the main obstacle preventing her from forgiving, and that she needed to nurture true humility in order to free herself from this vicious cycle. She awoke

from this dream with an overflowing feeling of joy. The next event occurred when a friend of hers, feeling that Lucy needed spiritual discern-
ment involving an important decision she was considering, brought her
to a meet a Spirit-filled Christian woman who was said to have the gift of
knowledge. Without knowing anything about Lucy but her name, the
woman told Lucy that she was filled with rage, and that she could not
forgive because of pride. She told Lucy many other things about her life,
which she could have known only through the Holy Spirit. Lucy said of
her reaction to this word of knowledge, "You could have knocked me
over with a feather."

At her next therapy session, Lucy gave the above account, and recalled
that the therapist had said to her at the outset of therapy that she was
filled with rage, but at the time, she had absolutely no awareness of what
the therapist was talking about, and thought he was wrong. Prayer,
dreams, and spiritual counsel all worked together with psychotherapy to
increase self-awareness and growth in this woman. One had to acknowledge the work of the Lord in this.

The client's resistance to interpretation was worked through by grace.
The therapist is convinced that he alone could never have helped Lucy to
see the extent of her rage, and therefore the degree to which it was ruining her life. Not only that, but insights were revealed to her in prayer,
dreams, and spiritual counsel which the therapist could not teach her.
The whole experience was therefore a lesson in humility and growth for
the therapist as well as for the client.

Discussion

The above approach to psychotherapy is clearly different from most
contemporary approaches. Some would say that it should not be called
"psychotherapy" at all, but stands somewhere between therapy and
spiritual counseling. Clearly it is a different approach because both
therapist and client confess that at the deepest level of their being, they
are spirit, not merely flesh. The goals of "self-actualization," or growth,
must therefore differ from those who do not confess this. The very concept of "self" is quite different in Christian therapy than in secular therapies, so it follows that self-knowledge and self-actualization will differ
from their counterparts in secular therapy. The self-awareness that
results from secular therapy does not go far enough. There is a depth of
self that can be fully developed only in relation to God. We are all more or
less blind to this reality, which is why we must be open through prayer to
what lies beyond. We can see only dimly, as Paul wrote (1 Cor. 13:12), and
it is only the Lord who can show us the way in our dimness of vision and

spiritual blindness. In the unchartered labyrinth that is the human psyche, it seems most prudent to ask the Lord's help in showing us the way. "For the word of God is living and active, sharper than any two-edged sword, piercing to the division of soul and spirit, of joints and marrow, and discerning the thoughts and intentions of the heart" (Heb. 4:12).

21

A Peace That Passes Understanding
Bryan Van Dragt

Anxiety is inescapable. This is true because anxiety is not something that we *have*, but is rather a reflection of what we *are*. It is, in effect, a message signalling that we are out of step with our own being and purpose in life. Perhaps nowhere is this purpose more clearly expressed than in Augustine's contemplation of the Divine: "Thou hast made us for Thyself, and our hearts are restless until they find their rest in Thee." Not until this purpose is fulfilled does anxiety relinquish its hold.

That anxiety is unavoidable does not, however, discourage us from seeking a "cure" for it. Our "solutions" take the form of dependency relationships with others or things outside of ourselves. These attachments express, on the one hand, our sense of alienation from love, in that our constant pursuit of love betrays our belief that we are separate from it. On the other hand, these dependencies demonstrate our alienation from ourselves, in that, rather than trusting to find love within, we seem determined to wrest it from those around us. In that any external attachment is at best only symbolic of that union which we seek with our own deeper selves and with God, each successive strategy merely postpones our confrontation with the meaning of our anxiety.

If all goes well, however, there comes a moment in our lives when everything goes wrong. That is, the structure of props and defenses (the "false" self) with which we have kept our anxiety at bay collapses and we are thrust unprotected into the direct experience of that dread. Christian mystics speak of this as the "dark night of the soul."

If we abandon ourselves to that experience rather than seeking to distance ourselves from it, we find the anxiety transformed into a most remarkable peace. This experience of the "dark night" and the ensuing peace tend to become a powerfully integrating focus that reshapes attitudes, feelings, and relationships.

As with all inner experience, this moment of transformation is ineffable and therefore more suited to contemplation and participation than to rational analysis. Any attempt to explain it must inevitably do it injustice. However, my own experience, the experience of many of those with whom I work, and personal accounts over the centuries in many traditions prompt me to examine this phenomenon from my own particular perspective—that of Christian existentialism. Following is a description of one individual's transition from anxiety to inner peace.

Case Presentation

By her own careful reckoning, Anita had a miserable life. The physical and emotional abuse in her childhood and the broken relationships of her adult life gave her just cause for bitterness. However, Anita hated herself even more than her mother, who had victimized her, or her father, who had failed to rescue her. She hated herself for not being able to rise above her own anger. Anita would allow herself neither to experience nor to express this anger, for she was convinced that it would betray her guilt and bring deserved rejection.

To compensate for the pain of her childhood and for her own self-rejection, Anita continually sought the approval of others. To earn this approval she tried to project an image of idealized perfection. If she were perfect, she would be loved. However, her basic belief in her own guilt would inevitably find confirmation in a word or a glance, and she would then respond with an explosion of righteous anger, as if to say, "You've no right to accuse me—I'm perfect!" It was, in fact, her intense anger with her family that first brought Anita into psychotherapy. Her marriage had failed, and her eight-year-old daughter reminded her continually that she was not the perfect mother.

During a three-week period of intensive therapy, in which she lived in seclusion, isolated from the ordinary distractions of life, Anita became preoccupied with thoughts of dying. In one dream she saw herself lying in bed and felt that she was sinking into death. She reached out to her parents. Her father took her hand, but could not hold on; her mother looked on contemptuously, not even offering to help. Before she could

sink further, however, Anita awoke in awful dread. Believing herself suicidal, she tried to distract herself from the thoughts. But dreams of death
continued, and even the sight of a dying insect would thrust her back into
her anxiety.

I encouraged Anita to re-experience the dream of her parents. As she
imagined herself sinking into death, she called out in desperation to her
parents to save her. But her parents slowly faded from the scene as she
realized that it was beyond their power to give her what she needed. Anger dissolved to overwhelming sadness as she became aware that no one
could save her from what she was about to face. She began to cry openly.

At length Anita's deep sobs were replaced by a long period of silence.
As she described this experience later, the frantic pace of her thoughts
suddenly ceased and the compelling sense of dread was replaced by a
deep sense of peace and joy. She found herself spontaneously envisioning herself and her mother embracing freely—something Anita could
not recall since before she was three years old. When she got up from the
couch, Anita felt relaxed, focused, and at peace. She also felt thoroughly
disoriented, as though seeing her surroundings for the first time.

The significance of this experience was that it precipitated for Anita a
radical and seemingly paradoxical shift in perspective and feeling. The
events of her past were not only unchanged, but Anita had allowed herself to experience more of their pain than ever before—and yet, she was
at peace. The painful facts of her life no longer mattered. What would not
yield to rational argument or years of conscious scheming was now
transformed virtually in a moment, without a word and with scarcely a
conscious thought. The forgiveness that Anita had for years denied both
herself and others was now an accomplished fact. She had let go. Anita
was subsequently able to return to and reconcile with her family. And
although the sense of wholeness was by no means permanent, Anita had
found inner quiet to which she was able to return again and again.

Discussion

The internal experiences leading to Anita's shift in consciousness parallel the accounts of many of those whose journeys I have shared. Although characters and situations differ, the path from anxiety to inner
peace seems to involve a common sequence of events.

The transition which begins as a deepening sense of alienation from
self, others, and (for some) God is met with more and more desperate attempts to secure from others or from circumstances the love which one
fears would otherwise be lost. One feels that this failure of dependency

supports and confirms an underlying belief that one is ugly and thus un-lovable, sinful, and deserving of punishment. The game is up. Certain that one is about to meet an awful fate, but unable to continue the self-deception, one falls headlong into the inner chasm of fear.

While the content of this experience varies from person to person with differing strategies or forms of dependency, the feelings reported follow a similar pattern. There is a sense of darkness, often described as a dark tunnel or black hole. Many speak of a sense of emptiness, hollowness, or nothingness. One feels lost, without direction. There is a deep feeling of abandonment, rejection, and utter aloneness. The core of this feeling is expressed in the agonized cry of Jesus on the cross, "My God, my God, why have you forsaken me?" One is overcome with hopelessness. One faces, in fact, the death of hope for love, for this hope has been misplaced. There is no acceptance from without that can overcome the determina-tion to reject one's own self.

But out of the ashes of one's crushed dreams springs a most beautiful awareness. To one's utter astonishment, all that has died is fear. Rather than finding oneself utterly cut off from love, the uninhibited plunge into despair transforms aloneness into an experience of "at-one-ness" in which no sense of separation exists. In this moment, all feeling of need or craving ceases, for one is no longer apart from that which one seeks. One has, in effect, *become* the peace.

Blame is no longer required, for the guilt (which, in existential terms, is one's choice to separate from one's "true" self) which prompted it is gone. Because the solution was found within, one realizes that the prob-lem must also be within. One sees that the sense of separation from love is self-inflicted. One forgives the other because it becomes clear that it is not he or she, but rather oneself who is ultimately responsible for the suffering. And as often as one forgets this, one must return through anxi-ety to that simple awareness that love is found within.

For some this experience is couched in traditional religious symbols and takes on religious meaning. One woman, for example, who had been sexually molested as a child, projected her fears of her father onto God and once dreamed of Jesus as an armed and threatening guerilla soldier. As she faced the incest of her childhood and relived those feelings, she spontaneously pictured herself cradled in the arms of a loving God. "As I get closer to the child in me," she later observed, "I get closer to God." Another person, who hated himself for hating his wife, upon giving vent to his anger, found himself envisioning Christ's hands placed over his own to bring healing both to himself and to the alcoholic woman whom he had only moments before imagined himself destroying.

At one point in her struggle with anxiety, when I suggested that she ask God to love her, Anita had said, "I don't even want him to *look* at me!" Following her "death experience," she could enter meditation and prayer unafraid, either of God or of her own depths.

In retrospect, like a stone skipping across the surface of a troubled pond, one has gone from this thing to that in search of a place to belong. Swallowed by the waves of anxiety, one sinks—only to come at last to rest. Here, within, where one stands, is the place where love, belonging, and wholeness are to be found. In the depths of one's own self is a footing that eliminates the need for self-destructive emotional attachments. In this moment of *non*attachment, true self-dependence is born.

What do psychology and theology contribute to this moment of existential forgiveness? At its best, theology points to the existence of an ultimate belonging, wholeness, "at-one-ment"—to the reality that, in the core of our being, we are not separate from love. But it cannot grant the bearer of that knowledge the existential realization that this love is for *me*. It cannot bestow peace. Psychology, with its careful cataloguing of the strategies we use to hide from our pain and guilt (i.e., of the ways in which we are lost) can help us discover the blocks to the awareness of love's presence. But it cannot make that intensely personal decision to set these defenses aside.

In the search for inner peace, man's experience is the primary source material. Psychology and theology are but abstractions of, or rational commentaries on this depth dimension of man. If one is to experience peace, one must at last lift the veil formed by the intricately woven fabrics of these disciplines and taste that which is only intimated by their rational contours.

To switch metaphors: Psychology and theology can lead one to the garden wherein peace is found, but they must wait at the gate— as must reason itself. Because the experience of inner peace relates most pertinently to man's depth dimension—that is, to one's relationship with self and with God—it is beyond explanation or cognitive understanding. It cannot be taught. As with the true self of which the mystics speak, inner peace is "hid with Christ in God"(Col. 3:3).

22

Earthly Father/
Heavenly Father
Frances J. White

Recently I had the privilege to hear a young man whom I had in therapy over an eighteen-month period speaking to a group about the positive impact that therapy had on his relationship with the Lord. Reviewing the session notes to try to isolate the factors that had facilitated his spiritual growth, I realized that at no point had we explicitly dealt with what might be termed spiritual issues per se. We had not prayed, referred to Scripture, or carried out any other "Christian" acts. There had been minimal discussion about his relationship to God. The sessions had centered primarily around his relationship to his parents, above all his father.

At the same point in time I was about to terminate a client with whom spiritual factors had been an explicit part of his therapy. He, too, had expressed a change in his view of God. Although there were very different situational factors involved, the dynamics were similar in both cases.

In both cases there were distorted object relationships. Both clients tended to see themselves as "bad" in order to maintain idealized parents. C and M expressed very early in therapy that they never could please their parents, particularly their fathers. They both manifested the nagging sense that it was their fault, that somehow they had not been "good enough." Both had intense anger at the rejection they felt by not measuring up to their parents' standards. Such reactions often surfaced when dealing with authority figures or, in fact, with anyone who had hints of their fathers' characteristics.

There was a very obvious searching for that perfect, all-accepting parent. This had hindered their individuation. They were both emotionally tied to their parents. They had transferred their perceptions of their human parents, particularly their fathers, onto God and resented what they perceived as his demands. Only as healing came in their responses to their earthly parents could they more fully experience God.

The parallel dynamics, in spite of personality and situational differences, coupled with the contrast between the explicit way I responded to religious factors with one and in implicit ways with the other, prompted me to interview them to delineate more distinctly the elements that contributed to the change in their perceptions of God. Both men interviewed were in their early thirties. M was a custodian in a large factory. C was an assistant pastor in a large church.

In both cases the interview included a complete review of therapy. The following extracts focus on the discussion of the spiritual issues involved in the course of therapy.

Interview One: C

Th: What brought you into therapy?

C: Jill, my wife, and I were thinking of going to the mission field. In the candidating process we had to take psychological tests. As a result of these tests, we were told that we would be recommended with reservations. My comment was, "What reservation?" The mission counselor said that I had unresolved anger that needed to be dealt with.

It was suggested that I take a year and go through counseling. I was skeptical. I had always thought that God, the Word, and the Holy Spirit were enough for me and any problem.

Th: What led you to me?

C: Skeptical, scared, hurting, hoping—we agreed, but not until we found someone who was competent and someone we could trust. They suggested you. I said, "Great!" We had heard you during a session on the African national and I told Jill that you really appreciate the African people as equals.

My conclusion was, if you could do that with Africans, you could and would for us. You wouldn't put us down either. We knew where you were coming from.

Th: You expressed a desire to see a "Christian" therapist, yet we did not talk about or read Scripture, pray, or even talk in Christian terms. Do you feel like what you have gone through is "Christian"?

C: You are right—we didn't do a lot of stereotyped Christian things. In fact, none. Yet I realize that what we did was deeply spiritual. I had been to victorious life conferences before with no result. I had prayed for years that God would change me, my depression, inconsistency, and so on. I had read books, confessed sin, had demons cast out of me. I had memorized books of the Bible, spent time with a Christian organization that was lay-discipled, but my problem still existed.

So the fact that you did *not* use all these things impressed me. You dealt with *me*. How I was feeling. You were the first person to ever recognize in me how much pain and hurt I had. Not even my wife knew how deep the hurt was. But you saw it, seemed to feel it and you were willing to listen. No preacher, no Christian worker, no one had ever tried to understand before. *I* didn't even understand.

Th: Would you describe your spiritual pilgrimage as you went through therapy?

C: What we have been through in these past eighteen months is the hardest thing we have ever done in our lives. But for me, it has been the best and most important thing to happen to me spiritually since I became a Christian.

We started meeting for therapy once a week in August of 1983. You always seemed to get us to talk about present incidents that happened to us and then somehow used them to get us to connect them to what I know now was "unfinished business in my past." There were times during those early months that the pain was so deep that I did not think I could endure it. There was one week that I refused to go—for fear of hurting more.

Looking back over my diary, I realize how hard therapy was. It grew harder and harder. Sometimes the emotional impact came soon after the session. Other times it was several days later. This had an effect on my spiritual life, on my family life. It was hard to pray during this time. It was hard to relate to others. I felt God was unreachable, unknowable, unapproachable. Was therapy alienating me from God? But maybe I have always felt that way, but never admitted it. I knew in my heart the right verses but did I ever really connect with God on a feeling level? The "aha" experience came during December of '83.

I went to my folks' for Christmas. I saw myself slipping into the emotional role of a child. I suddenly felt lonely, distant, like I did not belong in my folks' home. I sensed a rift, a distance from my folks that I had never felt before. I was petrified.

Then, when I met with you in January, February, and March, many things started to come together—lots of emotion and tears—yet release and freedom. I started to see that my problem, the rift, over Christmas was the "breaking away" (something that normally should have happened years ago) now crystallized in a few months. My allegiance up to this point was to my parents. In fact, my wife says that when I spoke of family I always talked about my mom, dad, brothers, and sisters; never about her and the children.

This "aha" experience gave me a perspective of my dad I had never had. He had always been perfect. I assumed all the blame. Now I saw a man hurting inside and lonely. I saw someone who had made mistakes. I saw good and bad. I could now love the good and accept the bad. And you know what? I could love the good in me and accept the bad. And most important—I could forgive him for the mistakes he made. In doing so, I could see the root of my anger, feel it, understand it, walk around it, accept it, and walk away from it.

Th: How did all this play a role in your spiritual life?

C: After the "aha" experience I realized that I had transferred the feeling of the immature dependence and anger I had toward Dad onto God. In therapy I sensed a need for distance from Dad. I also did from God. As I drew away from Dad I drew away from God. I experienced real depression, real feelings of failure as a Christian during those early weeks of therapy. I felt God had abandoned me. I was searching for that father I could finally please. So I couldn't do enough to earn God's love and acceptance and it got to be too much.

When I made the emotional break with Dad and became his adult son rather than his child, spiritual things that were only intellectual truths began to become feelings. I was acceptable to God. I could enjoy him. I could thank him and praise him—not just clingingly ask him about decisions that were acceptable for me to make. Sometimes, though, I miss the intensity with which I tried to please him. Nonetheless over this past year I have experienced the greatest freedom I have ever known—like the difference between a sprint and a marathon. Instead of sprinting 100 yards and giving up with outbursts of anger or depression, I have settled into a fairly steady pace of enjoying God, my wife, children, and even authority figures. I don't want to give the impression that it's all uphill. I have to fight a lot of feelings yet but now it's not all heaviness and defeat. The theologian in me wants to call it sanctification. The Lord has used therapy to remove blocks that were preventing spiritual growth.

Interview Two: M

Th: What brought you into therapy?

M: My boss said I'd get fired if I didn't come. I got mad at him. I told him I was sorry and would pray about it but he said, "Counseling or goodbye." So I told my minister and he called another minister for a name to make sure no worldly guy got hold of me.

Th: Your pastor wanted you to go to a Christian therapist. Do you think you had Christian counseling?

M: Yeah, but you know I looked around for a Bible the very first visit. It was the *Living* one. We don't use that one but you said I could bring my own. You said, "You look scared. Like something terrible is going to happen to you." I think I said, "I'm not worried about me but I don't want you to hurt my Jesus." You said something like, "I love Jesus, too. Shall we ask him to let us feel his presence in counseling?" Now, was I relieved! In later meetings, though, we didn't talk as much about God—just sometimes. Sometimes I'd go home and remember that we didn't even look at verses. Then sometimes you'd come up with a good one. Like the time you showed me the difference between honoring my mom and dad and still being their little child.

Th: So you see prayer, Scripture, and talking about God as important aspects of your counseling?

M: Oh boy, yeah. If you had not prayed I don't know if I'd have come back. My Jesus, he's important to me. Now with God, I wasn't so sure. He seemed more like my dad. I think all that's changing now though.

Th: M, would you tell me about the way God has changed for you?

M: Well, you know how I told you—it was like God had puppet strings on me and I had to do it all his way? Sort of like the way we found out I felt about my dad. He controlled me, too. But I love my dad, you know, I used to tell him everything. Now Jesus, I tell him even more. He's okay. More like my mother who hears what I say. But I didn't do anything without asking Jesus if it was okay first.

Th: And now?

M: Well, a lot seems different. Like in the beginning of therapy we talked more about Jesus. That felt okay. Then one day I said to myself, "Hey, all we talk about these days is my family. You know, me as a boy growing up and my dad's way of beating me when he got mad. That part of counseling didn't feel good. Almost quit. Then one time

you showed me how Jesus had a dad and a Father. Something like a
dad to help him feel better and a Father who could take care of everything. What was that verse? Had 'dad' and 'father' in it. Anyway, you
gave me a whole bunch of verses to look up about God's love—. But
just when I started to feel good again you got me so mad at my parents. [Laugh] I mean I got so mad. I felt all alone—except for you—
cause I was too mad to talk to them or God or even Jesus. Boy, was I
scared.

Th: How did it all end?

M: Well, remember when my mom and dad came with me? Now that
was a bad scene.
   But after that something started to change. Don't know why.
Guess 'cause the Holy Spirit worked. I started to feel better about
my dad. He don't call me an ass as much and Mom, well. She still
cries when I don't call her. That bothers me. Anyway, God thinks I'm
okay. I don't mix him up as much with my dad. You know I'm his son
just like Jesus. My dad, now, he still wants me to ask him about
everything. Sometimes now I don't. And sometimes I don't pay attention to Mom's tears. That's still hard.

Th: It sounds like those puppet strings have loosened up some, though.

M: Whew, yeah. And I don't get so mad either. Maybe I'm growing up.
You know that verse that talks about meat instead of milk? My wife
likes me better this way. Maybe my dad does. I don't know. God does.

Discussion

   As I analyzed my overall approach to these clients, I became aware
that my perspective of persons and God afforded me the freedom to incorporate or not to incorporate spiritual issues as an explicit part of the
therapeutic process. Understanding individuals as total integrated beings and not as discrete parts implies that what happens in therapy automatically affects every aspect of my clients' lives. Therefore, therapy
must of necessity deal with spiritual components because these are the
very essence of a person's humanness, permeating all of his identity. The
issue is not whether I deal with spiritual issues but rather how I can do
so in a way that facilitates rather than hinders the healing process in the
total person.
   A principle that was re-emphasized for me was to let the clients themselves give the cues whether to incorporate spiritual issues into the
therapeutic process in an explicit way. Letting the client lead helps me to
avoid my own preferential or even possibly compulsive "Christian" re-

sponses. It also frees me to be sensitive to the more subtle client messages that indicate a conscious or unconscious readiness, or lack of readiness, to deal with a spiritual facet of a conflict. For example, C communicated both verbally and nonverbally that he felt anger toward God for letting him down. He had tried and failed to overcome his problem through the spiritual disciplines. At this point in time he had no clue what the block was but had little expectation to find release through his Christianity. I had to respect his freedom and responsibility to know when and if he wanted to introduce overtly spiritual discussions into the process.

On the other hand, M's every mode of expression betrayed his fear that the therapeutic process would undermine his faith. He was asking for reassurance that I was indeed a Christian. I did what in his case came naturally in the situation, that is, express my love for the Lord and pray with him. Reduced resistance was a natural by-product. In fact, throughout therapy M needed to draw openly upon the strength he found in the expression of his faith, however many unhealthy components it contained, in order to have a source of comfort and courage as we slowly opened up the crippling wounds of his background. As the exploration of the role of others in his life unearthed too many traumas, we would plateau for a time, allowing him to savor the stability and nurturance he found in his Christianity. These more prolonged rest periods were occasions to examine the unhealthy elements of human relationships that had been transferred onto his concept of God. As his way of relating to God underwent changes, however small and undetectable at first, it became an even stronger base from which to deal more profoundly with past conflictual relationships. This seesawing process fostered health in all relationships. Had I discounted his Christian resources by ignoring them or poorly timing the interventions because I perceived the neurotic elements as growth inhibiting, I not only would have increased resistance but also eliminated the most powerful authentic source of strength and coping mechanisms he had. They allowed him to look at other relationships without disintegrating. A negative or even neutral therapist position might have undermined his relationship to God.

C, on the other hand, possessed a greater degree of inner strength. He had less need to cling to God, perhaps due to healthier individuation in earlier developmental stages. He could deal with background factors without seeing therapy as secular and, therefore, in his eyes, unspiritual. Nonetheless, I was aware of what his Christianity meant to him, the healthy and unhealthy way it translated itself in his total functioning, and how it was affecting or being affected at any point in time by the therapeutic process. His spiritual struggles were following an expected course. He was working outside of the sessions on his relationship to

God. Therefore, at no point in therapy did there seem to be a reason from the client's or therapist's perspective to intervene in a specific way.

Interestingly, C as well as M automatically seemed to expect that my values would affect the therapy process by virtue of the fact that both men had taken steps to investigate my basic Christian stance. Then, as I guided the sessions with these young men, I became aware how trust in my values, once reinforced through the therapeutic relationship, predisposed them to be sensitive to the way I perceived God. Once again I am impressed with the responsibility I have as a therapist to identify the beliefs and values I hold. This implies the use of bona fide hermeneutical principles to permit me to verify my understanding and application of Scripture. Only through such an ongoing process can I adequately control the messages I give about God.

I had to be particularly cognizant of what I communicated in the case of M, whose religious expressions were not always those with which I was comfortable. I found it necessary to work harder to identify the religious mores that were not injurious to his total health and those that were impeding growth. In either case I had to resolve any personal negative reactions so as not to contaminate the relationship.

There were times when I had to recognize how M slowed down his progress in therapy by using Scripture to avoid individuating from his parents. Sometimes a "reframe" that gave a more accurate view of reality to the meaning he gave to a verse helped to remove the block (e.g., in referring to Rom. 8:15: "You, like Jesus, have a dad who loves you but aren't you glad he is also called a father, a word that helps us know he's in control even when we make choices?"). In C's case a high-level, empathic, interpretive intervention often was enough to break through the impasse. For both, the resistance was used in the service of guiding the client to recognize those attributes of God which he needed to internalize for healing. Resistance thereby became a channel to develop a more biblical perception of God, which in turn fostered health.

What contributed to a healthier view of God became more apparent to me as we reviewed therapeutic experiences together. The reviews helped to concretize the changes that had taken place in all relationships, not the least of which involved God. It helped to clear up lingering confusion as to how unresolved issues had affected their perspective of God and how this view in turn played into their pain. They were able to realize changes in their spiritual practices. For example, in his prayer time C recognized that he was interceding more for others, thanking, praising, and worshiping God rather than primarily praying for himself. M has grasped more and more that God is not a magician but more often than not works through a process that permits us to learn.

Neither client has wholly "arrived." Growth is a process. M still struggles with giving up the comforting familiarity of a more clinging, less differentiated way of relating; C still misses the intense feelings that he had equated with spirituality. Therapy for them has not cured every neurotic element in any relationship, but is a major thrust forward in the life-long process of sanctification.

Summary

No two cases can address the many factors promoting a healthier client-God relationship. In these particular instances the following factors have been identified as contributors.

1. The therapist worked on what she believes is a biblical assumption: Persons created in God's image are whole beings who cannot be separated from the all-penetrating effect of the spiritual component.
2. The therapist followed the client's cues—that he wanted, was ready for, or needed, at any point in time, a more explicit or implicit intervention around a spiritual issue.
3. The therapist guided the client to draw upon the resources he already had developed in his relationship to the Lord. This relationship was a base to promote healthier all-around relationships.
4. The therapist, expecting her beliefs and values to affect the client, worked on being aware of how scripturally correct they were to the client.
5. The therapist tried to be alert to clear up her own reactivity that came from personal spiritual issues.
6. The therapist used resistance in the service of growth by "reframing" misused passages.
7. The therapist attempted to be aware at all times of the spiritual movement of both clients whether explicitly dealing with the God-relationship or not.
8. The therapist encouraged the clients to include in a natural way their relationship to God as part of the final debriefing process.

23

Fathers, Provoke Not Your Children

Gail M. Price

Sexually abused children accommodate themselves to abuse in several predictable ways. Summit (1983) refers to the pattern of accommodation as the "sexual abuse accommodation syndrome." The child responds with enforced secrecy, helplessness, feelings of entrapment, unconvincing attempts to reveal the secret, and, finally, retraction in the face of adult pressure. Summit points out that children cannot protect themselves because of a conflicting command to obedience. Demands that the child accept responsibility for disclosure and self-protection ignore the "basic subordination and helplessness of children within authoritarian relationships. . . . Children are required to be obedient and affectionate with any adult entrusted with their care. . . . A corollary to the expectation of self-protection is the general assumption that uncomplaining children are acting in a consenting relationship" (182). Summit further states that when the perpetrator is an adult that is supposed to be loving and nurturing to the child, the helplessness of the child is increased. In addition, the child is often told that he or someone close to him will be killed if he betrays the secret, leaving him chronically terrified.

Guilt is added to terror since the adult perpetrator gives the child responsibility for the betrayal and for the safety of self and others. Further, the child wishes the abuse to end and can imagine no solution other than the destruction of the perpetrator. The child may also attempt to convince herself that she is the cause of the abuse, as a way of gaining some control over an untenable situation. Guilt from these varying sources leads the child to fear punishment for her pervasive badness. To atone, she surrenders or destroys parts of the forming self. This lowers self-esteem to the point that further abuse is expected as the just due of the bad child. The cognitive and affective confusion inherent in experiencing a betrayal of the magnitude of sexual abuse adds to the helpless position. As Summit points out, without therapeutic affirmation of her innocence, the child becomes filled with self-condemnation.

Effective treatment of abused children requires the restoration of belief in benevolent, caring authority figures, and reduction of internalized guilt and rage. Paul's instruction regarding family relationships found in his letter to the Ephesians provides insight into the limits of obedience and into parental responsibility for children's emotional responses. He states "Children, obey your parents in the Lord, for this is right. 'Honor your father and mother'(this is the first commandment with a promise), that it may be well with you and that you may live long on the earth. Fathers, do not provoke your children to anger, but bring them up in the discipline and instruction of the Lord" (Eph. 6:1–4). These insights may be used as guidelines for interventions aimed at reducing the child's guilt and the unavoidable rage abuse creates in the victim, rage that often has no outlet and therefore distorts the personality which struggles to contain it.

The purpose of this case presentation is to summarize the clinical manifestations and therapeutic management of rage in a preschool child whose personality was undergoing major distortions as compensatory structures were forming to manage the experience of abuse. Many other issues were the focus of intervention during the two-year period reviewed. However, they are omitted in the interest of emphasizing the management of rage.

Marie was four when she was brought for consultation for disobedience, poor socialization, and somewhat bizarre infantile behavior. Marie's father had sexually exploited her from about eighteen months of age until the cause of her behavioral dysfunction became apparent in therapeutic doll play. Marie's mother had left her husband when Marie was two, and had remarried when Marie was three-and-a-half. Visits with Marie's father continued until the sexual exploitation was discovered. From that time, the father was required to see Marie under the supervision of her mother. He refused to accept this limitation, and did not see her, with one exception, for over a year. Almost from the moment

Marie learned that she would not see her father alone, that she would be protected from further sexual exploitation, she began to show improvement in all areas of functioning.

For several sessions following my discussion with Marie and her mother of her need for protection, she refused to enter the consultation room, and remained in the waiting room. I suspected she was testing me to see if I would use my power to make her obey, as I had made her father and mother "obey." I chose not to wait for her in my office, as I might do with a child who is clearly manipulating my behavior, wanting to know if I can take charge, should the child's impulses become out of control. Where sexual abuse is the issue, it is not the child's but the parent's impulses that are out of control. As Summit points out, the child has no choice but to "submit quietly and keep the secret" (1983, 183). In order, therefore, to circumvent the issue of power and control, and to avoid forcing her into submission, I went into the waiting room and sat on the floor by Marie.

I wanted her to know I had no interest in controlling her, that I knew the "secret" that she had struggled so valiantly to keep, and that I, an adult, was now going to take responsibility for protecting her so that she would no longer have to experience this overwhelming trauma. I gently approached several subjects before arriving at one we could talk about. Using information previously given to me by her mother, I asked her about the weekend which she had spent with friends while her parents took a brief trip. She began to talk in a somewhat animated fashion about the adventures she had. When she had calmed considerably, and the issue of her own self-determination with me was established, I asked why she had not visited her father this weekend, as she had done in the past when her mother and stepfather were away. She began to pound the floor, and then threatened to overturn a chair in a brief regression. I repeated the question, indicating that it had upset her, but I thought she should understand why so she would know it was not her fault. She thought for a moment, then got up and went into the consultation room where her mother was sitting, and asked her. Her mother responded by turning the question back to Marie. Marie thought again, and then said, "Because he makes me mad."

I asked about the things that made Marie angry. As with many children who have been sexually abused and who are still fearful of both parents' responses, Marie refused to talk about her experiences. I began to speak openly about the details I then knew, realizing I would add to them as I gained additional information during the course of therapy with Marie. I spoke about the tickling and fondling that her father had forced her to accept. I indicated that she was right to be upset by these things, that they were wrong for her father to do, and that they were not her fault. In an effort to help her understand the source of the shame she experienced, I said that when her father tickled her and touched her, it might have made her body feel good, and that she might have liked the special attention that she got, but that it also made her feel bad and that was why she wanted to hide her face. Because of these reasons, it was important that she not be alone with her father until he learned how to play games that she liked, and until he learned that it was wrong to fondle her private areas in that way. Throughout this discussion, Marie nodded her head in confirmation. Occasionally, she would look at me, and show in her eyes the real gratitude she felt at being understood.

I asked her why she thought her father did these things. She did not know. I told her that I thought her father did these things because he was sad. She nodded in agreement. I added that while it was okay for fathers and mothers to do the things together that her father did to her, it was not okay for fathers and daughters. She then further elaborated her experience by picking up a stuffed bear and its baby, putting them together, and making pelvic thrusts, staring into space and beginning to breathe heavily. She looked very sad. I asked if she was wondering if her father loved her. She nodded. I told her again that it was not her fault that her daddy wasn't loving with her, that other people loved her, and that her daddy had some problems that made it hard for him to love lots of people, not just her. Telling Marie that her father was not loving with her helped her to accept her rage at her father's self-centeredness and his tendency to use others as objects to gratify his own needs in a highly narcissistic manner.

These interventions were designed to help Marie reality-test her experience so that she could begin to integrate the splitting that developed in her images of self and father in order to manage the rage. Shengold describes such splits as vertical splits which are not manifestations of schizophrenia, but are the "establishment of isolated divisions of the mind that provides the mechanism for a pattern in which contradictory images of the self and of the parents are never permitted to coalesce" (quoted in Summit 1983, 184). One image is designed to preserve the parent as a loving object, and requires a bad self. The other part of the split contains the experience of the hurtful parent and the victimized, good self. In her regressive behavior, Marie became the bad person, manifest in whining, clinging dependency characterized by a marked inability to accept "No." This self-image returned her to infancy, prior to the onset of the abuse, but also mirrored her father's refusal to accept "No" if she tried to protect herself from his abuse. In this way, she manifested both the problem and a desperate attempt to preserve the self. When negative, regressive behavior is designed to preserve the self and to inform others of the trauma, albeit in disguise, no form of discipline will remove it, because it is life-preserving. Marie demonstrated this when she was discussing discipline meted out by her stepfather. He had spanked her when she became obstinately infantile, to no avail. "I used to cry," she once said when talking about his spankings, "but I don't anymore. It doesn't hurt like it did."

The good Marie was bright, polite, and entertaining. At times, efforts to sustain the good child were disrupted by anger leading her to make mistakes. When she made a mistake, she would berate herself, and then attack herself with blows to the head. No amount of soothing remarks or interpretations could break through this until one day she and I were drawing together. As she filled the paper with color, she engaged in a constant outpouring of self-disparaging remarks. I talked to her about why she was unkind to herself when she made a mistake. She said nothing, but hit her head only once. I then made an error, and called it to her attention with the words, "I made a mistake." With genuine kindness and in a soothing tone, she told me not to worry, that it was alright, that nothing bad happened, that everyone makes mistakes. I wondered aloud why she could be so kind to me, and so unkind to herself. She looked thoughtfully at me, but did not reply. After this encounter, her self-criticism in the sessions ceased.

Marie's hard-won improvement was temporarily lost around the time her father insisted on seeing her, and agreed to supervision (which was only partial because Marie's mother had an emergency that required her presence at her office). In the next session Marie told me she knew she could be safe if she was "Daddy's girl" and began to perform a very seductive dance. At the session's end she refused to relinquish her toys, and held them tightly to her, then looked at me with utter terror. I told her I was not going to be angry with her if she did not want to give up the toys or leave, and I was not going to be angry that she had done sexy things with Daddy, that she did those things because Daddy threatened to hurt her or kill her if she told, and that she was holding onto the toys the way she wanted to hold onto people who care about her when she is afraid and the way she wanted to hold onto her private place and not let Daddy or anyone else touch her there. She smiled, put down the toys, and ended the session.

Marie split the image of her father into two people, one of whom she admired and needed, and the other that terrified her and filled her mind with sexual imagery and fears of death. She described the confusion of these two images in a drawing. "I'm going to draw Ruler I and Ruler II," she announced. "One is a good guy and one is a bad guy. I can't tell which is which." The good father was one who helped her make things and repair things that were broken. He helped her build airplanes and cars and houses out of her Lego set, and taught her how to fix her tricycle when some part of it stopped working. The frightening father was condensed into a displaced image of a mean man who lived next door to her father and was going to steal children and kill them.

Marie tried to defend herself against the terror that she might be killed by attempting to make herself physically strong. She took gymnastics, and enjoyed demonstrating how fast she could run and how strong her arms were. She wanted to learn wrestling, and practiced karate, imitating things she saw on television, and things she could persuade older boys to teach her. She was uncertain as to whether she wanted to be a girl or a boy, but thought she preferred being a boy, and wore her hair short. She did not like dresses, and sometimes preferred to wear jeans with sweat pants over them. Dressing this way made her feel strong and safe.

Gradually the seductiveness and the regressions became reactive to events creating insecurity in her life with her mother and stepfather, such as their occasional weekends away or to the infrequent times when her father telephoned her or sent her a card. Generally, Marie responded with calmness and a burst of creativity when I could explain what I thought was happening and why she was so confused. She began to feel safer, and began to integrate the various parts of herself and of others. The integration first involved her peers. One afternoon she went skating with two friends. They had been "mean" to her in the past, wanting to make their own choices and escape Marie's tendency to control others the way she had been controlled. Even though they were mean, she told me, they helped her to skate better. She revealed the beginning integration of her image of her father in a drawing in which she again drew Ruler I and Ruler II. One was a "bad guy" having a mean face with huge red eyes. The other had pleasant features and a smile. She then asked for tape and taped the pleasant face over the hostile one. The integration became evident one day when she picked up a doll in session and wondered aloud if it was showing anger or fear in its face.

In her individual sessions in the second year of therapy she began to talk with me about her experiences with her father in an open and direct manner, and to express her understanding of the limits of her responsibility. One day she came in at peace with herself. She picked up a toy that had been broken for some time, commented that she did not break it, that someone else had, and that it was an old toy, and old things sometimes break. She would not like it if other toys were broken, however. I commented without thinking too much about it that it was okay to break some things, and not okay to break others. "Yeah," she said, "and there are some places it's okay to touch and some it's not. It's not okay to touch my private place." She then told me in some detail what her father did.

"I'd open my legs like this and he'd tickle me here and here and rub me like this." I asked how it felt. She replied, "It felt good, but I didn't like it!" She paused. "But it doesn't happen anymore."

Reference

Summit, R. C. The child sexual abuse accommodation syndrome. *Child Abuse and Neglect* 7(1983):177–93.

24

Cognitive Therapy with Spiritual Dimensions
Christine V. Bruun

Psychotherapy usually occurs at a time of crisis, during an extremely turbulent period in a person's life. Often this is a time when habitual coping strategies and customary solutions are ineffective at best and perhaps even destructive. The decision to make changes in therapy, sometimes painful, frequently follows the awareness that it would be worse not to change. At this critical juncture the person is likely to be open to many sources of help and new internal resources that might otherwise not be considered. It is precisely in this stage of need and malleability that traditional theological beliefs can be re-examined and access to personalized spiritual positions can be gained. In response to intense fear and anxiety, God may become less of an intellectualized concept and more of a personal bastion of acceptance and strength.

Three themes, each with a respective time component (past, present, and future) seem to recur in individual contexts when spiritual help has been recognized as a cornerstone of treatment. First, the past is replete with negative views of self due to painful experiences, negative labeling from others, and committed acts which have left residual guilt. Often there is buried, unresolved grief. Present crises often cause these to re-emerge in psychotherapy with fresh intensity and distressing sharpness. It is in the midst of painful, past injuries that the healing love of Christ can provide an absolving sense of forgiveness, comfort, and deep acceptance of the core person. Second, the acute emotions of the present, such as fear, guilt, sadness, and anger, frequently seem to be too overwhelming for the person to tolerate, much less to process therapeutically. It is often in this immediate "living out" process that the spiritually sensitive person is receptive to the empowering resources of the Holy Spirit. This help may come in varied ways: a new approach and frame of reference by which to perceive the problem; relaxation and renewal when anxiety and exhaustion dominate the picture; or the ability and strength to confront avoided grieving. Third, as the capstone of this triad of time-related dimensions, the future is reframed as the significance of the upheaval in the person's life comes to be seen. The course in which specific events have evolved, shaped the person, been reworked, and transmuted can provide a sense of redemptive suffering and a view of how the future can take on a new direction. The following case, using a cognitive therapy approach, may serve as an illustration of these therapeutic aspects.

Case Presentation

Mrs. C. was a thirty-two-year-old married woman with two children, a son seven and a daughter five years old. She and her husband had been married for nine years. Although there had been problems of trust and intimacy between them for most of their marriage, these had become more intense in the past two years. She discovered that he had been having an affair for two years, and she was unable to believe his explanations when he came home late. Mrs. C. felt increasingly anxious. She felt guilt-ridden about not being a better wife and mother and barraged herself with self-blaming and belittling messages; she also blamed her family and others for disappointing her. She became fearful of talking to people outside her family as she felt that others would perceive her anxiety and inadequacy and in turn would regard her in a negative way. Also, she believed that she had lost control over much of her behavior as she had become self-destructive in her overeating, indiscriminate spending, and increased smoking.

Her family background showed a history of alienation and negative self-perceptions. She was the middle of three daughters, each only a few years apart in age. She felt that her parents loved and approved of her sisters more than her, perceiving that her mother and father treated them with warmth and recognition and her with criticism. She described herself in childhood as shy and withdrawn, her mother as critical and aloof, and her father as blatantly rejecting toward her. She recalled one traumatic memory when she was six years old. She had climbed onto her father's lap, and he had forcefully pushed her off and told her to leave him alone. The bitterness and hurt from these early family experiences caused her to look for supportive, nurturing relationships outside of her home. She put her trust in several men whom she saw as protective yet who ultimately exploited her sexually. In one of these relationships she became pregnant and decided to have an abortion, an act for which she continued to feel a gnawing guilt.

At the time therapy began, Mrs. C. was undergoing a personal religious experience. Therefore she was quite receptive to the idea of incorporating her relationship with God in the working through of psychological issues. It became readily clear that coming to terms with the past was an essential prerequisite to successful treatment as her early experiences had spawned negative views of herself, an assumption that she was unacceptable to others, bitterness, hurt, and a tendency to be distrustful.

Early in treatment, a powerful experience initiated a healing process in the way she perceived herself. At the beginning of the fifth session she reported that she felt trapped and out of control. A period of relaxation was followed by her visualizing the images surrounding her trapped feelings. She described in detail being trapped in a clear, flexible, plastic cube in which there was no door, but she could see through the transparent material. She felt her back was gripped in an iron, viselike apparatus which conformed to her rib cage and allowed her only shallow breaths. She then saw Christ opening a door in the cube and beckoning to her. As she stepped out she heard the iron brace clang to the floor and Christ saying to her, "You are okay; you are loved." Following this visual encounter, she started to weep and said she felt like a little bird that had been released from its cage.

This experience laid the groundwork for the realization that she could explore and integrate the painful events of the past with the comfort and support of Christ within her; she was not alone. She was able to do this with the feelings of guilt about her abortion. To this point she had stifled her feelings about this loss and her sadness and had only acknowledged her feelings of self-blame and failure. She began to treat herself with compassion, understanding her needs and fears surrounding the decision, and allowing herself to mourn for the part of herself that had died. She began to see that, rather than being condemned by God, her loss and sorrow was acknowledged by him with gentle, loving support. The experience of this event provided a powerful prototype for managing her current problems.

A major source of her feelings of inadequacy with her husband, children, and others was the steady stream of negative self-messages, a pattern which had recurred for most of her life. It was necessary to identify these toxic cognitions and challenge them with more accurate and self-nurturing ones. She was able, with assurance, to replace self-statements such as "You are an unlovable person" with ones like "There is much sensitivity and warmth in you which draws others to you" because she could now use Christ's loving position toward her as a model for a way to treat herself. This approach not only helped her raise her self-esteem but also changed her sense of self-blame and failure. As she became less defensive and ashamed, she was able to respond actively to her husband and children in a more relaxed, self-assured way, which channeled the interactions among them in a more positive direction. This newly gained ability to talk to herself as a supportive, affirming companion helped her confront her fear of going out and being with people. She was able to desensitize herself with exposure to public situations by reassuring and coaching herself that she was competent to handle the circumstances and that others were probably seeing her in the positive ways that she was trying to see herself. The feelings of self-worth and competency that were generated helped establish an effective line of defense against the impulsive behaviors of excessive eating, smoking, and spending. These became less consistent with the ways she was seeing herself and, therefore, were more difficult to sustain.

Finally, Mrs. C. came to regard the future with more hope and meaning. She believed the events in her life had given her a sensitivity to the pain of others and that without the intensity of her own suffering she would not have been motivated to struggle with her distress to the point of an encounter with the loving Christ. This redemptive transforming of her emotional turmoil gave her a sense of purpose in the entire process. She turned to preparations for starting a self-help group for women who faced problems similar to her own. It is not that she no longer confronted the same fears and self-doubts but that she now had a new template with which to challenge negativity and to perceive and encourage herself.

In summary, Mrs. C.'s case illustrates some of the innumerable ways and time-frames in which God intervenes to buttress the person, in conjunction with the generally recognized principles operating in psychotherapy. Therapeutically, it is vital for the person to construct a positive self-image, to relate directly and constructively with others, to break into the pattern of self-defeating thoughts, to confront avoided situations which have fostered dysfunctional behaviors, and to mourn and resolve grief experiences. These issues are customarily managed with effective and potent psychological techniques. Yet the action of the Holy Spirit within the person seems to be a necessary and powerful force in the genuinely anchored healing of each of the above dimensions.

25

Postconversion Symptom Regression
James R. Beck

Conversions of all types, including Christian conversion, provide fascinating areas of investigation for psychologists of religion. Conversions are intriguing examples of sudden or rapid change, and thus they provide a unique window through which scientists can view the human psyche and personality. The focus of interest is as much in the results of a conversion as it is in the process of the conversion itself. Results vary from mild to radical, from superficial to pervasive, and from subtle to noticeable.

The results of religious conversion are most often positive in nature. Subjects may report a new sense of purpose, a burst of creativity, a heightened feeling of confidence, or some other growth-enhancing result (Batson and Ventis 1982). Such reports of significant improvement are not only public or written testimonies but are also heard in the offices of therapists. A husband whose temper sometimes raged out of control toward his wife may experience a dramatically improved ability to control anger after his conversion. Addicts may report a postconversion absence of cravings. Shy persons may describe an encouraging growth of social confidence. The list is endless.

Christian therapists are not surprised by reports of psychological improvement after conversion. Theologically we are prepared for such results because of the very definition of conversion—a setting right of issues previously askew, a settling of accounts with God, an answer to the deep cravings of the lost soul for meaning and purpose. Indeed, much of our evangelistic outreach includes promises of the integrating and healing results salvation will bring.

It is harder to understand why conversion may not be followed by any behavior change at all or why, in rare cases, psychological symptoms may worsen subsequent to conversion. The former issue is treated elsewhere (Johnson and Maloney 1982); the latter is the subject of this chapter.

Three cases from the author's experience reflect postconversion symptom regression. All three persons experienced an adult religious conversion and reported a history of pre-existing psychological symptoms of sufficient severity so as to have necessitated professional care. Their conversions were profound, enriching events. These converts all felt grateful for their religious experiences and expressed no regret that they had embarked upon the Christian journey. However, in addition to the positive benefits of salvation, they experienced a worsening of some of their symptoms or a regression toward a more entrenched cluster of disabling psychological problems. The following case illustrates some of these elements.

Case Presentation

Janet grew up as the only child in a lower-middle-class home. Her father was a civilian clerk on a nearby military base while her mother supplemented normal household activities with several interests—daytime card parties and an occasional night out to play Bingo. Additionally, both parents ran a part-time jewelry business which necessitated several trips per year to fairs and trade shows. Janet's parents seemed to have well-developed social structures to meet their own needs, but Janet's social life usually centered around the adult activities of her parents. Peer relationships were few.

Janet reported her father as a somewhat private man who engaged in only infrequent interactions with her. Her mother established a warmer relationship with her daughter and was Janet's chief confidante until adolescence. It was then that Janet began to experience problems. Her childhood had been uneventful, free from trauma, serious illnesses, or accidents. But Janet's teen-age years took on a soberness and sadness. For weeks at a time she would seem to be lost in low moods. High school friends soon introduced her to "reds" and her increasing use of stimulants would relieve the low moods.

In spite of Janet's intermittent down times, she managed to sustain an extensive network of friends, both male and female. Toward the end of her high school years, Janet became sexually active with several boys in successive relationships. Her mother, unaware of Janet's sexual activity, nonetheless became concerned because of her daughter's low moods and because of suspected drug use. Janet's mother arranged for her to see a local psychologist with whom Janet met for ten sessions as a senior in high school. Janet's initial resistance to the idea of therapy was not strong enough to sabotage her sessions. In fact, Janet seemed to appreciate her therapist's concern and the talks they had regarding her low self-esteem.

While Janet was a college freshman at an out-of-state school, some Christian dormmates shared their faith with her. Janet eventually made a personal commitment to Jesus Christ. She experienced some initial euphoria which led to a six-month period of tranquil feelings and peaceful moods. Janet worshiped at a local church and gradually shifted her friendships into a new circle of students. She abandoned her previous sexual style of relating to men and, perhaps as a result of this change, she began to date less and less often. Periods of low mood reappeared. At times Janet's depressive periods would be harmless in their effect, but at other times her moods would interfere with final exams or other school responsibilities.

After graduation Janet obtained employment as a graphic artist in her hometown. Her periods of low mood continued but on an intensified basis. Her struggles were soon evident to her employers. When she entered therapy for the second time, she was on a forced leave of absence because of a prolonged bout with depression. Eventually she resigned her position, and after a year of absence from the active work force began a rehabilitation program for a clerical job.

Discussion

This case illustrates some of the essential features of postconversion symptom regression: a prior history of treated psychological distress, an adult conversion, and a subsequent history of worsening symptoms or a shifting of symptoms to a more regressed cluster. This regression occurs in cases where the ameliorative benefits of conversion have affected other areas of the person's life but not those psychological areas surrounding the symptoms. The integrating benefits of Christian conversion do not seem to touch the very areas of the client's life where one would expect to see, and often does see, great benefit.

Christian therapists can deal with postconversion symptom regression in any number of ways. First, one could say that the emotional worsening is merely coincidental with respect to the conversion experience. The two events have no necessary relationship to each other. This solution to the problem lacks theological credibility since we cannot posit coincidence as an explanation of substance in situations where God is active.

Second, one could maintain that these conversions were not genuine. The converts may have made gestures toward real faith, but the actual process did not occur. The main evidence for this explanation would be the fact that psychological improvement had not followed the supposed conversion. This argument in turn is based on the assumption that conversions always result in a greater degree of psychological health. Such an inference is difficult to substantiate biblically.

In the third place, one can argue that these symptom regressions are so rare as to be statistically insignificant. As such they do not give us any particular insight into the interactions between theological events and psychological health in the human personality.

Finally, one can say (as does the author) that these infrequent occurrences give us a rare glimpse into the interaction of faith and affect and that we can learn about how psychology and theology interface by examining these cases. These clients may regress psychologically because of external changes which conversion triggers. In other words, Christians may possess poor abilities to relate to an emotionally disturbed newcomer with the result that the new convert suffers from declining social support networks which in turn leads to poorer mental health. Or it may be that Christian living requires more of a person rather than less, and the resulting drain depletes energy previously used to prop up emotional functioning. Or conversion is just the beginning of a lifelong struggle, and one cannot necessarily expect to see results in all areas of the new convert's life until several years have passed. Hence our observations of regression may simply be premature. Or conversions may initiate minor, temporary regressions which are not usually observable in normals but which become more noticeable and permanent in certain types of symptom clusters. Whatever explanation may prove most accurate, further investigation into this phenomenon seems warranted.

References

Batson, C. D., and W. L. Ventis. 1982. *The religious experience: A social-psychological perspective*. New York: Oxford University.

Johnson, C. G., and H. N. Malony. 1982. *Christian conversion: Biblical and psychological perspectives*. Grand Rapids: Zondervan.

26

A Case of
Congregational Healing
John H. Court

It is common for congregations to offer prayer support for the be-reaved and for those who are physically ill (though some disorders are more stigmatized than others), but a discreet silence commonly blankets those suffering emotional difficulties. For many the shame of consulting a psychologist or psychiatrist is still so great that this is either avoided altogether or at least not publicly admitted. Many Christians demon-strate a peculiar double standard: emotional problems are supposed to be resolved through prayer and faith alone, though such expectations do not apply to measles or broken legs.

The case reported here is unusual because part of the healing process involved a public declaration by a pastor's wife to the congregation. It illustrates the personal healing of memories in a case of dissociation, us-ing hypnosis for exploration and resolution, together with strong reli-ance on the spiritual resources of prayer and Scripture (cf. Shepperson and Henslin 1984). Perhaps most importantly, a willingness to share a personal experience of healing with the local church family led to others daring to come forward and seek similar help. Several families have al-ready been profoundly affected.

Background

Y, a pastor's wife, age 36, presented following a distressing period in
the local church during which she had been receiving letters making
ugly sexual allegations regarding her unsuitability for her role, in spite
of her obviously godly and dedicated life. The congregation shared her
distress, praying for her, while the inevitable finger of suspicion moved
around, with everyone wondering who would write such indictments.

Exploration using age regression in hypnosis revealed a number of serious, traumatic experiences in Y's childhood, which were gradually resolved through abreaction, cognitive restructuring, and prayerful
involvement of Jesus bringing healing to those events. The major breakthrough came when Y became conscious that *she* was the letter writer.
This awareness was followed by deep depression and distress for a period during which anti-depressants proved helpful. Her husband had to
come to terms with this revelation, and did so magnificently. There was
an extended period of disturbed dreaming which also provided a focus
for therapy.

Gradually Y integrated the shadow side of her personality, abandon-
ing her earlier denial and dissociation in favor of acceptance of herself
and forgiveness of those responsible for her childhood traumas. Two
years after her first therapy session, the elders of the church agreed to
call a meeting of those in the church who had been aware of the earlier
letters, so that a full explanation could be offered by Y.

Y Speaks for Herself

It is exactly two years ago now that anonymous letters were being sent
to me, letters which expressed considerable criticism of me as a person,
and were none too kind in the way they were worded. Receiving letters of
that type, with such blatantly expressed accusations, was very hard to
take, not only for me, but also for many of you, who, because of your
close proximity, were also aware of the contents of some of the letters. I
think especially of those who were in the choir at the time.

On the last Sunday in August 1982, it was announced from the pulpit
that the flow of letters had ceased, and that the problem was being dealt
with. At that time, no explanation was given. I have no doubt that there
were many people who could not help wondering who that letter writer
could have been. . . . I have asked for this meeting to be called so that I
could tell you that I was that writer!

I need to say that there never was a time when anything took place
from the perspective of a cold and calculating, or premeditated decep-

tion. I say that, not to minimize the impact of the revelation, but rather to explain to you that the problem was a deep, psychological one—one of which I was not the least bit aware at the time, and one which, when it finally hit, left me fearing for my very sanity.

I've asked for this meeting to be called, because I feel the need to express my heartfelt regrets to you all, for the suffering—for some of you, quite considerable suffering—that this situation caused. The sense of shock and dismay, even distress, that was expressed ("How could it be that someone in our congregation could do such a thing?") was indicative of the heartache felt by many. For those things, I am truly sorry, and I want humbly to ask for your forgiveness. I have not, until now, been able to be open and honest to the degree that I have wished. I really value the opportunity to share with you something of the incredibly gentle and loving way that the Lord has brought me through this dilemma to a point where I know a wholeness that never was part of my experience prior to these traumas. I took my wedding ring off that first mortifying day, because I felt unworthy to wear it, only to be confronted with the Romans 8:28 reference engraved on the inside. Now I had to exercise my faith, and believe that God would be faithful to his Word. But how?

I read of Paul's imprisonment, and how he believed that he was in that place in order to bring about "the defense of the gospel" (Phil. 1:16). I was in prison, too—a psychological and emotional prison. Could I dare to believe that that, too, could be for the greater cause of the gospel?

At that time, everything about my life, my conversion, my ongoing commitment to the Lord, and my involvement in Christian things was bowled over in one devastating blow, but the Lord gave me encouragement: "Your words have upheld him who was stumbling, and you have made firm the feeble knees. But now it has come to you, and you are impatient; it touches you, and you are dismayed. Is not your fear of God your confidence, and the integrity of your ways your hope?" (Job 4:4–6) In working through problems, I had to face, in some cases for the very first time, some very traumatic problems from my childhood and teenage years. Traveling back through some of those horrific memories was very painful and very hard.

Depression closed in, to a depth that I would never have thought possible. And so began a period where I had to battle with thoughts of suicide. I asked the Lord, "Can't you see that enough is enough?" His answer came, loudly, clearly, quickly. "You who seek God, let your heart revive." Slowly, lovingly, the Lord helped me to pick up the pieces, as he showed me more of his faithfulness to me and his healing.

It is certain that my life will never be the same again, but I know that I can honestly thank God for what he has taken me through in the last two years. I have a far deeper understanding of the unfailing reality of God's presence, come what may. I can categorically testify that God can and does heal painful memories. No, he doesn't take them away, but because he knows and understands, and because of all that he achieved on the cross, he can remove the sting. I also believe that through this experience, he has given me a new and deeper understanding and sympathy when others are hurting. Now I know that this experience has been allowed for the greater cause of the gospel.

Therapist's Commentary

Let me first say a little about the unusual aspects of the case and then proceed to the elements to which we can all relate as familiar. First, it is unusual for anyone to do something and to have no conscious awareness of having done it. The separation between the conscious and unconscious we call *dissociation*. It occurs when one part of the personality so strongly disapproves of or rejects what is occurring in another part, that there is a total denial of the unacceptable part. Some people, like Y, wrestle with internal conflicts which present so great a contrast that sanity is preserved by dissociating what we might call the "bad" part from the "good" part. Such complete dissociation can be easily produced experimentally through hypnosis with certain people. From such experiments we learn how there are different levels of consciousness in all of us, and we can move between them according to circumstances.

It is very unusual for someone who has written what might be called "poison-pen" letters to be publicly identified, even by accident, let alone by personal choice. It is easier to keep quiet and hope the memories will fade. You have heard why Y chose to take the harder way. From very early in therapy we discussed the need for taking this step eventually—for her own integrity and for the sake of those who might otherwise be inadvertently hurt by what had happened. Healing, to be complete, does require sorting out the tangle, not only within one's self and before God, but also with those who have in any way been involved. This is a clear biblical principle in relation to sin, and I believe the same to be true in psychological dysfunction.

I wish to emphasize that among Christians the load of guilt, shame, failure, or worthlessness arises very often not from our own misdeeds but through suffering at the hands of others, especially when we are young and relatively helpless or vulnerable. How we deal with those traumas makes all the difference—whether we are destroyed by them or grow through them.

An important verse of encouragement for Y has been that wonderful declaration by Joseph to his brothers. They did so much to harm him, but in Genesis 50:20 he says, "As for you, you meant evil against me: but God meant it for good, to bring it about that many people should be kept alive, as they are today." What a triumphant response!

Paul, in Romans 7, describes the universal dilemma:

> We know that the law is spiritual: but I am carnal, sold under sin. I do not understand my own actions. For I do not do what I want, but I do the very thing I hate. . . . For I do not do the good I want, but the evil I do not want is what I do. . . . So I find it to be a law that when I want to do right, evil lies close at hand. For I delight in the law of God, in my inmost self, but I see in my members another law at war with the law of my mind and making me captive to the law of sin which dwells in my members (vv. 14–15, 19, 21–23).

Paul is not writing about unbelievers. He writes of his own Christian experience. He writes of your experience and mine. He describes an ongoing conflict which every Christian faces. Most of us settle for some sort of compromise. Y, however, was faced with a real dilemma. On the one hand, there were traumatic moments in her past that she wanted no part of. On the other, she had a high view of God's calling. The "shadow" side of her personality was anathema, yet kept coming back to haunt her. But how could she *ever* be good enough? One day, surely, she would stand accused. And sure enough, the shadow, the traumas of the past, sought to demolish her with accusations of worthlessness and allegations so unthinkable they could not be ignored. She, with the rest of you, was quite properly horrified.

I share with you what I believe to be the turning point in the resolution of her dilemma. It was for me an exquisite moment in working with someone and seeing how the Lord can heal the scars of the past. It encapsulates the integration of professional techniques and God's loving intervention to facilitate true healing. Under hypnosis she became able to recall some early events that had distressed her and then said, "Last Friday I became incredibly angry." I asked if she could begin to identify the source of the anger, but Y was four steps ahead of me. She said: (1) "that I should suffer such indignity; (2) that there was nobody to help; (3) that I couldn't give thanks to God; (4) I was angry at God for allowing it."

I responded, "I suppose Jesus could have said that about his sufferings."

The result was a reframing of her experiences to understand them not simply as her own personal pain but something that Jesus could enter into with her and indeed, by his own suffering, came to heal.

My final general reflection is this: In most congregations we support one another prayerfully and lovingly if someone suffers a serious physical illness, or breaks a leg, or becomes unemployed, or is bereaved. We rally round, and the support is greatly appreciated. But if one of you has an emotional difficulty, can you share that? Broken legs, yes; broken hearts, no. Pregnancy, yes; impotence, no. Death, yes; suicidal depression—we'll hush it up as much as possible.

In this congregation you are privileged to have a pastor and his wife able to be honest with you. They dare to share their own struggle with you, for your good, realizing they make themselves vulnerable before you. My prayer is that their trust in you is warranted. May their experience of healing enable many of you to know that the Lord is risen—with healing in his wings (Mal. 4:2).

Follow-up

This public confession was a deeply moving occasion for all concerned, bringing a new sense of fellowship and love to the congregation. Y has been able to develop a personal ministry along with her husband, enabling others to seek help for problems they had never shared before.

Conclusion

Psychological and spiritual healing can proceed closely together not only for the individual but also corporately where there is the courage to be open with others in genuine love which seeks mutual growth.

One might question whether hypnosis was a necessary part of this client's treatment. It certainly illustrates that hypnosis can be an appropriate adjunct to Christian therapies, in contrast to the dire warning against its use offered by Bobgan and Bobgan (1984). Since formal treatment was contained within only eight consultations, a case can be made for saying that hypnotic techniques can greatly expedite what might otherwise have been a much more lengthy process.

We often struggle to understand suffering and at times find meaning in the ways whereby evil can be turned around for good. For Y, a peculiarly poignant encouragement came to her during therapy through the words of Genesis 50:20. She chose to make her own pilgrimage public, so that others might also be healed. Her integrity is being rewarded.

References

Bobgan, M., and D. Bobgan. 1984. *Hypnosis and the Christian*. Minneapolis: Bethany.

Shepperson, V. L., and E. R. Henslin. 1984. Hypnosis and metaphor in Christian context: History, abuse and use. *Journal of Psychology and Theology* 12(2):100–103.

27

A Christian Dimension to Holistic Care in Family Practice

A. Fraser-Darling

Case Presentation

It was Easter Saturday. As a rural family physician, I was seeing emergency patients in my surgery that morning. A patient whom I shall call Elsa called me and told me that she was feeling faint and giddy, and complained of various other somatic symptoms. I remembered that two months before, she had delivered a stillborn baby. Listening to her over the phone, I sensed this girl's distress and invited her to come and see me.

When she came, I became aware that the real problem was that she was still mourning deeply for her child. So we talked at length about the baby and she was able to have a good cry. She had only one person to whom she could talk, as she lived in an isolated village. The other woman had also lost a baby. People had expected Elsa to have "gotten over it" by now. Worse still, she could not tell her husband how she felt because he had enough worries with his business. I made plans to see her again but, more important, she realized that she needed to reveal her feelings to her husband for I sensed that he might be feeling his own sense of loss and they needed to share their sorrow together. Then, almost by accident, an even deeper sense of loss became manifest when she said, almost shyly, "I don't know, I always used to go to church but I feel I have lost my faith." And so we talked about faith and doubt and how even in the face of this apparently senseless loss, God was still there, waiting for her. I do not recall that we formally prayed or that I quoted passages of Scripture but the Holy Spirit seemed very close as we shared these things together. I suggested that she might like to come to the communion service in our village the next day. As a lay helper, I would be administering the chalice. Elsa accepted and the next day as she came up to the altar and knelt down, we smiled briefly at each other and I had the joy and privilege of offering her the blood of Christ.

A few days later she came to see me, a quite different person, smiling and telling me that she had told her husband who had responded with great love and concern for he had not realized before the depth of her loss.

Discussion

This case study illustrates a number of issues in the relationship of psychology and the Christian faith that are of general importance and from which we can learn valuable lessons. The first lesson that Elsa teaches us is to remind us of the first basic principle of effective counselling: empathy. This empathy exists at three levels: the mental, the emotional, and the spiritual. As we worked together on the loss of her baby, Elsa must have sensed my own Christian faith without it ever being mentioned verbally. So she was able to talk about this other loss to which I was able to respond. But in responding, I was careful to do so at her level; I made no attempt to quote Scripture or pray with her. Instead, to paraphrase Ezekiel, I, for a little while "sat where she sat" and my own prayer was that I should be a vessel for his grace.

The second lesson was to stay with Elsa, to accept her doubts and fears and sustain her as she struggled to grow to a new and deeper faith. Bonhoeffer, in *The Cost of Discipleship* (1959), draws a distinction between cheap grace and costly grace. It is far easier to dispense cheap grace. There is a great temptation for Christians to use Scripture and prayer inappropriately (i.e., nonempathetically) as a sort of panacea. It allows us to feel we are doing something for our clients. Costly grace requires us to sit beside and be with our clients to share their pain and sorrow as well as their joy and gladness. Bonhoeffer also points out that Christians are often so busy talking that they forget to listen not only to their brothers but to God!

These issues of faith and belief, doubt and uncertainty arise quite frequently in my work with patients both as family physician and counselor. Not only must you listen to the client but you also need to listen for the *ruach*, the Spirit of God. So the quote from Scripture, the formal prayer, the laying on of hands, or the kiss of peace must be used only when clients feel they can accept it. Here, it was more important for me to listen, to accept and stay with Elsa where she was. Her subsequent decision to come to the Lord's table was her own and perhaps enabled her to find that her gloom was "after all, Shade of His Hand, out-stretched caressingly" (Thompson 1969, 24).

My personal Christian faith is a vital resource in my life, but because it is so important, in counseling its dosage and administration need to be accurately assessed. Balint (1963) writes of the importance of the drug, "doctor," and how the dosage of this powerful drug needs to be regulated since one can easily overdose patients with too much doctoring. I feel this analogy applies also in the field of counseling.

A third lesson Elsa teaches us is the temptation for Christians to become judgmental. Williams (1982) writes of his experiences when he had an acute mental breakdown, how his fellow clergy in particular became very angry with him because, despite all their ministrations (including anointing with oil) he did not get better as fast as they thought he should. I know instances where a Christian healing group prayed for and laid hands on a person and because that person was not healed, recriminations would occur with an emphasis on that person's sins. So the poor suffering soul has even more guilt piled on him because he has not been able to respond as expected. Much harm has resulted and I have, on several occasions had to work to repair the damage from this inappropriate emphasis on sin when the paramount need was for compassion and sustaining love. St. John of the Cross reminds us that "when evening comes, we will be judged on Love."

The fourth lesson that Elsa teaches us is to beware of the dangers of professionalism that we can use to distance ourselves from our clients to be the experts who know all the answers or to place ourselves in the role of parents who tell their children what to do. I hope I worked with Elsa in a professionally competent way using the skills I have learned and even though it took place in my consulting room, I tried to be a fellow human being who could stay with her compassionately and with sustaining love as she groped her way toward the light. This requires humility and a deep respect for the uniqueness of the client.

Conclusion

It is always pleasing to tell a success story but for me, the main purpose is to illustrate how essential it is for doctors and counselors to think and practice holistic care. As Elsa said to me the other day when I asked her permission to use our experience, "I was made whole again." And the wholeness would not have been complete if we had not recognized and worked on her doubts and loss of faith. In humanistic terms she could have been helped to work through her grief and mourning for her baby and that would have been considered to be proper handling of her case. But failure to grapple with her loss of faith would have resulted in an incomplete gestalt and hindered her growth as a person.

Jung stressed the importance of spiritual values and my experience with Elsa illustrates this clearly. Working with spiritual things in this moment of crisis and asking for the power of the Holy Spirit enabled healing to take place and resulted in the client's spiritual growth.

References

Balint, M. 1963. *The doctor, his patient and the illness*. 2d ed. London: Pitman.

Bonhoeffer, D. 1959. *The cost of discipleship*. London: SCM.

Thompson, F. 1969. *Poetical Works*. Oxford: Oxford University.

Williams, H. 1982. *Some day I'll find you*. London: Mitchell Beazley.

28

Starting Over: What to Do When a Bad Marriage Gets Worse
Darrell Smith

The Couple

Brent was thirty years old and Juanita twenty-four when they came to me for therapy in response to the referral of a common friend of Brent and the therapist. He was a Ph.D. aeronautical engineer who tended to be controlling, analytical, and a bit chauvinistic. Juanita was a highly competent computer expert and eager to pursue her own career as a professional woman. Although both of them came from homes that taught Judeo-Christian values, neither chose a Christian life-style as adults. They considered themselves to be liberated from restrictive traditional values, yet their supposed liberation had not brought them the personal and marital fulfillment that they both desired so much. While the outward appearance suggested academic and professional success, inwardly they were quite miserable. In their words, without Jesus in their lives they knew neither how they got themselves into the situation facing them nor how to remedy it.

The Relationship

Brent and Juanita met in an engineering consulting firm of which Brent was a co-owner and director of research. Juanita was a computer data analyst and worked under Brent's supervision. Juanita's intelligence, independent flair, feminine beauty, and kindness were the characteristics that initially attracted Brent to her. She liked Brent's professionalism, intellectual sharpness, and the interests that she was led to believe he shared in common with her. Their dating relationship developed casually out of daily interactions at work and related activities such as taking lunch together. Both of them had been sexually active in previous relationships, and sexual intimacy became routine early in their relationship.

After one year of living together, they were married. Brent attempted to convince himself and Juanita that he loved and cared for her deeply, but he often related to her as his inferior/subordinate both on the job and in their relationship. Brent, arrogant and selfish, tended to neglect, verbally abuse, and dominate her. Brent's abusiveness intensified and eventually found expression in physical violence. Juanita was intimidated by Brent's violent behavior. Although she would occasionally strike him physically, Juanita usually deferred to Brent in a self-defeating, nonassertive manner. Living with Brent became progressively more difficult and painful.

During the second year of their marriage, Juanita decided that she could no longer live with Brent's violence, arrogant put-downs, and neglect and still have respect for herself. She moved out of their home into her own apartment, secured a new job, and pursued an independent life while contemplating divorce.

Brent, with his world falling apart, began to look for help in a source that he had been fighting so long. He became a "born-again" Christian after Juanita separated from him and prayed earnestly that they could be reconciled. God was working in Brent's life and revealing to him many of his selfish and hurtful actions. Juanita was suspicious of Brent's new-found religion, believing that it was probably nothing more than a crafty gimmick to hook her back into an unhealthy relationship. Also, she openly pondered whether Brent's efforts to effect reconciliation were more an exercise to reduce his sense of rejection than a genuine caring for her. Brent was threatened, nearly to the point of panic, by the growing possibility of losing Juanita.

When Brent and Juanita came to me for help, it was quite clear that two unhappy people were traveling divergent paths. Their marriage had begun on a fragile, hedonistic base and was headed for collapse unless a new foundation could be laid.

The Therapy Process

The marital relationship had deteriorated to such a negative state that Juanita refused to participate in any therapy sessions that included Brent. Therefore, I began seeing them weekly on an individual basis.

Juanita felt "beaten down" both emotionally and physically and considered divorce a much better option for her than reconciliation with Brent, but she was ambivalent about the whole situation. Much of the focus of my sessions with Juanita was on the venting of a gamut of emotions. On the one hand, she was filled with hurt, anger, and resentment from Brent's abusive and condescending behaviors. Yet, she experienced guilt and sadness because of the separation and was hardly prepared for the trauma of divorce. At the same time, however, she had a feeling of elation and emancipation that followed the distancing of herself from Brent. She also was excited about the possibility of an affair and eventually a relationship with a man who would treat her with kindness and respect.

I helped Juanita identify all the options available to her and consider the likely consequences of each. Attention was given to the recognition, declaration, and management of her personal and sexual boundaries with both Brent and other men at this crisis time in her life. This required some assertiveness training.

As therapy progressed, Juanita appeared to move more in the direction of divorce. Thinking that her parents, who adhered strongly to traditional values regarding marriage, would not support her getting a divorce, Juanita decided to keep Brent waiting and guessing until she could win her parents' approval. I confronted Juanita with the phoniness and unfairness of her position. I challenged her to be willing to pay the social and emotional price for the freedom she desired.

Juanita perceived that I was siding with Brent in his wanting to work toward reconciliation and wasn't sure that I would be fair and objective in her therapy sessions. I suggested that I refer her to my wife who is also a psychologist. Juanita made an appointment to see my wife but later broke it.

In my last individual session with Juanita, she indicated a complete change of mind and shared that she truly loved Brent and wanted to have a good relationship and marriage with him. Shortly after that session, however, I learned from Brent that Juanita had visited her parents and then filed for divorce. I concluded that Juanita had been effective in winning her parents' support and was now ready to seek legal release from the marital bonds. Had she pulled off a masterful snow job in our last session, convincing me that she had a genuine interest in making her marriage work? I didn't think so then nor do I now.

In my sessions with Brent, he readily acknowledged his abuse and neglect of Juanita and disclosed that he knew very little about women. He
appeared to be sincere in his desire for a second chance with her to form
a solid Christian relationship and marriage.

The early stage of Brent's therapy centered on his working through
his guilt and pain from mistreating Juanita and coping with his fear of
losing her. He despaired at the thought of divorce. I helped him to see
that the best way to lose Juanita would be to attempt to hold on to or
possess her and the best way to keep her would be to give her freedom to
leave. I sought to facilitate a patient and nonpushy demeanor on his part
with Juanita. I helped Brent simultaneously to hope for the best (a reconciliation with Juanita) but to be prepared for the worst (a divorce). I used
the old Yogi Berra technique repeatedly with him: "It isn't over 'til it's
over." He was not to give up on Juanita until the last glimmer of hope had
vanished. Until that moment arrived he was to seek to love her redemp-
tively and avoid any coercion, hooking gimmicks, and overdoing-it
actions.

I encouraged Brent to accept personal responsibility only for the good
and the bad *he* had contributed to the marriage and to seek forgiveness
of God, Juanita, and self for the wrong he did to her in their relationship.

I sought to nurture Brent's new Christian faith and aid him in his
struggle with the will of God. I supported him through recurring bouts
with depression, loneliness, and longing for Juanita's companionship
while agonizing over the possibility that she might be seeking another
man for intimate pleasure. I helped him deal with his anger toward
Juanita for her not seeming to care at all when he was now willing to do
whatever was necessary to make the marriage work. Brent also had to
work through his being confused and angry in his relationship with God.

Often I assumed the role of a sharing, compassionate friend as much
as I did that of a professional therapist. At times I volunteered to disclose
my own personal experiences that I judged to be therapeutic for Brent; at
other times I shared my experiences at Brent's request. I suppose there
were times in our therapeutic dialogue that an observer would have
found it difficult to discern who was therapist and who was client. More
than once, I could have been seen as a pastoral counselor when we were
using portions of Scripture to throw light on particular concerns or
issues. Biblical readings and Christian literature were used as biblio-
therapy sources.

Somewhat to my surprise, Brent related to me that Juanita was debat-
ing whether to go ahead with the divorce and later start afresh with him
in a totally new relationship. Her mood had shifted more toward reconciliation after lots of painful discussion, attending church together, praying, and engaging in social activities. God had not only been working in

Brent's life, but also in Juanita's. During her personal struggle, Juanita realized that a relationship with Jesus was the answer, and she rededicated her life to the lordship of Jesus. Still, she was confused about whether God wanted her in a bad, abusive marriage. This gave Brent a renewed sense of optimism regarding the possibility of regaining an apparently lost marriage, but it left him confused, too, about how he could fit such a divorce and remarriage arrangement into their desire for a Christian life-style. We explored the possibility of seeing divorce in the legal sense as the declaration of the death of a bad and unwanted marriage and remarriage as the beginning of a brand-new marital commitment with God's blessings.

As Brent and Juanita spent more time together, the option of stopping the divorce proceedings and having instead a special ceremony in which they renewed their vows to one another was explored. While the divorce proceedings were in process, Brent and Juanita had a long talk, not about divorce, but about the course of their lives in Christ. Juanita, who had been seeing another man socially, began to find good qualities in Brent. She ceased socializing with the other person and her interest in Brent and desire for reconciliation with him grew. As mutual trust increased and they experienced the forgiveness of God and one another, they decided against the divorce and planned a renewal of their commitment vows. Juanita continued to attend church with Brent, share a new set of friends with him, and enjoy other mutually rewarding social and spiritual outings.

Before the renewed vows were exchanged, Brent and Juanita began working with my wife and me in couples' therapy. The early phase of therapy dealt primarily with completing unfinished business and learning how to communicate effectively. We helped them learn how to give and forgive; how to plan, play, pray, and relate as equals; and how to negotiate and share sex role tasks. Later, the focus was on how to experience creative, spontaneous sexual intimacy; how to live together without deference and denial; how to harmonize dual careers; and how to develop individual and mutual devotional activities. Overall, we sought to help them to integrate the spiritual, mental, physical, and social dimensions of both their personal and married lives.

The final outcome of Brent and Juanita's relationship is still pending, but it appears that a bad marriage that began on a flimsy foundation and grew progressively worse has had a new beginning and rests on a Christian foundation.

29

A Tardy Pilgrim
H. Newton Malony

"**A** Tardy Pilgrim" is the title of an autobiographical account of a person who rediscovered his religious heritage after many years of searching (Malony 1978, 97–110). I gave this chapter the same title because it tells of another person who returned to faith because of what happened to him in psychotherapy.

Andy was single and in his mid-twenties when he first called for an appointment with me. He spoke rapidly, in a voice that had a breathy, forced quality. He said that he was experiencing recurring, troublesome thoughts that he had committed the unpardonable sin and would not go to heaven.

In my early interviews with Andy, it became apparent that these preoccupations with guilt were not part of an active religious experience for him. Instead they were separate, compartmentalized thoughts off to the side of a secular life-style. Andy was a sports announcer for a professional basketball team. He had a somewhat unstable, but at times intimate relationship with a woman who worked in the team's business office. He did not attend church nor was he involved in any other religious activities.

Although he lived in his own apartment, he had a close relationship with his widowed mother. She had never remarried after divorcing his father when Andy was three. His father had maintained regular contact with him to the time of his sudden death when Andy was twelve. Andy's response to the loss of his father came to be the central issue in therapy. He put a "religious" interpretation on his father's leaving. Like so many children whose parents divorce, Andy took much of the responsibility on himself. During the period from ages three to twelve, he dealt with his anger at the loss by suppressing it, but dealt with his perceived guilt at causing the divorce by trying to be good. He thought that if he was good, his father would return.

When his father died suddenly, Andy's plan was tragically aborted. His good behavior could no longer pay off. At this point the struggle between his anger, disappointment, hope, and sorrow became almost unbearable. Once again, he turned to a religious solution to the dilemma. Of course, it should be noted that during the preceding five years, religious concerns were always on his mind. So, when he attempted to resolve his confusion with religious answers it was simply a reinvestment in what he was already doing. Only this time the resolution did not work. His anger and his self-doubts dominated his thinking. Andy yearned for his father but realized that his only hope was in getting to heaven where he could be reunited with his father. He realized that getting into heaven would require much more than just being good. He had to be perfect!

It was at this point that the seeds of Andy's obsession began with a vengeance. In his search for direction, he stumbled across Matthew 12:31–32: "Therefore I tell you, every sin and blasphemy will be forgiven men, but the blasphemy against the Spirit will not be forgiven. And whoever says a word against the Son of man will be forgiven; but whoever speaks against the Holy Spirit will not be forgiven, either in this age or in the age to come."

These words became his "bear," as he called it. Try as he did to be perfect, these statements from the mouth of Jesus haunted Andy throughout adolescence and young adulthood. Although he probably railed at God for the injustice of his father's death—especially since he had been trying to be good—Andy did not directly connect his anger at God with his sense of having committed the unpardonable sin as he perceived it in the passage from Matthew 12. In a somewhat compulsive manner he would return to the passage again and again and feel judged and despairing about it. He could not remember having committed the sin, but in a strange way would feel compelled to commit it right then and there. So, he would often say such things as, "Damn you, Holy Spirit." Thus the repetition of the sin would be accomplished along with a continued suppression of the real dynamic related to the feeling that God had violated an agreement by taking his father's life.

During all these years neither Andy nor his family were involved more than nominally in a church. Nor did Andy seek counsel from a pastor or other religious persons except once at sixteen when he consulted with a Presbyterian pastor.

By the time Andy came to me for counsel, the above dynamic was deeply ingrained and well practiced. He was completely cut off from any awareness of how this long-standing obsession related to his father's death. He only knew that the obsession was tormenting. It had become increasingly intrusive and handicapping in his daily affairs. The "bear" was almost "unbearable."

Psychotherapy followed a fairly traditional course of history taking, empathic listening, and symptom exploration. Andy had originally sought out my counsel because I was a religious person. Therefore, I tried to show my prowess in these matters by engaging in discussions about the nature of God in general and the meaning of the passage in Matthew 12 in particular. I communicated to him my conviction that God is all-loving and he will forgive our sin if we repent and ask for forgiveness.

Although a discussion of these issues was what Andy desired, I now question whether these discussions were appropriate. On the one hand, they often became highly rational and we may have been doing little more than intellectualizing. I often felt like a teacher with a pupil who, incidentally, always had a reason for not fully believing what I was telling him. His obsession persisted. The symptoms did not abate. His "bear" did not lessen its grip.

On the other hand, these discussions did establish our relationship. I always listened to his struggle as it expressed itself in his relationship with his girl friend, in his radio announcing, and in his dependency upon his mother. He felt heard and supported. Our discussions about Scripture and faith were interspersed with dialogues about his daily life. I do not think that he felt overwhelmed although he resisted the giving up of his conviction that he had, indeed, done something for which God would not forgive him and that he would not go to heaven.

The feeling that the "bear" had him and that his situation was basically hopeless continued. However, he did experience some release from the generalized compulsiveness which had come to characterize his life. His penchant for having everything in its place, and his concern for exact matches in dress slackened in intensity.

Only when we began to explore the dynamics relating to the loss of his father did he experience any release from his obsession. Through fantasized remembering, I led him back to the time of the divorce and to early memories of loneliness after his father had gone. He was able to re-experience some of the sorrow and some of the early decisions he made to be good in hope that his father would return. Memory of his father's death became suppressed. Suppression had given way to repression because of the pain of the event. However, Andy was able to date his concern for having committed the unpardonable sin. He became aware of it in his mid-teens, at about age fourteen. By this time the preoccupation was fairly full-blown. He became convinced of the possibility that the obsession was related to his decisions at the time of his father's death.

I say the "possibility" because true obsessions never fully leave clients. They have lived with them for so long that when they come to us for help those obsessions have become part of their psychic structure. About the most that we can hope for is that they will consider the idea of a dynamic explanation seriously enough that it will relieve the pressure of the symptom. If this happens, the stranglehold that the obsession has had will lessen and the preoccupation with the symptom will fade into the background. This is exactly what happened to Andy. According to Andy, even more important was his broader understanding of the Lord and of what the Bible really said. He began to report less frequent thoughts about Matthew 12 and his unpardonable sin. The "bear," as he called it, lessened its grip upon him.

I interpreted these changes in two ways. First, insight doesn't heal. I had no illusions that giving a dynamic explanation to Andy's symptom would make it go away. It didn't. He could see the logic of connecting his obsession with his reaction to the loss of his father, but he still wondered whether he could be forgiven. Second, what does heal is redecision. Andy decided to live in a new way and he found relief from his symptoms.

As I noted earlier, during all this time Andy was preoccupied with religion but was not religious. He had accepted Christ before "bear," however, he had not actively practiced faith. I confess I became rather bold in encouraging him to rededicate himself to Christ and to rejoin the church, and to engage in prayer and Bible reading. I justified these encouragements on two grounds.

On the one hand, I feel that any therapeutic decision, such as Andy's decision to understand his situation in terms of his father's death and to trust the love of God, should be buttressed by action. Becoming a Christian by joining the church and practicing godly habits were, from this point of view, simply actions which firmed up his decisions. To have just depended on his insight would have been counterproductive. I would have done the same thing in encouraging certain actions for estranged spouses, phobics, or neurotics.

On the other hand, I firmly believe that psychotherapy involves the sharing of wisdom as well as advice for adjustment. Wisdom refers to the best way to live. It is like the treatment of choice in other settings. I would be in error if I did not affirm and encourage a client in doing those things which I feel are part of the good and the best. I would be derelict if I did not recommend these things regardless of whether they are part of the cure for a symptom or not. This is what I did for Andy. This is what I would do for anyone. In Andy's case it had direct relevance for his obsession.

My encouragements were singularly unsuccessful. Andy would come to therapy week after week and report that he had not gone to church or begun Bible reading and prayer. I pressed the point because he kept saying this was what he wanted to do. In his presence I called a pastor near to where he lived and made an appointment. According to Andy he fully intended to follow through on a confession of faith and on joining the church. He did neither! The pastor was nice. Andy just did not feel it was a church he would feel comfortable attending; he still wasn't ready to decide.

At this point therapy ended. His "bear" had become bearable. The obsession only rarely bothered him and his life seemed to be progressing nicely. Some months later he returned for two sessions to discuss his anxiety over losing a new job to which he had gone near the end of therapy. At this time, the problem seemed more situational than dynamic and he reported that the "bear" still did not bother him.

Several more months passed during which I did not hear from Andy. One day he called. Things were going well. He still did not have a new job but was managing to make it on the basis of some television contracts he had. He said, "I have something to tell you and I'd like to come in for a session." Much to my surprise, he reported that he had found a church, that he had confessed his faith, and that he had become a regular member. His face literally glowed with the account. He seemed truly excited and joyful. Interestingly, the church he joined was one that he had attended as a child. It was like going home.

Most important for the therapeutic process was his statement, "I owe much of this to you and I wanted to come in and tell you face to face." I confess I was humbled and pleased. Andy is now doing what he should be doing. He has been released from the obsession that he committed an unpardonable sin and has abundant life—both this life and the life to come.

Reference

Meadow, M. J. 1978. A tardy pilgrim. In *Psychology and faith: The Christian experience of eighteen psychologists,* edited by H. Newton Malony. Lanham, Maryland: University Press of America.

30

Andrew's Anxiety
J. Harold Ellens

Andrew was a bright, vigorous Caucasian male about thirty-five years of age. He seemed highly motivated to undertake therapy; he had made the appointment himself, and had selected me for his counselor because he had heard that I was a Christian therapist. He appeared on time at my office, neatly dressed and apparently at ease about entering therapy. He had lost his father at age five, and his mother five years before he appeared for therapy. He was the youngest of nine, having seven sisters and one brother; he was married and the father of a son and daughter, both under ten years of age.

Andrew's initial four or five sessions involved mainly an intense catharsis of traumatic reactions to various domestic and employment experiences over the last eight years. He indicated a repetitious pattern in which each year, from Thanksgiving to the end of the year, he would become unusually agitated, depressed, and anxiety-laden; this pattern was associated with a mild paranoid reaction with regard to authority figures, particularly men, in which he feared that his supervisors would find him inadequate or unworthy and terminate his employment. Andrew typically managed this depression by looking for ways to quit his job and find another one. During the eight years of his employment history, he had held four successive jobs as a banking executive at the managerial level. Despite his apparent pathology he had been consistently

253

successful in investment banking and was highly esteemed. As a result it was not difficult for him to change jobs and in each change he, in effect, achieved a promotion. He came for therapy because he found himself again in the year-end depressive state and was fearful that he would spoil his current role as vice-president of investment banking for a large corporation, a significant position for a thirty-five-year-old man. He had begun to recognize the syndrome as pathological and self-defeating and had finally decided to get help with his feelings of inadequacy, inferiority, depression, and anxiety, as well as with his self-defeating dysfunction.

Initially it seemed that Andrew suffered the fairly common holiday depression syndrome so frequently encountered with children of troubled families, namely, the chronic feeling that anything really good is going to get smashed. Consequently, the child does something self-destructive so that he can introduce predictability into his impending trauma and not let someone else be the victimizer. This gives the person control over his/her own destiny. "If things are going to get smashed I will do it myself so no one can do it to me." This depression is associated with holidays because good things seem more impending for children and things get smashed more frequently in troubled homes at holiday times than otherwise.

It soon became clear, however, that the difficulty had deeper and more profound sources. There seemed to be some question whether Andrew's problem was a borderline syndrome resulting from the dissociation related to preoedipal ego impairment and its associated defenses or whether he suffered from the neurotic patterns associated with the defensive process of repression of some unusual early trauma. As the first month of therapy played out we spent a great deal of effort to uncover a developmental history. Andrew was very resistive, particularly with regard to his experience before he joined the Marines at age eighteen. It became clear that he had an intense bond with his mother during childhood and adolescence, largely undisengaged before his enlistment in the armed forces. His mother proved to be an extremely dependent person whom all the children spent much energy attending, but who provided little gratification or affirmation, and who, when the children reacted in frustration and withdrew, merely lapsed into silence. She seldom expressed emotion of any kind to the children. The children saw her as very needy, vulnerable, inadequate, and fragile. Andrew had a love-hate relationship with her but would never, even in therapy allow himself to acknowledge the hate side. Andrew was the youngest child and had excellent relationships with his sisters though virtually no relationship with his brother.

Andrew did not readily speak of his father but when pressed to do so he indicated that he had been a famous chef at a major hotel restaurant and that he had left the family destitute so that they had to live in "the project," a slum area of fifteen apartment buildings built by the city and provided to destitute slum families on a subsidized low-rent basis. Andrew assumed an extremely flattened affect when speaking of his father.

The entire family attended the Missouri Synod Lutheran Church and Andrew had been well instructed in the faith. He continued to attend that church with his own children, though his wife was Roman Catholic. His church life and faith were important to him.

Andrew talked with some animation about his years in the Marines. When we finally got down into his adolescence and childhood, he soon became comfortable with those memories, often reporting with some delight what proved to be typically amusing childhood events, pleasant experiences of friends and comrades while growing up, despite the rather stark overall pallor that apparently hung over the family desperately trying to survive. Andrew could not remember anything prior to five years of age and the loss of his father. He vaguely remembered his father, he thought, and the fact that Andrew was "the apple of his father's eye," though he could not be sure that this was something the family had told him or a real experience.

In the tenth week of therapy Andrew reported that he had been having a recurring dream, that he had the dream occasionally all his life, but now nearly every night, and that it was intensely distressing to him, leaving him awake and overwhelmed with depression and anxiety. It was a dream about being pursued by a great threat, the nature of which he could not make out. He indicated that during the pursuit he always felt helpless and hopeless, certain that he would be killed. I encouraged him to cultivate the dream process, in so far as possible, by consciously giving himself permission, as he lay down to sleep, to dream the dream again that night and to try to carry it further along so as to discover more about the nature of the threat. He reported regularly on the dream and seemed to develop a great ability to induce it and to advance the development of it by the method I had suggested to him. He dreamed the dream frequently and also had a good deal of other dream activity. The other dreams seemed routine and unrelated to the pursuit dream in cognitive and affective content.

Little progress was made on the dream for a considerable time so we concentrated upon Andrew's situation at home and at work. His catharsis seemed to virtually eliminate the depression and anxiety; we had now moved past the holidays into the new year. I was unsure whether we were really getting to the cure. The dream continued. In the twenty-second week of therapy Andrew reported that the identity of the threat in the dream seemed to be clearing somewhat. He felt that it was some kind of monster but he had never actually been able to see it in the dream. He continued to feel helpless, hopeless, and overwhelmed in the pursuit, and always found himself "losing out" and on the verge of being destroyed when he would abruptly awaken in an intense panic, often crying out in a nightmarish way.

I decided to urge Andrew to counterattack the monster to see whether he could martial any assertive ego strength against whatever primal power the monster represented, acknowledging that I was taking a risk of introducing into the dream process extraneous material which might throw the whole thing off-track. Andrew was intrigued by the idea and agreed. One week later he reported that he had been attempting to follow my suggestions. They had not worked at first but the night before something had happened that seemed to be a result of the idea of counterattack. The dream had progressed as usual for just a little while when it abruptly changed to a military situation. He was again a sergeant in Vietnam and was leading his patrol of soldiers when they were overwhelmed by an enemy attack. He thought that they had all been killed but himself. He suddenly awoke crying. He had not had such an experience in Vietnam, but there was material from his real experience. I felt we had gotten off the track, but I decided to let this play out its own course simply because I did not know what else to do.

The military dreams continued and Andrew gave himself permission in the dreams to counterattack the enemy. The enemy was now a very tangible military enemy led by a larger than life commander. Eventually Andrew began to report that in the dreams he found himself with his soldiers searching out the enemy, feeling far less panic, hopelessness, and helplessness. I was not sure whether we were making progress or merely dealing with extraneous dream material which had to do with situations with which Andrew was familiar and which he knew he could handle. Then Andrew told me that the reason he had joined the Marines was that throughout his childhood he had felt terribly inadequate and fearful that he would never grow up to be strong and especially that he would not be a real man. There seemed to be no confusion of sex role identity but an inadequate role model identification and great anxiety about being a responsible adult male figure. He had overcompensated for his fear by enlisting as a Marine and retained to the present something of a macho style. He hated the Marines because of his experience in Vietnam but liked the Marines because of the masculinity that identity gave him.

This led me to feel that perhaps the shift in the dream from the monster to the military was not off-track. Andrew reported that he found himself standing up to the enemy in the dream and he felt little hopelessness and helplessness, though the anxiety persisted. This seemed like progress and I encouraged Andrew to continue that course, but the therapy shifted again to identity, role clarification, affective resilience, relational dynamics, and the like.

Shortly thereafter Andrew's report of his dream activity seemed to indicate an intensification of the process and an impending breakthrough. He said that he was actively countering the threat force and feeling some exhilaration from it. The following week he reported that the dream had shifted back to the monster. He had been in a military situation, had vigorously attacked the enemy, and had finally encountered the leader of the threat force. As he was in the act of killing him the dream had shifted back to the old monster situation. Andrew had panicked and run away. I encouraged him to attack the monster if he appeared again.

Two days later at 6:00 A.M. on a Saturday morning, Andrew called me at my home and seemed extremely distraught and begged for an appointment immediately. He seemed to be decompensating rapidly and was confused, perhaps even somewhat suicidal. I agreed to see him at 7:00 at my home. He arrived at 6:30 in an apparently profound depression and somewhat dissociative. He began immediately to spill out the story that he had had the dream, and had met the monster. It turned out to be a very large, horrible man; he had attacked him, and just as he had struck him with a heavy club to kill him, the man turned toward him and it was his father.

There followed a four-hour marathon of anguish, crying, despair, hopelessness, helplessness, and gasps of broken sentences about his first five years. For the first time Andrew began to recover the memory of his early years and was able to piece together crucial early developmental experiences which now came flooding out. His father had been a heavy drinker who came home regularly in a drunken stupor and beat Andrew's mother and the children, though he never struck or abused Andrew, "the apple of his eye." Frequently his father was absent for long periods of time; the family was deprived, hungry, fearful of the father's return, poverty stricken, and forced to live in the slum. One day when Andrew was five his father returned drunk after being absent for what Andrew thought was probably six weeks, and began to beat Andrew's mother. The other children were not present and Andrew recalls feeling desperate. He went to the kitchen, got his mother's butcher knife, went into the back room, taped the knife to the broom handle, and came out and speared his father as he was attacking Andrew's mother. His father was struck in the shoulder and sustained a superficial flesh wound. He turned on Andrew, and chased him out of the apartment with an ax with which he threatened to kill Andrew. Because of his father's drunken state, Andrew escaped down the street and hid for two days in a friend's house until he was finally discovered by his favorite sister. His father left home and the family never heard from him again.

Andrew was overwhelmed with guilt for destroying the family, for "killing" his father, for depriving his mother and siblings, and for destroying his own chance to have a normal life. By the end of the four-hour marathon he was able to translate some of that guilt into anger, but he was extremely afraid of his anger. The root of his inability to confront authority, his need for the macho style, his confusion of his own identity, his anxiety about his masculinity, and his need for self-destructive behavior any time he became really successsful, now seemed to be clear. It also seemed clear that his pathology was the anxiety neurosis associated with repression rather than a borderline syndrome.

Andrew had often spoken with me of his faith and his longing for a clearer sense of God's love for him and his desire for a more "heartfelt" spiritual experience. After we had spent four or five sessions analyzing the breakthrough dream experience and Andrew was able to recover more of his early memory, he was able to see his father in human dimensions and begin to deal with him somewhat objectively as a fractured and pathological person who was the product of his history just as Andrew was of his. This line of discussion led, in later sessions, to the matter of forgiveness. Andrew was understandably resistive. We discussed forgiveness in terms of its psychological dynamics and effects as well as its spiritual processes. That led to a discussion of the way God forgives us and the meaning of the unconditional, radical, and universal nature of God's grace to us. Andrew was visibly relieved as he grasped the way in which God accepts us as we are at any given moment in our struggle with our humanness and growth process and affirms us as wholly acceptable just as we are at that place and time, unconditionally. I suggested to him that forgiveness is redemptive because it frees the forgiver even more than the forgiven from the burden of needing to carry around the grief, guilt, anger, loss, and depression. His spiritual orientation led him to an immediate perception of the import of that and he easily internalized it.

As Andrew was able to accept his father's humanness and pathology he seemed able to accept himself as well. There was a discernible decrease in his need for exaggerated masculinity, a complete elimination of his need for self-destructive behavior, and a discernible sense of relief and quietness about him. At this point, however, he began to experience his negative feelings about his mother. Associated with this, moreover, he was able to get in touch with long repressed deficits in his relationship to his wife. The marriage went through a brief crisis as he began to reconstruct his manner of relating to the prominent females in his life. He had been dependent upon maintaining a secure relationship with them, from mother on, because that was the only secure and nurturant thing in his life. He had repressed all negative factors in those relationships and assumed a skillfully masked dependent and childlike role. After the break-through experience he began to actualize his own real self, a new and sometimes scary experience for him.

I encouraged Andrew to try to discover whether his father was still living. He spoke with his sisters about it, and his oldest sister indicated that for some years she had been attempting to track him down and had been able to determine that he had gone to a western mountain state, but had left there five years earlier. He had remarried, raised five more children, and had been in good health the last anybody knew. She had a contact in a southern state which she thought was where he had gone. Two weeks later the sister was able to determine the town to which the father had moved. I urged Andrew to go to see him. He resisted. Through the local sheriff's department of that small rural southern town Andrew's sister finally contacted her father's second wife by letter. The woman wrote back to indicate that Andrew's father had died after a year-long illness, on the night on which Andrew had had the breakthrough dream.

Andrew was again emotionally devastated but recovered quickly because he was consciously able to feel that there was no need to reprocess the whole loss experience and he could forgive his father for the entire misfortune, as well as forgive himself for the anguish of his own reaction. This case more than any other I have seen illustrates what seems to me to be a fact of life for the helping professions, namely, that the insight of God's unconditional grace and acceptance is a profoundly healing experience. If seen as a reality constituent to the nature of things in this universe, it must be one of the most significant elements of sound psychological theory and practice.

31

Dependent Personality Disorder: A Case Conference
C. Markham Berry

Case Presentation

Kitty was a forty-five-year-old divorcée with three children, ages seventeen, nineteen and twenty-four, successfully employed as an office manager in a small business. The two older children were on their own while the youngest, a daughter, remained in the home.

Kitty's chief complaint was, "I'm completely messed up and don't know what to do." She described severe depression and anxiety extending over several years, but much worse during the last two weeks, a time which coincided with her discharge from the hospital. She was hospitalized for a basilar skull fracture, fractures of two fingers and several ribs, along with internal injuries. These were sufficiently severe that on the night of admission the family was told she might not live.

The injuries were inflicted by her husband, Dave, in her own home two months after she had sued him for divorce. Her decision to divorce him had been a difficult one to make even though he had beaten her on previous occasions and had been painfully insensitive to her and the children for years. In addition, he had affairs with other women on several occasions. She had finally decided to divorce him when she learned he had attempted to seduce their seventeen-year-old daughter. In spite of all of this she tried to avoid breaking up the marriage, hoping "he would go into counseling, because I love him and didn't want him to leave."

The marriage had begun well, and she remembered their courtship and the first year after their wedding as being very happy times. Dave was in the navy and seemed satisfied with his career. When their first child, a daughter, was born, things changed. He was intensely jealous of the baby and became more and more dissatisfied with the navy. He ultimately resigned his commission, having been passed over several times for promotion. Kitty thought this was occasioned by his "bad attitude and heavy drinking." At home during this time he was very difficult to live with, being very critical of her and angry at the limitations of a life which now included the responsibilities of a wife and child.

Things improved briefly after Dave got a civilian job in a large aircraft factory though he soon became disenchanted with this work, resenting being moved around the country. But he performed well enough to receive regular promotions. When it looked like their life would stabilize in Atlanta they had two other children.

During these years they both renewed Christian commitments they had made as teen-agers and joined in the life of a large and enthusiastic church. Kitty felt good about their life at this time, though Dave remained critical and unreasonable much of the time. She had to work full-time outside the home to maintain the life-style he demanded, yet he expected her to do all the housework as well as be responsive to all of his needs. He belittled her in many ways, "calling women inferior beings, like his father does."

He kept the checkbook, and managed all the money without consulting her, including her salary. She paid the household expenses with an allowance which Dave doled out to her weekly. Kitty didn't like this but didn't complain since this was the same as it had been in her own home, and she considered this basically "the lot of a woman." At this time there were a number of seminars around Atlanta which encouraged women to be submissive to their husbands, promising them that this would heal and strengthen their marriages. Kitty did her best to follow this teaching, to conform to all of Dave's wishes.

Several things happened, though. Instead of increased love and appreciation for her, things went the other way and he treated her "more like a piece of furniture than a wife." The two older children also began to act like their father, insulting Kitty, ordering her about, and complaining when she did not instantly meet their needs. Only the younger daughter seemed to understand her, resenting the way the others treated her. But she also became angry at Kitty for allowing all this to happen.

Physical abuse had been rare up to this time, and usually occurred when Dave was "in a temper, and drinking too much." Then the company he worked for began to lay people off and he thought he might lose his job. With this stress he became morose, drank more heavily, and on several occasions beat her up badly, "although he never broke any of my bones before this!"

As time went on and things deteriorated Kitty finally considered a divorce, primarily to give the younger child a more stable and pleasant home environment. This had been a terrible decision since she thought of divorce as the ultimate symbol of defeat, that she had failed and was therefore extremely shameful. In addition, Kitty had always felt dependent on Dave for both her emotional and financial support, an impression which he kept alive by repeated threats of leaving her destitute. It was only after she had seen a friend go through a divorce and survive, and also when Dave threatened to sexually abuse their daughter that Kitty finally made her decision.

Following the divorce, Dave moved out into an apartment, but otherwise their lives went on as though nothing had happened. He spent most of his spare time in the home and continued to harass both the mother and the girl. In addition, he was derelict in making support payments, and spent much of his time going from one person to another alienating family and friends toward her, telling them how badly Kitty had treated him.

The incident which precipitated her seeking help began when she finally became angry enough with him to do something. She threatened to call the police to put him out. In the argument which followed, Kitty threatened him with a large kitchen knife. Dave called the police who came promptly, took the knife away from her, and ordered him to stay away from the house. When they left he followed her into the bathroom and attacked her, beating her nearly to death. They made so much noise the neighbors called the police again. Kitty was taken to the hospital, but nothing was done to the husband, because she would not press charges against him.

During the intake interview in the Christian counseling center Kitty sought out, the counselor learned that Dave was still living in the house, and that Kitty's parents, knowing all that had happened, had come to her berating her for the miserable way she had treated him, urging her to let him return to her as her husband. Moreover, both older children, the nineteen-year-old son in particular, had joined in this tirade. When the counselor asked Kitty why the husband was still around, she said, "I don't really know. . . . I love him, I guess."

The remainder of the initial interview centered on Kitty's feelings of helplessness, her tremendous guilt, and her overwhelming sadness at losing the husband she loved so much. She was extremely confused, occasionally irrational, and even had noticed that her memory was failing her and many of the events of the past six months or so were indistinct or completely forgotten.

The counselor suggested a working diagnosis of exogenous depression, with a secondary diagnosis of dependent personality disorder. The therapist felt that the masochism would probably turn out to be the most critical therapeutic issue in counseling, though she wondered if Kitty might not have been more responsible for her problems in this marriage than was apparent thus far, suggesting that she might have a passive-aggressive personality disorder.

The counselor felt that Kitty needed help to sort out all that had happened to her, to help her understand why she found it so difficult to deal more firmly with Dave, along with some simple supportive therapy to encourage her to set up a new life. She wondered if a course in assertiveness, and perhaps one in communication, would not help Kitty deal more effectively with her friends, her family, and the children.

Discussion

Kitty is familiar to all who provide professional counseling. People we think of as unassertive, passive, weak, self-punishing, having poor self-esteem or addictive personalities, and who are abused in adulthood are often people very much like Kitty.

Many analytic thinkers would agree that the central dynamic issue in Kitty's situation was the masochism demonstrated in her history. The typical object-relations configurations of narcissism were also apparent even though Kitty did not demonstrate the insensitive, self-centeredness or vanity we usually associate with narcissism. Some analysts make sadomasochism the target of their treatment for all narcissism, even when it is not obvious (Gear, Hill and Liendo 1981). Others focus their attention on the conflicts centering around the narcissism.

One would expect to find evidence that the intrapsychic part-objects of "good me" and "bad me" have not properly fused into a coherent self which incorporates enough infantile idealism to give healthy self-confidence and self-esteem. In many different ways the difficulties arising in this early maturation failure make such patients exceptionally vulnerable to insult and injury. At one level they feel intense guilt that they have failed. Punishing part-objects of "bad-me" from childhood inner experiences accentuated by those of a bad marriage are reflected in a critical superego and patients therefore derive some relief for having received proper punishment. To this extent they identify with the accusations of spouses, agreeing that they are indeed bad. This process then locks into projective sadism, encouraging relationships to continue on their course as devastating as they are.

In an alternate formulation, the masochism represents a partially comfortable retreat for patients from the fear of damage to fragile self-esteem. Abuses may in some way be projections of the spouse's self-hatred of the split-off bad part-objects of his own fragmented self, and by dealing with them as though they were defects in the patient, he wards off threats to his own grandiose self (Storolow 1975a, 1975b).

Such patients were probably treated in much the same way as children, not receiving the kind of empathetic and encouraging parenting which would have helped them develop more internal coherence and appropriate self-esteem and assertiveness.

Another psychoanalytic way of considering a person like Kitty is to see the pathology as originating in the "depressive position." Winnicott (1955) has described the pathology seen in this kind of masochistic dependency in the schizoid personality disorder. He calls attention to an extremely important developmental maneuver which takes place in early infancy when the infant gives something of importance to the mother and it is received happily by her. At first, this giving may be limited to a smile or a touch on the mother's cheek. Later it will involve more complex gifts, but the normal growth process requires some response from the mother which indicates that this has been received and that both the gift and the child are valued. An important component of the self-esteem of the healthy infant comes from this experience of being appreciated. In many homes a mother's attention can be so fully demanded by her husband that she is not free to respond in this nourishing way to her infant. Even when the mother is responsive to the child, her denigration from the powerful one in the home often weakens her importance in the eyes of the child and dilutes her effectiveness in nurturing the child.

When one is doing psychotherapy with someone like Kitty, it is wise to keep all of these possibilities in mind. The most influential of these dynamics in the life of the particular person in treatment will emerge in the material presented and also in transference as therapy moves along.

The diagnosis of a dependent personality disorder has been made more objective in DSM III (APA, 1980) by requiring the following criteria. This patient "passively allows others to assume responsibility for major areas of life because of inability to function independently." A second requirement of DSM III is that the patient "subordinates own needs to those of persons on whom he or she depends in order to avoid any possibility of having to rely on self, e.g., tolerates abusive spouse." And third, the dependent personality "lacks self-confidence, e.g., sees self as helpless, stupid." These are clearly demonstrated in Kitty's history. However, patients who have this kind of masochistic dependency sometimes choose mates who require them to do everything, and assume the dependent role themselves. So the pattern is not quite as precise here as it is in the other criteria.

A more certain finding in the dependent personality is a focus on relationships as being the most important element of reality. Many who see relationships as the center of all being will not tolerate abuse. Others soon realize that the pathology of the person they want to love is so deep that a really loving relationship is not possible. So we must assume that patients like Kitty have a defect in their ability to know and judge the people close to them. Until they are aware of this problem they will almost inevitably either return to abusive spouses or even find similar partners.

The fundamental dynamics of narcissism will often surface. The splitting is already suggested by pathological self-depreciation. The grandiose side of the split, equally unrealistic, is seen in the lofty hope maintained to the end, that of being the great lover who can heal the beloved by absorbing his pain.

Even more clearly, narcissism is demonstrated by confusion as to what a truly sound relationship involves. Such patients' view of a loving relationship focuses almost exclusively on efforts to give, to minister, and to heal by absorbing. To expect to receive in this process is hard to see, as they have not learned the place appropriate assertiveness should have in a real relationship.

A distinction must be made as to how much of a person's narcissism arises in his childhood, either from defective parenting or a failure to see an inspiring model of a good relationship between parents, and how much comes from a congenital anxiety disorder. Kitty's narcissism came from the former predominantly while Dave's demonstrated some serious genetic pathology. In any case, those patients who are more largely influenced historically than genetically will be more amenable to therapy.

Treatment is more difficult than it would appear at first, since without encouragement from the counselor, the patient will feel guilty about requiring this kind of attention. I have found it helps to keep the fundamental principles of the making of healthy relationships before me during the entire therapy, even spending time teaching them to the patient. Supplementary experiences such as marriage communication courses and assertiveness training would be, as suggested, helpful, bringing these issues into the therapeutic hour to help make them a part of communication patterns.

Psychoanalysts and other theorists have a tendency to unlimber their sadism in encounters with this kind of person. When a survey of the literature is made, it is apparent that a good deal of this hostility has been loaded onto the concepts of *dependency, passivity,* and *masochism.* They are bad words. Should we demonstrate hostility in therapy we will find a slippery tendency on the part of the patient to agree with us. When this occurs, it is vital to the effective course of therapy that the whole issue of sadomasochism be dealt with. It is probably better for us to work through these problems ourselves before dealing with others. I have become convinced over the years that the conceptual model of relationships as described in the Bible, whether in the life of the church, or the marriage and family, or the community at large, offers us a much richer understanding of relationships in general. It is the task of Christians who do therapy to give persistent and thoughtful attention to this model. In knowing the nature of good, mature biblical relationships we will serve our clients much better. In making one of our tasks in life the full use of the riches of this biblical revelation, we will serve our community and our professions more fully.

Thoughtful, patient, skilled and loving therapy with people like Kitty will be rewarding not only to patients, but to therapists as well. In the process one learns that deeply hidden beneath the surface of pathology is a profound biblical truth. We all are called to be lovers. There is in this process of loving in the fullest Christian sense, an important element of absorbing abuse unjustly. Our model is the Lord himself whose entire life was an expression of the kind of love which absorbs the full impact of sin into himself and gives back an overflowing wave of grace. Pathology is a distortion of this truth. In understanding it we'll know more about the pathology we all share as sinners.

References

American Psychiatric Association. 1980. *Diagnostic and statistical manual.* 3d ed. Washington, D.C.: American Psychiatric Association.

Gear, M. C., M. A. Hill, and E. D. Liendo. 1981. *Working through narcissism.* New York: Aronson.

Storolow, R. D. The narcissistic function of masochism (and sadism). *International Journal of Psycho-Analysis* 56(1975):441–48.

_____. Toward a functional definition of narcissism. *International Journal of Psycho-Analysis* 56(1975):179–86.

Winnicott, D. W. The depressive position in normal emotional development. *British Journal of Medical Psychology* 28(1955):89–100.